Making Policies for Children:
A Study of the Federal Process

Cheryl D. Hayes, *Editor*

Panel for the Study of the Policy Formation Process
Committee on Child Development Research and Public Policy
Assembly of Behavioral and Social Sciences
National Research Council

NATIONAL ACADEMY PRESS
Washington, D.C.   1982

Library of Congress Cataloging in Publication Data

Main entry under title:

Making policies for children.

1. Children--Government policy--United States.
2. Children--Nutrition--Government policy--
United States.   3. Family policy--United States.
I. Hayes, Cheryl D.
HQ792.U5M34   353.0084'7   82-2218
ISBN 0-309-03241-5   AACR2

Available from

NATIONAL ACADEMY PRESS
2101 Constitution Avenue, N.W.
Washington, D.C.   20418

Printed in the United States of America

Panel for the Study of the
Policy Formation Process

Laurence E. Lynn, Jr. (Chair), John F. Kennedy School of
Government, Harvard University
Lewis H. Butler, Health Policy Program, School of
Medicine, University of California at San Francisco
Sherryl Graves, Department of Psychology, New York
University
Sheila B. Kamerman, School of Social Work, Columbia
University
Thomas Kiresuk, Program Evaluation Resource Center,
Minneapolis, Minn.
William A. Morrill, Mathematica Policy Research, Inc.,
Princeton, N.J.
Constance B. Newman, Newman and Hermanson Company,
Washington, D.C.
Fernando Oaxaca, Resource for Communications, Inc., Los
Angeles, Calif.
Martin Rein, Department of Political Science,
Massachusetts Institute of Technology
Harold A. Richman, School of Social Service
Administration, University of Chicago
Carol B. Stack, Institute of Policy Sciences, Duke
University
Carol H. Weiss, Graduate School of Education, Harvard
University

Cheryl D. Hayes, Study Director
John R. Nelson, Jr., Research Associate

iii

Committee on Child Development
Research and Public Policy

Harold A. Richman, School of Social Service Administration, University of Chicago
Roberta Simmons, Department of Sociology, University of Minnesota
Jack L. Walker, Institute for Policy Studies, University of Michigan
Robin M. Williams, Jr., Department of Sociology, Cornell University
Wayne Holtzman (ex officio), The Hogg Foundation for Mental Health, University of Texas; Chair, Panel on Selection and Placement of Students in Programs for the Mentally Retarded
Sheila B. Kamerman (ex officio), School of Social Work, Columbia University; Chair, Panel on Work, Family, and Community

Contents

Preface

This report is the product of a 30-month study sponsored by the Administration for Children, Youth, and Families of the U.S. Department of Health and Human Services. The Panel for the Study of the Policy Formation Process, established by the Committee on Child Development Research and Public Policy of the Assembly of Behavioral and Social Sciences, had three objectives: (1) to develop a better understanding of how federal policies affecting children and their families are formulated; (2) using the framework of that understanding, to identify factors likely to influence the content of such policies in the near future; (3) to offer observations concerning how participants in policy debates concerning children and their families could most effectively pursue their interests.

From the outset we recognized that many critics would question whether a committee created to address issues relating to children and families should establish a panel, under the sponsorship of an agency with sectarian interests in these matters, to pursue study objectives of this character with anything approaching the detachment expected of the National Research Council. While we leave it to the readers of this report to draw their own conclusions as to our success, we want to make clear why the panel undertook this study, how we sought to maintain the necessary detachment, and what we feel was achieved.

We undertook the study for three reasons, the first of which is straightforward. A primary purpose of the parent Committee on Child Development Research and Public Policy is to synthesize, coordinate, and propose research relevant to public policy affecting children and their families, and therefore the study was of interest. As researchers, we wanted to see if we could achieve deeper understanding of a vital aspect of social decision

making. As a panel concerned with public policy, we
wanted to see if we could derive operationally useful
insights from that understanding.
  A second reason for undertaking the study is related
to the first. An aspect of the parent committee's
mission is forging links between research and policy
making and developing an understanding of policy making
to serve as a foundation for its other ongoing studies as
well as its future work. While several of us had been
actively involved in policy making and most were familiar
with the literature on children and family policy, all
recognized the value of an opportunity to examine the
policy-making process collectively and develop a shared
perspective.
  A third attractive feature of this study was the
opportunity it afforded the panel to study policy making
from the perspective of many professions and social
science disciplines. A major premise underlying formation
of the parent committee was that its broadly interdisci-
plinary membership, which comprises individuals with both
research and governmental and professional experience,
would produce reports of greater depth and creativity
than if the same work were approached from narrower
perspectives. A panel study of policy making that seemed
to invite contributions from several research traditions
and perspectives seemed an ideal vehicle to test this
premise.
  The parent committee was concerned, however, with
potential problems of intentional and unintentional bias.
Accordingly, members of the panel were chosen primarily
for their professional competence and experience in the
field of policy making in general. Only a few had prior
identification with policy positions concerning children
and families. Although panel members were not chosen to
represent any particular mix of political views, in fact
they exhibited considerable diversity in their views of
the appropriate role of government with respect to the
well-being of children and families. Indeed, it would be
impossible to predict even now how the panel might come
out if polled on such partisan issues as enactment of
comprehensive child care legislation or the proper role
for the agency sponsoring the study.
  Because our study represents a departure from the usual
National Research Council approach, a word of explanation
is in order. In the first phase of the project, we
reviewed the literature on policy making as it affects
children and summarized the findings and conclusions it

contained. We also reviewed representative literature from the broader field of public policy determination. We attempted to see if we could discharge our obligation by showing the policy implications of preexisting social science research, an approach that is characteristic of National Research Council studies. On the basis of these reviews, we concluded that the most useful contribution we could make to the subject we were asked to investigate was to gather additional data on the policy-making process as it affects children and to interpret it in the light of what we already know but, if appropriate, with a fresh perspective. Accordingly, we undertook three new case studies of federal policy making affecting children and their families, presented in Part 2 of this volume, and completed the analysis contained in Part 1.

As to the results of the study effort, while we took seriously our obligation to offer observations useful to participants in policy making, we rejected as altogether inappropriate any notion that we should provide a field manual for children's advocates or agency officials. Rather, we believe we have provided a framework for participation in policy making that will be useful to individuals and organizations of a wide variety of political and programmatic orientations. We regard this framework, described in Chapter 4, as the report's main contribution, with implications that are both general enough and operational enough to be useful to groups such as the Committee on Child Development Research and Public Policy.

The members of the panel met 10 times during the course of the study and formed an unusually close-knit working group, with each participant contributing to the effort at numerous points. Several drafts of the report were begun and discarded in the process of arriving at the approach presented in this volume. As chairman of that panel as well as of the committee until 1980, I welcome the opportunity to express my gratitude and admiration for the enthusiasm, creativity, and effort displayed by the panel members throughout the study. The study also benefited at its earliest stage from the advice and insights of the following individuals, who served on an ad hoc panel to devise a work plan: John D. Steinbruner, Ronald G. Havelock, and John M. Seidl. Appreciation is also due the members of the Committee on Child Development Research and Public Policy, who constituted a sympathetic-ally critical audience and valued advisory group for this study. In addition, I wish to thank the numerous individuals outside the National Research Council who took the time to read and comment on the case studies and the early drafts of the report.

The study director for the project was Cheryl D. Hayes, who played an outstanding role in translating the panel's ideas and directions into a plan of work and then into a report. Special acknowledgement is also due John R. Nelson, Jr., research associate, who did the research for and drafted the three case studies and assisted in their analysis. Wendy E. Warring, research assistant, also assisted with the research for the case study on the child care and dependent tax deduction credit. Special thanks are due David A. Goslin, executive director of the Assembly of Behavioral and Social Sciences, for his advice and assistance throughout the project. Christine L. McShane, the Assembly's editor, did her usual outstanding job in preparing the report for publication.

Finally, the committee and the panel owe warm thanks to Edith Grotberg, director of research and evaluation at the Administration for Children, Youth, and Families, for initiating this study and providing support and encouragement throughout.

Laurence E. Lynn, Jr.
Chair, Panel for the Study of
the Policy Formation Process

Making Policies for Children:
A Study of the Federal Process

Part I:
Report of the Panel

Introduction

Government action to protect children, principally those
who are orphaned, abandoned, neglected, or otherwise
dependent, is part of the American heritage. In recent
decades, however, government has acted to meet more of
the social and developmental needs of more children--not
only those special needs of children whose families are
unable or unwilling to provide adequate care. This
expanding public role is reflected in the growing number
and variety of federal initiatives for children and
families. Although estimates vary, there are more than
260 programs administered by 20 agencies of the federal
government that benefit children either directly or
through professional service providers, parents, and
other adults (U.S. Department of Health, Education, and
Welfare, 1979; Family Impact Seminar, 1978; Rose, 1976).
These programs include a broad range of activities: tax
benefits and income supplements for families with dependent children; health, education, and specialized services
for needy children; regulations governing the delivery of
aid and services; personnel training, technical assistance, and institutional support for agencies serving
children; and a wide variety of research on the problems
facing children and families.

Because federal efforts to support children and their
families are extensive and varied, it is difficult to
identify any overarching goals or purposes. Programs
have been enacted piecemeal over an extended period of
time with little apparent attention to their collective
impact or their interrelationship. As Gilbert Steiner
has noted, "Public involvement in [this] field is a
federal agency-by-federal agency, congressional
committee-by-congressional committee, state-by-state or
city-by-city assortment of unrelated decisions that are

3

as likely to be contradictory as complementary" (Steiner, 1976:vii).

Critics frequently draw attention to significant problems of efficiency and coordination among existing programs. Yet, even if greater efficiency and coordination could be achieved, advocates for children would still contend that the level of government effort is inadequate. In promoting their own interests and positions they would continue to propose increased public expenditures for a wide range of activities, such as preventive health care, early childhood education, special services for the handicapped, aid for abused and neglected children, foster care, day care, income supplements for families, and more jobs for parents.

Advocates for children are not alone in seeking larger allocations. In recent years the competition for federal resources has become more intense, and, by all indications, the trend will continue. Human services experts predict that in the next decade the demands on the federal budget will be greatest for income maintenance, health benefits, and other services for the aging population (Lynn, 1978:26). In the face of this competition, how can programs and resources directed toward the welfare of American children and their families be improved? How will the necessary trade-offs among various proposals be made? How can the proposals that are most needed, most effective, or most politically feasible be identified and pursued?

There are no easy answers to these questions. Clearly, however, better services and benefits for children or increased efficiency and coordination among existing programs are unlikely without greater systematic knowledge of the process by which public resources are allocated. Despite the best efforts of concerned individuals and groups both within and outside government, a more effective public policy toward children will be difficult to produce if we lack understanding of how and why decisions concerning programs and budgets are made and how these decisions can be directed to meet the needs of children.

Existing studies of policies affecting children and families provide little insight. Several descriptive accounts of federal policies and programs have been undertaken recently (U.S. Department of Health, Education, and Welfare, 1979; Snapper et al., 1975; White House Conference on Children, 1970; Lash and Sigal, 1975; Wakefield and Wakefield, 1978, 1979). Such comprehensive descriptions of programs, agencies, congressional committees, statutes, budgets, research agendas, and court decisions attempt to uncover the significant participants and the forums, the channels of communication, and the influence involved in identifying and resolving issues related to children. Other studies have presented typologies of federal programs, distinguishing the ways in which they benefit children (Family Impact Seminar, 1978; Rose, 1976). Still others have evaluated specific substantive policy proposals (Bane, 1977; Steiner, 1976; Keniston and the Carnegie Council on Children, 1977; deLone, 1979). These studies are sometimes valuable for their accuracy and rich detail in explaining particular outcomes, yet they are limited in the understanding they provide concerning the conditions and constraints that will influence the directions of policy in the future. To obtain this type of knowledge, policy makers and advocates alike require an understanding of the process of policy formation that goes beyond what is currently available in the literature on policy for children.

OBJECTIVES OF THE STUDY

The Panel for Study of the Policy Formation Process undertook its work in an effort to create a better understanding of federal decision making affecting children and their families as a basis for more effective action by key participants in that process. The study had three major objectives.

First, the panel sought to gain some understanding of how federal policy for children is made. We examined what we called "concrete expressions of the formation of policy": programs, legislation, budgets, regulations, and court decisions. We identified the principal governmental and nongovernmental actors in the policy-making process and explored how these individuals and organizations influence policy outcomes. We uncovered some of the significant forces that interact to shape program content, regulation, and budget size. Moreover, we examined how these interactions vary in different kinds of government actions: direct service programs, regulatory promulgations, and tax provisions.

Second, the panel attempted to identify some of the conditions and constraints that characterize federal policy making affecting children and their families. By tracing selected policy developments through their political and socioeconomic environments, we discovered a

variety of factors that are likely to influence trends
and future directions.

Third, we tried to understand how the participants in
the formation of federal policy for children influence
the decision-making process. Through an examination of
the dynamics of policy formation in selected areas, we
made several conjectures concerning how and when various
participants can influence federal policy. Our purpose
was not to map strategies for achieving more or larger
policies and programs.

These objectives reflect the needs of our intended
audience. First and foremost, we hope to inform the
research community and to stimulate a new direction for
future study. In addition, we hope to provide useful
guidance to policy makers both inside and outside
government who participate in federal decision making
affecting children.

APPROACH OF THE STUDY

At the outset of the study we reviewed much of the literature on policy determination in order to examine existing
theories of policy formation and assess their potential
as analytic frameworks. We then developed three case
studies of federal policy developments as the body of
evidence for our analysis. Finally, we analyzed the data
from the case studies and drew conclusions concerning the
nature of federal policy making affecting children and
families and effective participation in that process.

The Policy Determination Literature

There is disagreement among experts over the precise
definition of policy. Greenberg points to the great
variety of boundaries (or lack thereof) suggested for the
concept of policy, including all government action, a
program of goals, general rules to cover future behavior,
the consequences of action and inaction, important government decisions, a selected line of action, and a declaration of intent (Greenberg et al., 1977). Because of its
inherent complexity, public policy is more difficult to
study systematically than most other phenomena investi-
gated empirically by social scientists. The policy
process takes place over time and therefore cannot be
explained as a simple unit or event. It generally

involves a large number of decision points--for example, a Senate vote, a presidential veto, and an appellate court decision. Although each of these "outputs" contributes to policy formation and might be predicted by existing theories, they are partial measures. In our review of existing literature, we have not encountered any model that integrates such events and distinguishes their relative significance.

A second characteristic of policy making, which renders it less susceptible to systematic analysis by traditional quantitative techniques, is that it inevitably involves the presence of a large, heterogeneous group of participants. The power to influence public policies affecting the well-being of children, or any other group, is shared by individuals and organizations at each level of government as well as in the private sector. The interests, perceptions, and values of those participants differ, as do the formal and informal roles they play in the decision-making process. The concerns and constituencies of the member of Congress, the departmental secretary, the agency director, the program administrator, the research manager, the project officer, the practitioner, and the parent often conflict in important respects. Policy making is a process of resolving conflicts of interest; the policy analyst must assign weights to the involvement of various participants. Such judgments are partially subjective, depending to some extent on the preconceptions of the policy analyst and to some extent on the perceptions of the sources consulted. The major difficulty involved is to assign significance to those perceptions.

A third relevant characteristic of policy making is the complexity of each of the events that contribute to policy formation. Just as the larger policy process is complex, occurring over time, involving a number of decision points and many different actors, each individual policy event--for example, a legislative vote, a court decision, or the appointment of a subcommittee chair--shares these characteristics on a smaller scale. Even an apparently simple government policy is likely to be the result of a complex chain of causes and relationships and to have many interrelated consequences. Such complexity is difficult to deal with systemically in the context of existing theories of policy formation.

Finally, policy formation is not susceptible to description by simple additive models. Policies are shaped by a variety of conditions, events, and actors

over a period of time. It is a dynamic process. Forces
interact in complex ways that are hard to disentangle.
The effect of a single government action on society
cannot be understood in isolation from others. The panel
believes that the dearth of cumulative understanding in
this area has not resulted from a lack of interest on the
part of policy makers or researchers; it reflects instead
the fact that there is no consensus on what is scientifically knowable about policy making or on how to acquire
useful knowledge. The crucial epistemological issues are
reliability and generalizability: On what scientific
basis can observations, information, and other data on
policy formation be integrated into a body of knowledge
on which social scientists agree? If such agreement were
reached, would it center on historically specific knowledge or that obtained from analysis according to a set
of general laws of policy formation? These two issues
are far from resolved.

The Case Study Approach

To collect, integrate, and interpret information, the
panel conducted case studies of federal policy making
affecting children and families. This method was
selected after a systematic review of its advantages,
disadvantages, traditions, achievements, and limitations
in public policy study. With the experience of other
investigators in mind, we adopted the case study method
because it seemed to provide the best opportunity to
explore both inductively and deductively the dynamics of
policy formation. We were nevertheless mindful of the
problems associated with this methodological approach.
   Properly conducted, a case study can integrate a vast
quantity of information from a variety of sources. It
can draw material from official documents, formal analytic
studies, interviews, journalistic accounts, and related
sources. In addition, it can explore a variety of interactions among relevant actors and institutions that make
policy. As a detailed, systematic presentation of how
particular policies evolved, a case study can provide a
context for testing and modifying existing models and
developing new hypotheses concerning the policy process.
Moreover, as Alex George suggests, the case study is a
valuable means of "discerning new general problems,
identifying possible theoretical solutions, and formulating potentially generalizable relations that were not

previously apparent" (George, 1979:17). The panel
believed that this method offered the most promising
means of learning more about the complexity of federal
policy making affecting children, assessing existing
theories, and, above all, developing an analytic framework
for understanding the policy formation process in a way
that will provide lessons concerning future participation
"in a systematic and differentiated way" (George, 1979:2).

We recognize, however, that this method, like all
others, has limitations and is vulnerable to criticism.
Time and resources precluded more than a few intensive
cases. Necessarily, our investigators had to be selective
in gathering information and weaving it into a coherent
narrative. In so doing they may have excluded important
data or have been unconsciously attracted to information
supporting a priori views. Significant factors may have
escaped documentaton, eluded interviews, or have had
their effects in ways that are not directly observable.
The investigators may have tended to identify with
participants to whom they had access or, for that matter,
with those having strong, articulate, or well-informed
views. In addition, since we adopted no existing model
of policy making, it was difficult to anticipate all of
the behavioral relationships of potential relevance to
policy determination. Finally, there is the issue of
generalizability, of how indicative the cases are of the
past or, a fortiori, of the future. Despite these limitations, we believed that the case study method offered the
most useful, methodologically sound vehicle for conducting
a study of federal policy making affecting children and
families.

Once the case study method was chosen, we turned to the
questions of content and subject. Because we wanted an
inclusive account of the policy formation process, time
and resources limited us to three cases. In light of the
difficulties of defining policy in a conceptually coherent
way, we chose instead to concentrate on the concrete mani-
festations of federal policy: programs, regulations,
budgets, and legislative revisions. Thus, our case
studies of policy formation became case studies of the
initiation and development of legal provisions, programs,
and regulations. The inquiry was guided by three
questions: Why has federal policy toward children in
these areas evolved historically as it has? What are the
conditions and constraints that shape the context of
future policy in these areas? How was federal policy
making influenced by concerned actors in the process?

We selected three case studies from an array of federal activities affecting children and families by applying several criteria. We agreed that the cases should represent activities carried out in different bureaucratic locations. We considered other cabinet-level departments in addition to the U.S. Department of Health, Education, and Welfare. We also agreed that the cases should include types of federal activities in addition to grant-in-aid programs, such as regulatory initiatives and uses of the income tax code. Furthermore, we did not want the case studies to be limited to programs or other legislative initiatives that were "successful" as measured by (1) the lack of opposition they encountered in the legislative process or (2) a rapid or steady rate of growth in program participation and budgetary appropriation. Hence we looked for initiatives that encountered opposition or even failed to be enacted.

The final choices rested on the judgment of panel members that each case should examine a different type of federal action: a categorical grant program, a regulation, and a tax measure. We selected three activities that appeared to offer interesting and varied examples of the federal policy formation process: the Special Supplemental Food Program for Women, Infants, and Children in the U.S. Department of Agriculture; the Federal Interagency Day Care Requirements in the U.S. Department of Health, Education, and Welfare (now the U.S. Department of Health and Human Services); and the Child Care Tax Deduction/Credit of the U.S. Department of the Treasury. Each case involves a different set of congressional and executive branch policy makers and nongovernmental interests and advocates. Presented in Part 2 of this volume, these case studies are a major product of our efforts.

Because they represent different types of federal actions on behalf of children, different goals, and different sets of actors and institutions inside and outside government, the three case studies offer a basis for comparison. Taken together they suggest many of the circumstances and events that have shaped the current context of policy for children. Since the initiation and implementation of the three policies cover roughly the same period of time, they were all subject to the same general social, economic, and political conditions. Moreover, the period of time over which each policy was examined was sufficient to allow extensive observation of the roles and influences of various actors, the resolution of conflicts in debate surrounding the policy initiatives, and the patterns of success or failure following the implementation of the program or regulations.

The primary goal of the case studies was to discover what occurred in the formation of each policy and why it occurred in the particular way it did. The cases focused on certain observable actions of the federal government: the enactment of statutes, the adoption of agency budgets, the promulgation of regulations and guidelines, the establishment of administrative units, the interpretation of the law by the courts, and the results of evaluation research. These actions constitute federal policy toward children in the sense that they are the observable and identifiable phenomena providing form to policy initiatives and influencing the behavior of the policy makers who support or oppose them.

To impose coherence and rigor in the preparation of the cases, we established three major criteria. First, each case is explicated historically, both to explore the context of policy development and to test the widespread hypothesis that policy making is incremental. Second, each case focused on the policy making process. Rather than ask what should have been done, we asked what was done, why it was done in that way, and how it affected what was done subsequently. Our emphasis was on understanding the policy formation process and not on judging it. Although we were concerned with all assessments of policies and programs related to the three case studies, we ourselves did not attempt to evaluate their effects on children and their families. Rather we examined the effects of existing program evaluations on the policy formation process. Third, we assumed that the relative power of actors influenced the achievement of their goals and that such power was exercised within social, economic, political, and ideological structures.

Each case study identified relevant actors and institutions, emphasized them according to their observed prominence, and explained their perceptions insofar as they were relevant to the policy process. If the history of an event was in dispute, the interpretation carrying the greatest weight of factual evidence was incorporated into the case. The emphasis accorded a decision affecting a policy varied with the controversy and the significance of the particular act to the policy process as a whole.

A fundamental issue was the thoroughness, validity, reliability, and bias in estimation of the body of evidence itself. Each case study is a report based on the verbal accounts (comprised of written documentation and interviews) relating to the policy but not to behavioral observation, ratings, or psychophysiological measures. A great deal of effort was devoted to checking for potential reporting errors or omissions and distinguishing between matters of fact and matters of interpretation. In several instances, members of the panel were actual participants in the decision-making processes described, and their direct observations contributed to our sense of the validity of the cases. In addition, cross-checking of methods (documents _versus_ statements, formal _versus_ informal documents and statements) and perspectives (using experts and policy participants outside the panel) went on continuously throughout the study.

The Analysis of the Case Studies

We were impressed by the complexity of the interactions within each case study. We attempted to disaggregate these interactions into their components and to understand the role of each in federal policy formation. These components can be grouped into six general categories: contextual factors, principles and ideas, actors and institutions, constituency pressure, media presentations, and research studies. This disaggregation, although useful in explaining retrospectively the roles of these components, offered little insight into their interactions in the formation of federal policies or their potential in future policy making.

The panel sought an analytic construct to relate these components and to provide general lessons concerning their interactions. Accordingly, we adopted an analytic metaphor with two qualities absent in other theoretical models we reviewed: (1) an enticing resonance in both the case studies and the panel's own experiences and (2) the potential for yielding some useful advice about federal policy making for children.

According to the metaphor, policy making can be visualized as occurring at three levels: high, middle, and low. At each level, differences in decision making can be noted along three key dimensions: the nature of the policy issues in question, the actors involved, and the type of government actions that result. Policy making at the high level can be said to involve the definition of major social problems, the formulation of solutions, and the resolution of conflicting social values--for example,

the legality of abortion or the federal regulation of
energy consumption. The main participants are policy
makers at the highest level of government: the President,
the congressional leadership, and the Supreme Court.
Policy making at the middle level involves decision
making affecting the allocation of authority and
resources—for example, the establishment of a new
compensatory education program or the authorization of
funds for a new program of research. Decisions made at
this level represent the means to achieve the ends
established at the high level. The key participants are
presidential appointees, members of Congress, or desig-
nates of either. At the low level, policy making involves
the technical design of means chosen at the middle level—
for example, the writing of regulations or congressional
legislation. The primary participants are the staffs of
the high- and middle-level actors.

The high, middle, and low classification scheme is not
meant to be pejorative. The stakes at any level can be
substantial. A high-level decision maker can become
involved in the low arenas and, conversely, under certain
circumstances, a low-level actor can participate in
high-level policy making. The classification refers
principally to the level of decision making necessary to
resolve the contested issues. Although the characteristics of decision making at each level are distinguishable, a complex policy issue could be contested in several
arenas simultaneously; the high level would not necessarily be the critical one for resolution. Similarly, as
events progress in the policy-making process, the level
of decision making can change, thus altering the nature
of the policy issues in question, introducing new participants, and creating new possibilities for government
action.

In Chapter 4 we detail the many nuances and caveats
concerning this analytic framework. For now the reader
should regard the metaphor as a tool we found useful in
studying the policy-making process. We stress that it
has numerous intellectual antecedents elsewhere in the
literature and that it still requires further examination
and verification by others in different contexts.

Once the framework was developed by the panel, its
usefulness was tested by staff efforts to apply it to the
cases. The original classification was found only
partially applicable and was modified. The method was
consensual, subjective, and interactive. No doubt this
review process will continue and will include individuals
outside the panel.

By applying the framework to the case studies and our experience, we discerned that the different characteristics of each level of policy making suggest particular strategic opportunities or levers that appear as keys to effective action. We attempted to ascertain the levers applicable at each level and to develop from them some advice to participants in the policy-making process who represent the interests of children and their families. In this way, we developed the substance of our conclusions and recommendations.

PLAN OF THE REPORT

The remaining chapters of this report present the findings and conclusions of our study. Chapter 2 is a summary account of the three case studies. Chapter 3 is an analysis of the components of the policy formation process revealed in the cases. Chapter 4 integrates our findings concerning the characteristics of policy formation at each level of the process and presents our general conclusions concerning the available levers to participants both inside and outside the federal government. Chapter 5 relates the framework and conclusions of Chapter 4 to federal policy making toward children and their families. It states our conclusions on how various actors in the policy-making process might alter their behavior to be more effective advocates for children and their families.

2 Three Cases of
Federal Policy Formation

In this chapter we present summaries of the three case
studies that comprise the evidentiary base for this
study: (1) the Special Supplemental Food Program for
Women, Infants, and Children; (2) the Federal Interagency
Day Care Requirements; and (3) the Child Care Tax
Deduction/Credit. Each summary distills significant
information from the case and organizes it into an
interpretive narrative. All detailed documentation is in
the case studies themselves, which are presented in Part
2 of this volume. Here we provide a descriptive
presentation of the data, highlighting the significant
factors contributing to these selected federal policy
developments.

THE SPECIAL SUPPLEMENTAL FOOD PROGRAM FOR
WOMEN, INFANTS, AND CHILDREN

Significant federal food assistance to children began in
the mid-1930s when Congress passed the Agricultural
Adjustment Act, giving the U.S. Department of Agriculture
(USDA) millions of dollars in surplus farm products. In
conjunction with the Work Projects Administration, the
USDA channeled some of this surplus food to schools and
relief programs. With the wartime disruption of international markets in 1939, the USDA expanded domestic
distribution outlets, particularly the School Lunch
Program. When America entered the war, the food surplus
was absorbed by allied and domestic needs. Nevertheless,
the USDA continued the lunch program as a wartime
exigency. In 1945 the lunch program drew political
support not only from farm interests but also from local
school districts, PTAs, state school administrators, and

15

health officials.   In 1947, Congress made the School
Lunch Program permanent.

Until the Great Society programs of the 1960s, Congress
enacted only one other food assistance initiative for
children: the Special Milk Program.   In 1965 a glut of
milk increased federal surplus holdings to unmanageable
levels.   With the support of the USDA and dairy interests,
Congress created a milk distribution program for children
in schools, summer camps, and other institutions to ease
the government's surplus holdings.   The Special Milk
Program was significant for two reasons.   First, the
programs represented the only postwar effort to provide
food assistance to children outside school.   Second, every
administration since Eisenhower had tried unsuccessfully
to curb the program on the grounds of an improved dairy
situation or the failure of the program to target aid to
needy children.

In 1966, Congress passed the Child Nutrition Act,
shifting food assistance resources to children in poor
areas, whose nutritional needs were presumably greater.
The act was part of a general movement in the mid-1960s
away from agriculturally determined food assistance
programs and toward programs specifically directed to
disadvantaged groups.   This movement reflected a growing
coalition of school interests and antipoverty and antihunger groups.   There was, however, no irreconcilable
antagonism between members of Congress representing either
farm or antihunger groups; indeed, several came to
represent both.

Among congressional supporters the idea of targeting
food assistance to poor, malnourished children grew in
the 1967-1968 period with repeated media exposés on hunger
in the United States.   Together with the civil rights
movement's new attention to economic equality and the
increasing political tensions within the Democratic party
over the war in Vietnam, these exposés induced expansion
of all federal food assistance.   Among the Johnson
administration's responses to these pressures was the
Supplemental Food Program.   Based in part on medical
research on the effects of malnourishment on fetal and
infant development and in part on the enormous political
appeal of feeding hungry babies and pregnant women, the
Supplemental Food Program supplied special food packages
to provide additional nutrition to this group.   Throughout
its life the program remained small--$10 to $12 million--
and was soon engulfed in the Nixon administration's
decision to replace all in-kind food assistance with

stamps. This decision was based on the administration's efforts to reduce delivery costs and prepare the food assistance programs for possible incorporation into an overall welfare reform: the Family Assistance Plan. To assess the viability of a changeover of the Supplemental Food Program into a voucher program, the USDA initiated in 1970 a pilot voucher program and commissioned Dr. David Call of Cornell University to evaluate it. Call found that targeting particular foods to family members, in this instance infants and pregnant women, did not significantly increase their nutritional intake because the additional food was shared by all family members. Presented with this evidence of failure and given the overall policy thrust toward food stamps, the USDA began phasing out the Supplemental Food Program in 1971-1972. Local welfare clinics and other advocates, however, protested the department's plans. Through the intercession of several members of Congress, the USDA halted its suspension of local programs in particular states, but the program as a whole remained in a political limbo.

In 1972 a staff member of the Senate Agriculture Committee, James Thornton, became aware of two local food and medical assistance projects at St. Jude's Hospital in Memphis and at Johns Hopkins University. Both projects provided specific nutritional aid and medical care to infants and pregnant women in poor areas. The projects produced significant reductions in anemia among the participants. Working with Rodney Leonard, president of the Community Nutrition Institute, Thornton drafted legislation creating a $20-million federal program in the mold of the Johns Hopkins-St. Jude projects. Senator Hubert Humphrey agreed to introduce it in the Senate. After a defeat in committee and some debate on the floor, the Senate passed the program as an amendment to the Child Nutrition Act. Despite USDA opposition, the House concurred. President Nixon signed the bill, and the Special Supplemental Food Program for Women, Infants, and Children (WIC) became law in December 1972.

Due to Call's findings on the ineffectiveness of targeting food to families, the USDA had initially opposed passage of the program. A Senate amendment, included at the department's behest, that mandated a complete evaluation of the program led officials to believe that WIC would be found ineffective--USDA thus acquiesced. The implementation of WIC, however, posed problems for the department. Unlike the Supplemental

Food Program, WIC had a medical requirement for participation and evaluation. The medical and health content of the program caused the USDA to try to transfer it to the U.S. Department of Health, Education, and Welfare (HEW). Failing in that attempt, the USDA continued in its indecision over the program's design and evaluation.

Nutrition advocacy groups became convinced that the USDA was deliberately delaying implementation in order to scuttle the program. They began pressuring the department through Congress. Redbook magazine ran an article describing the St. Jude's project and urging readers to write in protest over the USDA's delay in implementing WIC. Finally, in spring 1973 the Food Research and Action Coalition (FRAC), a public interest law firm, brought suit in federal district court against the USDA to compel it to spend the funds authorized for WIC.

A combination of circumstances, most of which were planned, allowed this and subsequent litigation to transform WIC from a $20-million pilot into a $0.5-billion program. Since they anticipated litigation when drafting the legislation, Thornton and Leonard had used entitlement language that legally mandated the expenditure of funds. In addition, they had stipulated that WIC draw its funds from Section 32 tariff funds—thus removing the program from normal appropriations channels in Congress. Armed with these provisions, the FRAC successfully obtained a court decision ordering the USDA to spend all the funds authorized for WIC in fiscal 1973. Since the fiscal year had nearly ended, the USDA was compelled to spend $20 million in 3 months. This order effectively annualized WIC's participation rate at $80 million.

The law and the litigation combined to produce a mechanism by which every delay, intentional or otherwise, or impoundment of WIC funds served only to compress the funds to be spent into a shorter time span and across a larger number of participants. When WIC's two-year, $40-million authorization expired in 1974, Congress faced a decision concerning a program whose annualized expenditures exceeded $100 million. Given a choice between quintupling WIC's funding or dropping thousands of pregnant women, infants, and young children from the program, Congress quintupled it. The following year, over a presidential veto, it passed a child nutrition bill that exceeded administration requests by $1 billion. Included was a $250-million authorization for WIC. Proponents justified this expansion on the grounds of participation rates and evidence of WIC's success drawn from committee testimony and surveys.

Despite the USDA's delaying of WIC's implementation, the Office of Management and Budget (OMB) impounded a quarter of WIC's 1976 funds by spreading the authorization over an additional fiscal quarter. The FRAC returned to court and obtained an order for the USDA to spend all authorized funds. The effect was to expand WIC to an annualized level of $440 million by the close of fiscal 1978.

Within a month of this final court decision the evaluation of WIC, which was to have determined its fate as a $20-million pilot program, was finally completed. The long-awaited evaluation was conducted by Dr. Joseph Endozien of the University of North Carolina. Endozien found that WIC infants evidenced increases in weight, height, head circumference, and mean hemoglobin concentration and that anemia decreased. Despite the evaluation's conclusion that the program was an unmitigated success, the General Accounting Office (GAO) and several outside reviewers found it fraught with methodological and conceptual problems. GAO went so far as to question whether an evaluation of the type WIC required was even possible.

Adding to the criticisms of Endozien's findings was a study of WIC's delivery system by the Urban Institute, which replicated Call's earlier evaluation with similar results concerning food sharing within the family. The USDA, however, could use neither of these studies to retard WIC's expansion. Committed to the administration's block-grant position in Congress, the USDA could not bargain for specific program reductions. The result was WIC's continued expansion and advocates' unchallenged use of the studies.

Where GAO saw bad science, WIC's advocates saw only positive findings. What the Urban Institute regarded as poor targeting, the advocates saw only as increases in clinic visits and a need for further participant education to prevent food sharing. A later evaluation of WIC by the Center for Disease Control reinforced, albeit with severe qualifications, Endozien's findings. Armed with their interpretations of these studies, advocates claimed that WIC was a demonstrable success; Congress agreed wholeheartedly.

The inauguration of the Carter administration meant new directors for the USDA's food assistance program. Drawn from the ranks of advocacy groups, these people supported WIC's expansion and made it a centerpiece of the department's nutrition policy. WIC easily rebuffed a

muckraking attack on its efficacy that appeared in the
New Republic and a futile attempt by HEW to have it
transferred into the Bureau of Community Health Services.
There was no significant support either for denigrating
WIC or for removing it from the USDA once these advocates
controlled its administration. Although in positions of
authority at the USDA, however, they still had to deal
with the OMB.

The USDA's initial proposal for the expansion of WIC
called for a $600-million authorization in fiscal 1979.
OMB scaled it back to $535.5 million and deleted the
entitlement language from the bill. In the Senate,
supporters introduced a bill similar to the administration's proposal but retained the entitlement language and
set authorization levels of $550, $800, $900, and $950
million, respectively, for fiscal years 1979 through 1981.
Both the OMB and the congressional budget committees
resisted the entitlement language at these authorization
levels. Proponents, however, managed to convince the
committees to make an exception for WIC, due to its
history of impoundments and litigation. OMB still opposed
the bill and recommended a presidential veto. Several
lengthy pleas from the USDA and a congressional promise
to reduce WIC's fiscal 1980 authorization to $750 million
induced President Carter to sign the measure in November
1978. The efforts of earlier administrations to restrain
WIC's growth created a context in which congressional
proponents and advocates could, even years later, expand
the program at a rate unprecedented for social programs
in the late 1970s.

THE FEDERAL INTERAGENCY DAY CARE REQUIREMENTS

Historically, federal policy toward out-of-home, nonparental child care has evolved in three separate but
related traditions: basic protection for a child without
parental care; care for a child to enable the (generally
female) parent to seek employment; and care for a child
to enhance physical, emotional, and cognitive development.
In a sense the first tradition underlies the others as
the basic responsibility of government at all levels
toward children outside their families. The second
tradition closely followed welfare reform measures that
stressed "workfare" and consequently entailed some
provision for child care while the parent or parents
sought employment. Salient examples of these measures

include the Welfare Reform Act of 1962, the Work
Incentives Program of 1967, and the Family Assistance
Plan of 1969. The third tradition, comprehensive child
development, emerged from research on early childhood
development and related demonstration projects that
indicated the salutary effects of specific intervention
upon a child's cognitive growth. This tradition
culminated in the Head Start Program of 1964. Though
divergent in their approaches, the latter two traditions
had in common the objective of breaking the poverty-
welfare "cycle."

At the close of 1967, three years of the most sustained
social welfare initiatives since the New Deal came to an
end. Urban race riots, swollen federal budgets, increasing inflation, unprecedented increases in welfare rolls,
and, as a backdrop, a seemingly interminable war in Southeast Asia had altered the face of politics in the 1960s.
In response to what was a severe crisis in the nation's
welfare system, Congress enacted the Work Incentives
Program (WIN). WIN simplified extant work incentives for
recipients: get a job or lose all benefits. Since
mothers with preschool children were included in this
program, some provisions for child care became integral
to its implementation. Fearing that WIN might entail
child care arrangements without regard for the child's
physical or cognitive development, liberal proponents in
Congress amended the WIN legislation to mandate a set of
interagency regulations for all federally funded day
care. They assigned this task to the Children's Bureau
in HEW, a bastion of the child protection tradition.

HEW Secretary Wilbur Cohen chose Head Start director
Jule Sugarman to chair the interagency panel that would
author the regulations. Sugarman had recently become the
associate director of the Children's Bureau as part of
Cohen's strategy to keep Head Start out of the U.S. Office
of Education. Because of both his past and present positions, Sugarman had a large stake in the compensatory
education approach to day care, which stressed quality
over cost. He also had to appease panel members from
agencies involved primarily with the employment aspect of
WIN, and the quality of day care concerned this latter
group chiefly insofar as it threatened to increase program
costs. Sugarman's solution to this deep-seated division
among panel members was to draft regulations containing
high standards amenable to the developmentalist position,
but sufficiently ambiguous in their specific provisions
and enforceability to allow agencies with different

priorities to acquiesce in their promulgation. Thus, there was little debate over the appropriateness or efficacy of the requirements.

Although the 1968 day care requirements set standards for many areas—health care, nutrition, physical settings in facilities, education levels for center employees, and parent participation—the focus of the requirements was child-staff ratio for preschoolers between 3 and 5 years old. Sugarman's panel chose staff ratios near the level of those of the Head Start program. Since child care is a labor-intensive undertaking, the more staff members required for a given number of children, the greater the cost. To mitigate the impact of these low ratios, Sugarman allowed all adult employees and volunteers in a center to count as care givers, and, like the other requirements, the enforcement remained at the discretion of the administering agency. It was the staff ratio more than any other requirement that became the touchstone of future controversies over the Federal Interagency Day Care Requirements. Soon after promulgation of the requirements, the Children's Bureau was stripped of its authority over HEW's day care programs (except Head Start) and the new administering agency, the Social and Rehabilitation Service (SRS), quietly reassured their clients in the states that the regulations would not be enforced.

The 1968 requirements lay dormant as a political and regulatory issue until the Nixon administration proposed its innovative welfare reform measure, the Family Assistance Plan (FAP). An integral element of FAP was its massive day care program. Within HEW a tentative decision was made to lodge the day care program in the Office of Child Development (OCD), the successor to the Children's Bureau. OCD's director, psychologist Edward Zigler, received authorization from HEW Secretary Elliot Richardson to revise the requirements in preparation for the FAP day care program. Zigler recognized the essentially symbolic character of the requirements and sought to draft a new set with enforceable, but tempered, prescriptions for federally funded facilities. He held conferences of advocates, care givers, and scientists to aid in the drafting process. By the end of 1971, Zigler had completed a substantially revised set of requirements.

During this period, congressional supporters of an enlarged child care program, apart from the FAP, introduced a bill to this effect. Sponsored principally by Senator Walter Mondale and Representative John Brademus,

the Comprehensive Child Care Act was the apotheosis of
the developmentalist approach to care programs. It would
provide child care services not only to the poor but also
to middle-income groups. Although the child care program
received the reluctant approbation of HEW, conservative
criticism and the attachment of the program to a bill
reauthorizing the Office of Economic Opportunity (OEO),
containing many features repugnant to the administration,
led to OMB and White House opposition. President Nixon
vetoed the measure in December 1971.

The veto transformed the political ambience surrounding
the Nixon administration: it came to be perceived as
antichild. Within HEW, Richardson and Zigler scrambled
to shore up their credibility among advocates on the
issues of federally funded child care. Their one
remaining card was the revised federal requirements,
which they believed might recoup their political losses
due to the veto. Advocates, however, were not placated
by any administration action. In addition, OMB produced
its own scathing attack on Zigler's revised requirements,
criticizing them as too costly and as an unwarranted
federal intervention. Promulgating Zigler's revision
promised no political gain for the administration; given
the internal dissension, it was simpler to bury the
revision.

The Federal Interagency Day Care Requirements remained
dormant until 1974 when a crisis over social service
spending led to the Title XX amendment to the Social
Security Act. Expansion of social service spending had
led HEW to propose strict regulations governing federal
matching funds to the states. Congressional opponents
blocked enforcement of HEW's regulations and instead
imposed a $2.5-billion ceiling on the spending. The
administration believed the ceiling was too generous and
pressed for the regulations. The consequent stalemate
led HEW's assistant secretary for planning and evaluation
(ASPE) to negotiate a compromise among the interests on
both sides of the issue. The result was Title XX, which
incorporated some facets of the administration's new
federalism, while maintaining some degree of federal
control over state allocations of funds.

As part of the price for their acceptance of Title XX,
the AFL-CIO, at the urging of the Child Welfare League,
demanded that the legislation mandate enforcement of the
1968 Federal Interagency Day Care Requirements. The ASPE
acquiesced and wrote such a mandate into the bill. The
specified means of enforcement was complete suspension of

day care funds to any state with centers out of compliance. In accord with its bargain, HEW promulgated a slightly revised set of requirements to take effect in October 1975.

The number of day care centers out of compliance with the requirements, particularly the staff ratios, was such that any serious attempt at enforcement would have resulted in a suspension of several hundred million dollars in federal aid to the states. Across the country, state agencies and centers lodged protests with Congress and HEW. Under this pressure the House quickly passed a bill suspending the staffing requirements for six months. The measure went to the Senate Finance Committee. Its chair, Russell Long, saw in the enforcement an opportunity to enlist liberal support for his perennial project: putting welfare recipients to work. Long and Walter Mondale, a leading Senate proponent of the day care requirements, struck a bargain. In exchange for Long's support of an additional $300 million in Title XX day care funds to ease state compliance with the staffing ratios, Mondale agreed to an amendment mandating the employment of welfare recipients in the additional staff slots. The requirements would then be enforced, the states pacified, and the welfare burden lightened. Congress passed the Long-Mondale bill in January 1976.

The Ford administration found the proposed bill antithetical to its policies. The administration opposed the increased funding, the earmarking for day care, the welfare hiring provision, and the enforcement of the requirements. At the urging of OMB and HEW, the President vetoed it. The Senate sustained the veto by a slim margin. Despite HEW's reservations, OMB conceived of the veto as an opportunity to wring some concessions from Congress on Title XX. OMB threatened to proceed with enforcement of the day care requirements unless Congress dropped the additional day care funding and revised parts of Title XX. As long as the administration could sustain a veto of legislation to provide additional funding, OMB believed that the pressure from the states could induce congressional compliance.

OMB's strategy failed almost as soon as it was implemented. In Congress, Mondale and his opponents struck a compromise over the vetoed bill. Their revised measure suspended enforcement of staff ratios for a year and reduced the additional $300 million for Title XX to $240 million; otherwise the bill remained substantially

similar to the earlier vetoed measure. The compromise
pleased the states; they would receive more money without
enforcement of the expensive staff ratios. More important, it satisfied enough senators to undermine Ford's veto
threat. Congress easily passed the compromise measure,
and the President had little alternative but to sign it.

Congress had justified suspension of the requirements
with a provision in the original Title XX legislation
requiring that HEW prepare a report on the appropriateness
of federal day care regulation. Until the report's
completion, any final judgment on the Federal Interagency
Day Care Requirements could be postponed. In HEW the
task of drafting the appropriateness report fell to the
ASPE. The drafting group within ASPE received little
guidance from Congress or from HEW. Progress was very
slow, and the report was still unfinished when the Carter
administration took office.

Under Joseph Califano's leadership the new administration at HEW decided to present a report that would inform
the public debate over the requirements but avoid any
specific policy determinations. Califano was simply not
prepared to commit HEW at the time the appropriateness
report was due. Under these constraints the final
document proved, politically at least, to be less than an
outstanding product. Advocacy groups and members of
Congress subjected it to harsh criticisms. The advocacy
groups anticipated that the report would present a
definite policy direction--but it gave none. Whatever
else it might have accomplished, the report allowed
Congress and HEW to procrastinate on enforcement of the
requirements. After its release the department returned
to the problem of the requirements.

Generally, the administering agency, in this case the
Office of Human Development Services (OHDS) and specifically the Administration for Children, Youth, and Families
(ACYF), is responsible for writing the regulations governing its programs. Although OHDS was responsible for HEW's
day care programs, Califano stripped that office of the
duty and transferred it to a trusted deputy, HEW General
Counsel F. Peter Libassi. Libassi's skill with controversial HEW regulations had made him an asset to Califano,
and in October 1978 he assumed responsibility for the
revision process.

During the preparation of the appropriateness report
and the transfer of responsibility for the requirements,
a major study of center-based day care was completed. In
1974 the OCD had commissioned Abt Associates to conduct

an $8-million study of the effects of regulatable center
characteristics on children receiving care. Specifically,
Abt examined the effects of child-staff ratios, group
size, and care-giver qualifications on the social and
cognitive development of the children involved. Abt
produced a set of findings that demonstrated that group
size had a more significant effect on the child than did
staff ratios. Such findings had strong implications for
the revision of the requirements. As long as there had
been standards for day care centers, the tacit assumption
of advocates and social scientists had been that low
child-staff ratios were the key to high-quality care.
Conversely, the chief argument against low ratios had
been their high costs. Abt now intervened with scientific
findings that lifted policy makers out of the dilemma.
Concentration on group size enabled HEW to subdue the
politically volatile issue of child-staff ratios and
their costs.

Decision makers in HEW found the Abt study relevant to
their revision of the requirements. Its findings spoke
directly to the key policy questions. Its completion
coincided with the timing of these crucial decisions.
Its results provided some comfort to all viewpoints:
deemphasis of the costly child-staff ratios, a significant
correlation between regulatable center characteristics
and children's performance, and an overall methodology
that, although not flawless, was at least palatable to
the research community at large. Above all, the Abt
study recommended staffing and group size requirements
with which the vast majority of centers were already in
compliance. Those centers not in compliance could comply
at relatively low cost. Finally, its recommendations
accorded in large measure with the direction that the
principal decision makers and interests sought to move.
Not surprisingly, HEW's preliminary revision of the
requirements incorporated to a great extent Abt's
recommendations.

The signing of the Federal Interagency Day Care
Requirements occurred in March 1980. By then Califano
had been replaced by Patricia Harris. The final regulations mandated child-staff ratios as stringent and, in
some instances, more stringent than those Abt had
recommended. The final version of the requirements was
in some respects more akin to the developmentalist
position and a rebuff to the proprietary centers.
Secretary Harris resisted a strong letter-writing
campaign mounted by the proprietary centers to implement

less-stringent regulations. Advocates of stricter
requirements convinced Harris that stiffer requirements
were better for the children. To avoid any undue
hardship for the day care centers, the requirements
provide for a two-year phase-in period. Presumably by
1982, the Federal Interagency Day Care Requirements will,
14 years after the first set was promulgated, be enforced
for the first time.

THE CHILD CARE TAX DEDUCTION/CREDIT

As early as 1939, taxpayers brought suit to contest the
Internal Revenue Service's disallowance of child care
expenses as an income tax deduction. After several
defeats in court, proponents of a child care deduction
marshalled their forces for the major codification and
revision of the tax laws in 1953. Proponents gave three
rationales for enacting a deduction for child care costs.
First, care costs, as necessary expenses to the employment
of parents, were deductible as business expenses. Second,
most working mothers were compelled by economic hardship
to seek work, and a tax deduction would serve a legitimate
relief function. Third, they argued, a tax incentive
would encourage mothers receiving public assistance to
work to support their families. Federal welfare outlays
would therefore decline. In their cause, proponents
enlisted several unions, whose female members would reap
some tax benefits, and some employer organizations, whose
largely female labor pool would receive a work incentive,
helping to ease labor shortages without raising salaries.
On the principle of tax equity in business deductions,
they also managed to garner the support of the American
Bar Association and the American Institute of Accountants.
Opposition to a child care deduction stemmed from two
sources: bias against labor force participation by
mothers of young children and its potential impact on the
tax structure. Simply stated, many members of Congress
did not want to create any incentive for mothers to
forsake primary care responsibility for their children
and seek employment. Though less concerned with this
ethos, the Treasury Department sought to avoid any
precedent in the tax code for expanding employee business
deductions. Moreover, the potential revenue loss of an
unrestricted deduction worried the department. One
solution to these concerns was the Eisenhower administration's proposal to allow only widows and widowers a

special deduction for work-related, child care expenses. The solution maintained the traditional parental roles in the nuclear family, precluded any precedent for an expanded definition of business expenses, and restrained potential revenue losses.

Proponents adjusted their rationale for a broader deduction to meet these objections. Seizing on the notion of economic necessity, which mitigated opposition to working mothers, they sought to demonstrate that most working mothers had taken jobs out of necessity; their husbands could not earn an adequate income to support their families. A few members of Congress argued for a deduction as a matter of equity for women, but their argument apparently lacked sufficient public support to be effective. Although married women with children were entering the labor force in unprecedented numbers in the early 1950s, the total number of working mothers in the labor force remained small. Only 2.25 million women with children under 18 worked--a scant 4 percent of the labor force. Indeed, proponents of a broad deduction lost in the House.

On the Senate side, they were more successful. Acceding to a $4,500 income limit and a $600 maximum for the deduction, proponents extracted a compromise provision from the Senate Finance Committee. The income limit reflected the rationale of economic necessity for the deduction; it was imposed only on dual-earner families claiming child care expenses. The limitation on the deductible amount assuaged the Treasury Department's concerns over revenue losses. Finally, the enactment of a special section in the tax code precluded use of the deduction as a precedent for future expansion of employee business deductions. The Senate's amendments were accepted by the conference committee, and the child care deduction became law in 1954.

Congressional and Treasury staff estimated that the deduction might reach 2.1 million households and result in $140 million in lost revenue--an average annual savings of $67 per household. The actual impact was limited to approximately 300,000 households and a revenue loss of $21 million. The average tax saving, however, was slightly higher, $70 per year. Obviously, only a small proportion of households with working mothers benefited from the deduction. Either most of those paying for child care were unable to claim it due to the restriction, or most working mothers were not using formal child care arrangements. Members of Congress appeared to have

assumed that the former was true and persisted over the
ensuing eight years in introducing legislation to liberalize the deduction. Their efforts, however, bore little
fruit. The only revision they managed to enact changed
the law to allow a deserted wife to take the deduction on
the same basis as a widow. Less than an innovation, this
revision merely redressed an oversight in the original
legislation.

Their fortunes changed when the newly elected Kennedy
administration brought with it a Keynesian approach to
fiscal policy, specifically a tax cut, and a renewed focus
on social problems. In his 1963 message to Congress on
tax revisions, Kennedy recommended liberalization of the
child and dependent care deductions. The administration
proposed to raise the income limit on dual-earner families
to $7,000 and the maximum deduction to $1,000 for three
or more children. The principal justification for these
changes was the rise in child care costs and median income
since 1954. In addition, the administration explained the
need for a larger deduction by citing the extant labor
shortages in professions filled predominantly by women:
nursing and teaching. Since 1953, little had changed in
the targeting or purpose of the child care deduction, but
by 1963 there were proponents in the executive branch as
well as the Congress.

There were, however, indications of a shift in women's
labor force participation. In December 1961, Kennedy
created the Presidential Commission on the Status of
Women. Though far from radical in its recommendations
concerning American women, it did suggest changing the
child care deduction along lines adopted in the administration's proposal. Other commission suggestions were
ambivalent on the larger question of working mothers and
dual-earner families. Members agreed that more child
care facilities were required because of the increasing
number of mothers in the work force, but they expressed
regret that economic necessity compelled women with young
children to seek employment. Thus, their recommendations
for the child care deduction emphasized aid to the needy.
Beyond this partial effort to understand the problems of
women, there were further portents of change. Most significant of these was the Equal Pay Act of 1963, which
prohibited employers from discriminating against women in
compensating them for doing work similar to men's.
Regardless of its efficacy, the act indicated that sexual
equality was coming to be a rationale for policy
initiatives.

In the House Ways and Means Committee, however, this rationale remained unpersuasive. Unwilling to risk offering an incentive to mothers for seeking work, the committee refused to accept any of the administration's proposals concerning dual-earner families. They made only one significant change: raising the deductible amount from $600 to $900 for single parents with two or more children. The House passed the committee's bill intact.

Wary of alienating the House Ways and Means Committee, Treasury demurred from lobbying in the Senate for a change in this relatively small section of the tax bill. Proponents of the original administration proposal were left to their own resources to change the House version. Senator Maurine Neuberger, a commission member, introduced a measure containing the administration's proposal. Neuberger argued that her measure acknowledged that the 24 million working women deserved more equitable treatment in the tax code. Although the Senate Finance Committee incorporated her amendment into their bill, they were persuaded more by the changes in child care costs and family incomes over the preceding decade than by Neuberger's plea for equality. The Senate version included a $7,000 income ceiling and a $1,000 limit on deductible child care expenses for dual-earner families. In conference the House pared it to $6,000 and $900, respectively. The measure became law in April 1963.

Although the revised deduction increased the average tax benefit per household to $83, the number of households claiming the benefit dropped from 272,000 in 1960 to 254,000 in 1966. Over the next four years the number of households claiming the deduction doubled, but the tax benefit dropped to $65 per household per year. Rising real incomes, inflation, and increases in minimum taxable income narrowed steadily those households eligible for the deduction.

In the 16 years since the deduction first became law, women had accelerated their entry into the labor force. By 1970, 32 million women worked and one third of these women had children under the age of 18. Between 1954 and 1970, the number of working women had nearly quadrupled and the number of working mothers had doubled. Although lobbying for a liberalized child care deduction by unions and professional organizations predominated by women persisted throughout the 1960s, it appears that the profound shift in the role of women finally eroded congressional opposition to liberalization. Ideological bias against working women in general and working mothers in particular was slowly crumbling under the weight of social change.

Among members of Congress, support for working women, even working mothers, became a politically attractive position in the light of organized lobbying efforts by feminist organizations and more diffuse constituent pressures. Media attention focused on the purported inequity in the tax code's severe constraints on the deduction of child care expenses. A successor group to the Commission on the Status of Women reflected the changing ethos in asserting a woman's right to choose to work at home or in the marketplace. The issue of the child care deduction was no longer framed as a question of maintaining some idealized nuclear family structure and became instead one of sexism in the tax code.

The declining social bias against working mothers undercut the principal justification for targeting the deduction on women compelled by economic necessity to work. Two other changes in federal policy further undermined this targeting. First, since 1964 the government had enacted several major categorical day care programs for low-income households. The tax subsidy to this group had been effectively supplanted by direct aid. Second, Congress had altered the tax structure itself to reduce or eliminate the tax liability of low-income households. The extant child care deduction was fast becoming an anachronism. Although members of Congress had since 1963 introduced many bills to change the deduction, not until 1971 did these social and political changes coalesce to effect any revision.

The revision issue came before Congress in the form of the Nixon administration's Family Assistance Plan (FAP). FAP stressed child care as a work incentive and liberalized the child care deduction by increasing the deductible amounts from $600 to $750 for one child, $900 to $1,125 for two children, and $900 to $1,500 for three or more children. It doubled the income ceiling to $12,000. After passing the House the measure went to Russell Long's Senate Finance Committee. Long separated the tax revision from the FAP legislation, and the committee reported out a substantially revised child care deduction. Renamed the Job Development Deduction, it increased eightfold the maximum deductible amount for one child, doubled the income ceiling, and included housekeeping services among the deductible expenses. Since a major purpose of the deduction was to promote the employment of low-income people in child care/housekeeping positions, the committee reduced the deductible amount for out-of-home child care.

On the Senate floor the committee bill encountered little opposition. Senator John Tunney proposed and the Senate accepted an amendment to convert the itemized deduction into an adjustment to income--i.e., an "above-line" business deduction. This amendment would allow all eligible taxpayers to take the deduction regardless of whether they itemized deductions on their tax returns. Tunney also offered successfully another amendment to raise the income ceiling to $18,000. When one senator objected to the amended bill on the grounds that it threatened the traditional family structure, Long--hardly a social radical--defended the changes. He asserted that maintaining disincentives against working women was no longer an acceptable social policy. The beliefs about women's proper place that had circumscribed the child care deduction for nearly two decades had apparently lost their influence in Congress.

When the Senate bill went to conference with the House, the Treasury Department intervened. Treasury objected to the domestic employment incentive and the new income ceiling. The increase in employment and the distribution of tax benefits to middle- and higher-income families did not justify the revenue loss. Above all, Treasury opposed the inclusion of child care costs among business expenses. The department feared the effects of an expanded definition of allowable business expenses on the structural integrity of the tax code. House conferees concurred; the final bill did not include the business expense provision. The other provisions of the Senate version, however, were signed by President Nixon in December 1971; in that same month, the Mondale-Brademus Comprehensive Child Care Act was vetoed.

The following year, Tunney again introduced and the Senate passed a bill to permit the child care costs to be deducted as business expenses. For the same reasons as before, the Treasury and the House Ways and Means Committee joined forces to delete the amendment in conference. In 1974 the Ways and Means Committee adopted most of a Treasury Department proposal to simplify the deduction. The amendment would abolish the distinction between in-home and out-of-home child care, increase the income ceiling to $30,000, and limit the deductible amount to $2,400 for one child and $4,800 for two or more children. As a result of a Rules Committee action, however, their revision was never considered on the floor of the Senate.

The fall of Wilbur Mills from his chairmanship of the committee and the House leadership's hope for a more liberal bill in the 94th Congress led to the Rules Committee's action.

In January 1975, during the worst recession since the 1930s, a new Congress took up a massive tax cut measure. The House passed the measure without making any changes in the existing child care deduction. On the Senate side, Tunney and Long allied themselves to revise the deduction. Their new version allowed taxpayers to deduct all child care expenses from their gross income as a business adjustment or to credit 50 percent of those expenses, up to $1,200, directly against their tax liability. The Senate accepted the amendment despite its estimated revenue loss of $1.7 billion. Potentially every dollar paid for work-related child care (and housekeeping) would be exempt from federal income taxes. With Treasury's strong backing, the House deleted in conference most of the Senate's amendment. They agreed only to raise the income ceiling on the present deduction to $35,000.

Despite this defeat the notion of a tax credit for child care expenses remained current. Proponents in the House and Senate believed that the credit was the solution to the problems associated both with the itemized and the business deductions. To claim the credit, taxpayers would not have to itemize deductions, thus eliminating the existing bias against households electing the standard deduction. And the Treasury would not have to acquiesce in a broader definition of business expenses. A credit would also simplify the current deduction--something the department favored. The House Ways and Means Committee approved a 20 percent credit on child care expenses up to $2,000 for one child and $4,000 for two or more. Committee approval was eased by the infusion of new members after Mills's departure and the presence of media representatives at mark-up sessions--a post-Watergate congressional "reform." Under these circumstances, opposition to a popular tax credit was not easy.

As passed by the House, the credit encountered Treasury opposition in the Senate. Without an income ceiling the department thought the revenue loss unjustified by the credit's large benefits to higher-income households. It shifted ground, however, when confronted by a Senate amendment to the credit-- refundability. On the Senate floor, Edward Kennedy introduced an amendment to the credit making it refundable to individuals whose tax liabilities were less than the

amount of their credit. Kennedy justified the measure as
a subsidy to families headed by women whose income
generated tax liabilities less than their allowable
credit. Although the Senate approved, the Treasury
Department and the House conferees refused to allow a
social program to distort the tax structure. The department was willing to accept a credit with no income
ceiling, but not a refundable one. The conference
committee deleted the refundability, and the credit
became law in 1976.

Without an income ceiling and therefore open to all
eligible households regardless of their decision to
itemize deductions, the child care credit expanded greatly
among households earning more than $20,000 per year. In
1975 only 134,000 households earning more than $20,000
claimed the deductions; in 1976, 959,000 claimed it.
Ninety-four percent of the additional tax saving provided
by the credit accrued to this income group. In part,
this distribution of tax benefits was an inevitable result
of the distribution of tax liabilities; higher-income
groups incur proportionally higher tax liabilities and
thus benefit more than low-income groups. They also tend
to spend more on child care. Many members of Congress,
however, believed that the credit would aid middle- and
low-income households more than the extant deduction
did. The data indicate that this did not occur. Indeed,
Treasury and committee staff estimates of the credit's
impact predicted the actual outcome, and the department
initially opposed a credit with no income ceiling on the
grounds that it would unjustifiably benefit higher-income
groups.

There are two explanations for the passage of the tax
credit despite its distributional impact. First, it was
easier politically to provide tax relief for all income
groups than to target that relief with an income ceiling.
Second, the information on the credit's impact across
income classes represented only a small part of the total
information generated by staff members on the tax revisions. The sheer quantity of data precluded their
effective assimilation by members of Congress, who relied
more on their own intuitive sense of the revision's
impact than on the data. A child care credit simply
appeared to accord greater tax relief to low- and
middle-income groups than did an itemized deduction.

Since enactment of the child care credit in 1976,
Congress has made only one change in this tax provision
affecting children. Largely as a result of constituent

letters and a widely circulated newspaper column, "The
IRS Is Unfair to Grandma," Congress lifted the prohibition
against a credit for payments to relatives not considered
employees for Social Security purposes. The change was
minor, and total revenue loss from the credit increased
by only 5 percent.

CONCLUSION

These case studies trace historically the development of
three federal policy initiatives on behalf of children
and their families. Each represents a different type of
government action: the Special Supplemental Food Program
for Women, Infants, and Children is a categorical grant
program; the Federal Interagency Day Care Requirements
are regulations governing the delivery of federally
financed social services; and the Child Care Tax
Deduction/Credit is a provision of the income tax system
for individuals. Each involved a different set of agency
and congressional actors and coalitions of interests,
inside and outside government. Though they share roughly
the same social, economic, and political context, each
addressed a different set of issues concerning the
appropriate role of the federal government in the lives
of children and their families. Furthermore, each of
these policy developments traced a different course from
its initiation to its implementation.

These three federal policy developments do indeed
share the common characteristics of policy determination
discussed in Chapter 1. Each took place over a period of
time and involved a number of important decision points
along the way. The Child Nutrition Act of 1966, the
passage of the $20-million WIC pilot program in 1972,
USDA's delays and OMB's impoundment of the WIC appropriations in 1976, and the several court orders requiring the
USDA to spend the available funds all contributed to the
establishment and growth of WIC. Similarly, the passage
of WIN in 1967, the failure of FAP in 1969, and the
passage of the Title XX amendment to the Social Security
Act all influenced the revisions and final signing of the
Federal Interagency Day Care Requirements in 1980. And
the initial passage of a child care deduction in 1954,
the Equal Pay Act of 1963, the expansion of a child care
deduction for dual-career families in 1963, and the
failure of the Comprehensive Child Care Act in 1971 all
led to the final passage and expansion of the child care
tax deduction/credit.

In each case, individual decisions were themselves complex policy events involving interactions among many actors, interests, and factors. Each case involved a large and heterogeneous group of participants having different interests, intentions, and perceptions of the policy formation process. To ask what each case is really about is to uncover the conflicting agendas of the individuals and institutions that played a role in the development of these three federal policies and to understand the coalitions among them.

The WIC legislation, for example, received the strong endorsement of powerful farm interests seeking markets for their surplus food commodities. The primary concern of the farmers was not the feeding of hungry children or the nourishment of pregnant women, yet their interests were joined with those of antipoverty and antihunger groups as well as school administrators and social service providers to support the establishment and growth of the program.

Similarly in the development of the Federal Interagency Day Care Requirements, the child development research community, the anti-welfare/pro-workfare groups, and the nonprofit day care providers approached the issue of federally enforced standards from different perspectives but had similar interests in the passage of strict regulations governing the delivery of federally financed day care services. The proprietary providers, for whom more staff means higher costs, lower utilization rates, and smaller profits, had a very different interest in the type of regulations established. The long delay before a final signing of the requirements in 1980 is testimony to the intensity of the conflict among these groups.

By putting low-income mothers to work in child care/housekeeping jobs, the Child Care Tax Deduction/Credit received strong support not only from women's groups but also from those who were interested in lowering the welfare rolls. Its development mirrored in many respects the changing ethos of American society regarding the role of women, as they joined the labor force in increasing numbers over the past 30 years. The case history of the tax credit reflected a movement from a categorical assistance approach to aiding children and families to an income supplement approach not wholly, nor even principally, founded on financial need.

Finally, in each case there were few, if any, direct and predictable sequences of events. The outcomes were shaped by complex interactions among a variety of factors

and forces: the roles and positions of key actors; the
role of the media and the timeliness of research findings;
the alignment of interests; the passage or failure of
important pieces of legislation; and the prevailing
social, economic, demographic, and political conditions.
In the next chapter we examine how several of these
components, both singly and in combination, influenced
the policy formation processes.

3 Components of the
Policy Formation Process

In each of the three case studies, a number of observable factors helped influence the policy outcome. From our analysis we conclude that these components can be grouped into the following six general categories:

1. Contextual factors, including those social, economic, demographic, political, and ideological factors, that shape the overall context of federal decision making at any given point in time.
2. Constituency activities, including direct and indirect pressure, exerted by both organized and unorganized constituencies outside the federal government.
3. Principles and ideas that shape a participant's vision or policy goal.
4. Actors and institutions, including those that participate directly in the federal decision-making process in the legislature, executive, and judicial branches of government.
5. Media presentations, including television, radio, and the popular print media such as newspapers and magazines.
6. Research, including knowledge-building, problem-exploring, policy-forming, and program-directing studies that are introduced into the policy process to support or refute the position of program proponents and or opponents.

Each case is in effect a narrative that describes how these components contribute, both individually and interactively, to policy formation. In this chapter we discuss these components as they are manifest throughout the cases in order to identify some of the salient forces shaping federal policy toward children and their families.

CONTEXTUAL FACTORS

Although the cases touch on events dating back to the New Deal, all three deal principally with events that occurred between the late 1960s and the late 1970s. During this period there were several important changes in the social, economic, demographic, political, and ideological factors that shaped the overall context of federal decision making affecting children. Inflation surged and unemployment increased. The birthrate slowed, and a growing number of American women, particularly those with children under the age of 18, entered the labor force. The civil rights movement and the war on poverty blossomed as liberals advocated social reform and the broadened participation of minorities, especially blacks, in the political process. And the United States engaged in a prolonged and unpopular war in Southeast Asia.

The influence of these changes can be observed in the cases, sometimes as direct effects but more often they are mediated through other components in the process. Hence, we observe, for example, that the increasing labor force participation of women and the growth of single-parent families influenced the liberalization of the child care tax credit and the growth of child care programs. Similarly, we note that the rapid economic expansion of the 1960s directly influenced the growth of social programs and federal spending. Conversely, sluggish growth and high inflation in the 1970s had the opposite effect on the enactment of new programs.

As an indirect influence, the increasing entry of women into the labor force created a broader constituency with a stake in policies benefiting working women, particularly child care assistance. Accordingly, this demographic change was reflected in political advocacy, media attention, and the shift in traditional beliefs about a woman's role. Similarly, declining dairy prices in the 1950s created pressure on Congress by farm interest groups for a new domestic program.

In addition to the social, demographic, and economic contexts, prevalent social values and beliefs also play a significant role. In all three cases, we observed, and sought in some instances to measure through public opinion surveys, the power of values and beliefs in molding policy. In most situations, these beliefs are manifest through other components of the policy formation process: constituency pressure, media events, research, and the perceptions of key actors. Thus, for example, hunger,

especially among pregnant women and infants, was regarded
as unacceptable in the midst of American affluence. On
the Senate floor, Humphrey's photographic display of the
effects of malnutrition on infants touched a humanitarian
chord and was undoubtedly crucial to the passage of WIC.
Support of WIC was classified more than once as a "Mom
and apple pie" political issue because of its target
population.

Beliefs and values were equally potent in the child
care tax deduction/credit case. Beliefs about a woman's
proper place consistently restrained congressional
liberalization of the child care tax deduction during the
1950s and 1960s. Socioeconomic change (women entering
the work force) slowly altered this belief and ultimately
led to the passage and liberalization of the deduction
itself.

The long-standing debate over the appropriate role of
government in the lives of children was a central element
involved in the Federal Interagency Day Care Requirements.
Although the obligation of government to protect children
from exploitive labor practices, fire hazards, physical
abuse, and the like has become an accepted principle,
federal intervention to ensure children's cognitive
development is more controversial. Supporters of the
child development research community and public day care
providers contend that the public obligation to protect
children extends to measures designed to enhance their
healthy growth and education. Critics, particularly
among fiscal conservatives and proprietary day care
providers, argue that such intervention threatens to
undermine the role of parents in childrearing and the
free market in social service delivery.

Finally, political factors incumbent on government
structures also shape the context of federal policy
making toward children. Legislation rests with Congress,
enforcement with the executive branch, and adjudication
with the judicial branch. Specifically in the cases we
examined, the fact that Senate bills, unlike House
measures, are usually open to floor amendments helps
explain why the original WIC measure and several efforts
to liberalize the child care tax credit were initiated in
the Senate. Liberal members were able to circumvent
conservative committees and bring their measures before
the entire Senate. Similar actions were not possible in
the House. The fact that HEW promulgated the 1968 day
care requirements without OMB's approval, while OMB
blocked the less stringent 1972 requirements, was due to

a change in administrative procedures. In 1968, OMB
(then the Bureau of the Budget) could not review agency
regulations; by 1972 it could. Similarly, the role of
the judiciary is a significant structural factor. During
the late 1960s and 1970s the courts adapted a more
activist posture in mediating disputes within and between
the other branches of government. Court rulings, for
example, were crucial in the expansion of the WIC program.
In another era the judiciary might have been less inclined
to interfere in a conflict between Congress and the
executive branch.

To summarize, we understand these factors to be
contextual by virtue of the fact that they establish the
settings in which other components interact in policy
making. It is to these other components that we now turn.

CONSTITUENCY PRESSURE

Constituency pressure is at once one of the most obvious
and most difficult variables to identify. It often takes
elusive forms, such as letters, informal meetings with
policy makers, and public opinion polls, as well as the
more orchestrated, organized lobbying efforts of interest
and advocacy groups. Most instances of constituency
pressure in the three cases examined here involved
organized groups, such as the Children's Defense Fund,
the AFL-CIO, and FRAC. We also encountered some instances
of unorganized pressure, such as letters from constituents
and public opinion polls. Overall, we observe that the
nature and influence of constituency pressure varies at
different points in policy formation. Even when it is
not an obvious component of policy making, constituency
pressure remains a significant backdrop. As we have
noted, it is often the medium through which changes in
contextual factors, for example, social, economic, or
political events, affect the policy process. In several
respects, constituency pressure has the characteristics
of a contextual factor: it is a constant, diffuse, and
largely uncontrollable force (by policy makers) in policy
formation.

Unorganized constituency pressure appears most
frequently at the point in the policy process at which a
problem is defined: letters to Congress on tax problems,
public outrage at widespread hunger in America, or public
opinion of expanding welfare rolls. We interpret it as a
reflection of the role of public opinion in the identifi-

cation of social conditions as social problems. For
example, until women's employment outside the home was
perceived as appropriate, the problems of dual-earner
families were not recognized as legitimate concerns of
public policy.

Unorganized pressure appears less frequently than
organized pressure when a specific policy is being
formulated. Thus, for example, public opinion supported
aid to hungry children, but the Community Nutrition
Institute suggested the specific programmatic form that
such an initiative might take. We interpret this as an
expression of the need for concrete policy proposals by
legislative and executive branch policy makers at that
stage in the process rather than an abstract sense of a
social problem requiring a government response. In
general, organized constituencies are better able to
marshall the necessary forces and propose concrete
initiatives than are unorganized constituencies.

When a policy is being debated and enacted, both
organized and unorganized constituency pressures appear
to affect the policy process. At this stage, both types
of pressure have a specific initiative focused on a
problem that they can support or oppose. Hence, for
example, once designed, WIC drew on diffuse public opinion
favoring such a programmatic approach as well as direct
support by organized groups.

For changes to be successfully promoted while a program
is operating and expanding, reforms must be proposed in
specific terms. Organized constituencies, therefore, tend
to be involved more frequently than unorganized ones. It
was an organized group, FRAC, that brought suit against
the USDA to change their handling of WIC program
operations.

There were several configurations of interests from
the first food assistance programs. In the 1930s, farm
interests pressured Congress to relieve their problem of
surplus commodities. Part of the attempt to resolve this
problem resulted in the food assistance programs. The
existence of the program created in Congress and among
outside interests an alliance between rural representatives and the school constituency: federal aid to farmers
in return for federal food assistance to school children.
Within this alliance the farm interest dominated programmatic initiatives until the 1960s. In that decade the
Democratic-liberal-activist coalition of the Great Society
seized the initiative from farm interests and educators.
An antihunger, antipoverty coalition emerged that relied

heavily on public sentiments and media presentations. Support for WIC itself came from advocacy groups such as the Children's Foundation and Community Nutrition Institute as well as local free clinics in the states. Producer interests became much less pronounced, with the exception of the infant formula companies. Nonetheless, it should be noted that WIC's initial passage and early extension depended on its status as an amendment to the multibillion-dollar child nutrition bills. These bills commanded support from powerful education interests throughout the nation.

The conflict over the Federal Interagency Day Care Requirements displayed no consistent alignment of interests in opposition. In support of the requirements were the various children's advocacy groups. The opposition tended to come chiefly from the executive agencies. Only when there was the threat of enforcement in 1976 under Title XX did interest groups express strong opposition to the regulations. The requirements have been employed by interest groups as vehicles to other ends: more employment opportunities in day care, revising welfare policy, increasing government spending on day care, and reducing categorical programs. Constituency pressures were often expressions of other conflicts that happened to touch on the requirements in a particular context.

We observe this symbolic use of the Federal Interagency Day Care Requirements more than once in our case study. They were originally mandated by members of Congress opposed to the WIN program. Unenforced, they lay quietly until the day care proposal of FAP led to a demand for more realistic requirements. In 1972, Edward Zigler, director of the Office of Child Development, responded with a revised version. Zigler's revision was buried amidst the advocacy groups' opposition to all Nixon administration initiatives and their emotional attachment to the 1968 version of federal day care standards. Revived once more in negotiations over Title XX, the requirements again became hostage to several strategies, including the promotion of workfare, the increase of day care funds, the decrease of Title XX funds, and enforcement of the day care requirements. The backlash created by organized interests was sufficient to destroy the requirements. Thus, constituency pressures focused on the shape of the day care requirements as a manifestation of the larger issue of federal responsibility for the well-being of children.

In the case of the child care tax deduction/credit,
constituency pressure demonstrated steady support for the
provision. Since it was first proposed in Congress,
organized interests uniformly supported it. This support
came from both employee and employer organizations,
although it was not a major goal of either. Not until
the late 1960s did any organized groups, such as the
National Organization for Women, make the tax deduction/
credit a major goal. In the 1960s, organizations promulgating the rights of women included the tax system in
their overall effort to end discrimination against women.
Still, congressional liberalization of the tax credit for
child care resulted from more than the growth of the
women's movement. By the time the movement became significant politically, the rapid increase in the labor force
participation of women had discouraged prevalent biases
against working mothers. Accordingly, the opposing forces
shifted after the 1963 revision. The issue of liberalization became less of a contest over a woman's proper place
and more an issue of tax equity versus tax structure--
political logrolling versus revenue loss. As with the
contextual factors, it is difficult to separate constituency pressure from the other components at work in the
process. They continually interact.

PRINCIPLES AND IDEAS

One component that appears significant in all three cases
is what we have called "vision"--a unique combination of
idea and principle that serves as a participant's policy
goal. We were consistently impressed by the powerful role
of vision in policy making. The principal architects of
WIC envisioned a food assistance program for pregnant
women and infants. They convinced Senator Hubert Humphrey
of the idea's merit. Losing in committee, Humphrey played
eloquently to the Senate with images of suffering children
and the simple act by which Congress could relieve them.
Victorious in Congress, WIC's architects had anticipated
administration opposition and the subsequent litigation.
The law was therefore written to maximize the probability
of success. Aided by FRAC, which also envisioned the
program as a major federal food assistance effort, WIC's
supporters managed to obtain court decisions ensuring its
rapid expansion. Supporters even anticipated USDA and
OMB behavior and won a court order that turned agency
ploys to the program's advantage. They succeeded in

expanding a $20-million pilot into a $750-million entitlement program in 5 years.

In the Federal Interagency Day Care Requirements we observe conflicting vision in policy formation. For proponents the regulations had an emotional, symbolic character, reflecting a long tradition in social work. The requirements represented an optimal goal that, with time and struggle, would one day be realized for all needy children. Opponents approached the requirements in more pragmatic ways: Were they enforceable, affordable, necessary? More interest-laden issues such as social services costs, welfare rolls, employment, and revenue allocation often established the context in which the debate resurfaced. Resolution of these issues, however, rarely depended on settling questions concerning the requirements themselves. Indeed, on more than one occasion, decisions concerning the proposal for FAP, the WIN program, and Title XX services brought about a de facto settlement of the controversy by postponing or resubmerging it in bureaucratic procedures.

Two general observations can be made concerning the role of vision in the case of the day care requirements. First, the attempt to embody the ideas of the child development research community in the regulations could not overcome or undo policies determined by substantive interests, primarily those of the states and proprietary providers. Vision, unsupported by interests, was unable to overcome these obstructions.

Second, apart from the requirements themselves, the case study offers evidence that policy making is more than a series of incremental responses to interest group demands—that vision is indeed relevant. The creation of Title XX is an excellent example of policy makers confronting a serious problem—the social service stalemate—with an imaginative solution. Building vision on interests, the assistant secretary for planning and evaluation in HEW was able to break the deadlock and broach a new approach to social service funding. Though unsuccessful, the proposal for FAP represents a similar blend of imagination and interests in its approach to a guaranteed income. A vision that comprehends interests is a potent factor in the formation of policy. It appears most effective when the ordinary mechanisms of incremental change through political brokering prove incapable of resolving conflicts among various interests.

In the child care tax deduction/credit case we also observe vision presented in the form of a principle in conflict: tax equity <u>versus</u> the integrity of the revenue system. Regardless of its legal definition, in the policy formation process, tax equity is a principle accorded substance by the alignment of political forces. Decisions concerning the distribution of the tax burden reflect the political pressures that various constituencies can bring to bear on Congress. Operationally, maintaining the integrity of the tax structure is the ideological safe-guard against tax provisions that threaten to seriously deplete revenue collections. Policy determination is thus a function of the interplay between the political benefits of appeasing constituent demands for lower taxes and the responsibility of lawmakers to ensure adequate revenues to operate the government.

The liberalization of the child care tax deduction/ credit in the 1970s reflected the increasing political pressure to reduce taxes and to make the tax code more equitable. This liberalization was aided by the departure of Representative Wilbur Mills--the unequaled congres-sional guardian of the tax structure. Once Mills departed, the more equity-prone decision-making process in the Senate approved an increase in the benefits of the child care tax deduction/credit. The check of the House Ways and Means Committee became less effective as its own decision-making process became more open following Mills's departure. In the executive branch, responsibility for maintaining the structural integrity of the tax system resides in the U.S. Department of the Treasury. Alone, however, Treasury was incapable of sustaining opposition to proponents of liberalization. The result was a steady growth in the size of the tax benefits and number of beneficiaries from the child care tax deduction/credit.

We observe that both vision and interest are signifi-cant in policy formation. Principle without interest seems impotent; interest without principle appears self-serving and manipulative. Although we hesitate to assign a primary role to either, we do note that vision has appeared dominant in the cases we examined. In the case of the Federal Interagency Day Care Requirements, vision that failed to account for prevailing interests proved incapable of realization. Successful vision, like that underlying the WIC program, is linked in some significant way to interests, and its power is enhanced by that linkage. Indeed, the most effective vision appears to be that which imagines the possible without forgetting the necessary.

ACTORS AND INSTITUTIONS

Key government participants appear at each stage in the policy formation process. Individuals and groups, who hold beliefs, seek changes, respond to others, and make decisions, shape policy. In each case study we discovered one or more key participants striving to realize a vision--some more successfully than others. Hubert Humphrey and his staff were able to bring the WIC program into being. Senate passage was in large measure a result of Humphrey's elan on the floor after defeat in committee. WIC's growth was fueled by advocates who used the courts, constituencies, and visceral appeals to create an effective lever against the USDA and the OMB.

In the case of the Federal Interagency Day Care Requirements, the cast changed several times as the policy debate moved in and out of the agencies and Congress. Many of the principal government participants in 1968 were replaced by new personalities in subsequent debates over revisions. Jule Sugarman, a principal in the 1968 requirements, did not participate in the 1972 revision or the 1975 Title XX controversy. In contrast, Edward Zigler, a principal in 1972, continued as a private advocate after he left government. Indeed, we find that some actors shift their roles over time but remain, in some capacity, participants in the policy process.

This observation is more complicated than the revolving-door notion of government-to-private-sector-to-government-service. We see in these role changes the opportunity of advocates to promote continuity in policy making that is typically attributed only to career civil servants. For example, in the case of the WIC program, Rodney Leonard's efforts to promote food assistance to special target groups did not cease when he left the USDA. He persisted in promoting such programs and with the help of others succeeded in establishing WIC. Participants are themselves frequently the agents of continuity in policy formation.

Institutions, too, represent actors of a sort. They exhibit certain general characteristics and behavioral patterns. Perhaps the most vivid display of institutional behavior patterns is the USDA and OMB response to the WIC program. Both executive agencies opposed the program during its early years of existence. The USDA believed target feeding to be ineffective and disliked the medical requirements of the program. The OMB believed WIC to be too costly, too rapidly expanding, and basically "bad" public policy. Both agencies sought to persuade Congress of their positions and, failing in that, both used their institutional resources to create delays and impoundments to restrain program growth.

It would be a gross understatement to suggest that their tactics were ineffective; rather, they served to expand WIC at many times the rate its congressional and private proponents had dared to hope. Because court decisions changed the character of the policy debate, these institutions, particularly OMB, were unable to respond effectively. As a practical matter, rapid expenditure of all program funds was the most effective means of restraining program growth. In WIC's case, the usual executive weapons against program growth, impoundment and delay, produced results that were antithetical to the institutional goals of restraint in spending.

In addition to general behavior patterns, institutions establish a context in which policy making takes place. As noted above, the role of an institution determines to a large extent where, how, and in what capacity an actor can participate in the policy formation process. The functional division among the three branches of government limits the power of any single participant to formulate, legislate, and execute policy changes. Less obvious is the administrator who uses his or her power to write regulations in order to control a program's development. Such an individual may hold a relatively subordinate decision-making role but through the form and content of regulations can exert an influence on a program greater than that of Congress or the President. An OMB budget examiner's power to change a program's direction may be limited to impounding funds, even if spending is not what the examiner wants to see changed. The President may not be able to effect a policy initiative without convincing Congress and the bureaucracy of its worth.

The "iron triangle" is a metaphor for the power of institutions and institutional actors in policy making: congressional committees, executive branch agency heads, and interest groups. Our cases reveal that these institutions are not monolithic, nor do they function in the same way from case to case. The committee structure results in a wide distribution of policy-making power in Congress: authorizing committees, appropriations committees, and revenue committees. Each must endorse a social service program in order for it to be established. An executive branch agency must take responsibility for its implementation. Other policies, such as tax cuts, can be accomplished in one committee of each house of Congress. Within an executive department the administering agency must clear its regulations with the general counsel and the assistant secretary to have them promulgated. Where one stands may indeed be determined by where one sits and, as the cases reveal, there are quite a few seats in each institutional setting.

MEDIA PRESENTATIONS

We identified in the case studies several examples of media presentations that influenced the policy formation process, including television, newspapers, and popular magazines and journals. (We do not include scientific research journals in this category.) Media presentations can affect the conception, debate, and expansion of a policy. Moreover, their influence on policy formation is frequently felt at later stages in the policy process as well as when a policy initiative is introduced. A CBS documentary on hunger, for example, helped define malnutrition as a serious problem. It also galvanized public opinion and facilitated the expansion of food assistance programs in the 1970s.

The response elicited by a media presentation appears crucial to its influence on policy formation. Respondents fall into one of two audiences: the public and policy makers. Policy makers are, of course, the key respondents, since they in fact initiate policy proposals. Their response, however, can be direct--evoked by the presentation itself--or indirect--evoked by public reactions to the presentation. A New Republic article criticizing WIC, for example, reached the President's desk in summary form; Carter responded to it directly. On the other hand, the Redbook article on WIC elicited 200 letters from citizens to the USDA. In this instance the media presentation was indirectly influential.

In our three case studies, media presentations served to define social conditions as social problems. They helped to frame issues for the political agenda. Presented in graphic form to millions of viewers, hunger became an emotional national issue. A working woman complaining of tax inequalities became symbolic of social changes when she aired her grievances on a television news program or in a newpaper's editorial pages. Furthermore, at times, media presentations can be very specific in affirming (or condemning) a program or policy initiative.

The Redbook article on WIC, for example, urged readers to write to the USDA and demand that the agency implement the supplemental food program. Similarly, a newspaper column complained of the exclusion of payments to relatives as tax deductible child care expenses. Both articles influenced policy formation.

Despite their influence in framing problems and issues, however, we observed no instances of a specific policy or program initiative's being conceived by the media. Vision and constituency pressure seem to intervene in the policy process even if the principal instigation is a media presentation. Hunger was a media issue, but the food stamp, supplemental food, and WIC programs were designed by policy makers. Again, there is a constant interaction between media and other components of policy formation.

RESEARCH

We observed in the three cases numerous instances of research and analysis playing a role in decision making. Research can be categorized as knowledge-building (contributing to fundamental understanding of social and behavioral processes), problem-exploring (contributing to the definition of social problems), policy-forming (contributing to the formulation of policies to address specific social problems), and program-directing (contributing to the design and improvement of established programs).* Each can have a different kind of influence on policy making. Knowledge-building and problem-exploring research, for example, is most often influential in defining a problem or providing supporting justification for the initiation of a policy proposal. Policy-forming research is similarly influential at the stage at which a social problem is recognized and alternative policy proposals are under consideration or when a particular policy initiative is being conceived. Program-directing research usually has its greatest impact when specific programs are being designed or refined. In the case studies we confined our collection of data and analysis of the impact of research to that which was relevant to the policy formation process in each case. We did not examine or cite studies that were not part of

*This typology is drawn from the National Research Council's Study Project on Social Research and Development (1978).

the documented history of the particular policy formation process. Although we observed several instances in which the results of research did not accord with the thrust of a policy initiative, all of the studies cited in our cases played some role in the decision-making process.

Our first observation on the role of research is that no single type of research appears to be inevitably influential on policy. We have an example of knowledge-building research on brain development and nutrition that was extremely influential in the WIC program's initiation, debate, and expansion. There appear to be mediating events in this instance, however. The Johns Hopkins and St. Jude's nutrition projects for pregnant women demonstrated to policy makers how research on neurophysiological development could be employed to deal with a social problem. After WIC's conception, this body of basic research remained a significant justification for the enactment and eventual expansion of the program.

Two examples of program-directing research, the Call study of the pilot voucher program and the USDA's study of the WIC program's delivery costs, had an influence on decision making. For a period of time they successfully supported opponents of the program's expansion. Research can thus affirm or deny the policy initiative and still have significant impact on the policy formation process.

On the relation of timing to influence, we note several examples of research having an impact at different points during the policy formation process. The more exploratory the research is, the more far-reaching its potential influence on the policy process. Conversely, the more directed toward specific programs the research is, the less applicable it is to contexts other than the operation and expansion of the particular program or immediate decision. Thus, even if program-directing research is more likely to directly influence policy operation and expansion, it seems less likely to influence decision making related to the formation of any other policy. Similarly, the more directly focused a piece of research or analysis is on the operation of a particular program or decision, the more crucial its timing becomes. Hence, the Urban Institute's evaluation of the WIC delivery system had relatively little impact because it was introduced in the policy process after crucial decisions concerning the program's expansion had already been made.

The conflict between research studies related to WIC's program operation and those related to its medical justification illustrates the interaction of research with

other components in policy formation. Generally speaking,
opponents of target-specific food assistance resided
principally in the USDA and the OMB. Although they did
not deny the medical evidence linking proper nutrition to
healthy infant development, they pointed to the two
evaluations of target-specific delivery systems (by Call
and the Urban Institute) as evidence of programmatic
ineffectiveness. Whatever its theoretical merits, they
argued that food assistance could not effectively be made
target-specific. In large measure the UDSA's determination stemmed from the overall administration policy of
replacing all direct food distribution programs with food
stamps and, ultimately, a unified, income-based welfare
system. Moreover, the administration sought to extricate
the USDA from programs with expensive delivery systems.
Within the department there was a general resistance to
taking on any new food assistance programs since those
already under way were dramatically shifting USDA's
traditional role of aiding farmers through price supports
and marketing. What research the USDA considered relevant
or influential depended on the larger policy imperatives
that were operative.

Proponents of target-specific food programs were
equally selective in their use of the research findings.
They discounted results that contradicted their assertions
about WIC's efficacy. They ignored methodological criticisms and other reservations concerning evaluations of
the program's impact on participants. Nevertheless, in
the debate over WIC's effectiveness, proponents of the
program were victorious. They had two factors in their
favor: one scientific and the other ideological. First,
research supporting the notion that proper nutrition is
esssential for optimal human development was unquestioned.
Second, feeding hungry infants was an activity that existing social values and sentiments reinforced. Congressional decision makers had an intuitive sense that a
programmatic effort of this type was good policy--
politically and morally.

During the development of the program, research and
evaluation generated ambiguous results concerning the
Supplemental Food Program and WIC. Scientific findings
introduced as evidence in the policy debate consistently
affirmed the strong link between proper nutrition and
healthy fetal and infant development. Equally consistent
were the evaluations of target-specific food delivery
systems: They did not work well. In sum, although
nutritional assistance to this group was certainly

warranted, the programs' delivery systems failed to
effectively meet their needs. There were further
complicating factors. Two studies had yielded results
indicating that a carefully administered local program
could produce measurable effects on fetal and infant
development. Yet one of these studies (by Endozien)
encountered severe methodological criticisms, and the
other (by the Center for Disease Control) qualified its
conclusions to the point of precluding any programwide
extrapolations. Research and evaluation thus became
relevant to the policy formation process only insofar as
selected results were useful to proponents or opponents
in advancing their causes.

We observe this use of research for advocacy purposes
again in the formulation of the Federal Interagency Day
Care Requirements. The principal research study in this
case, Abt Associates' National Day Care Study, was
appealing to both supporters and opponents of strict
regulations. Its results provided some comfort to all
sides in the policy debate. For advocates concerned with
cognitive development, it affirmed the link between
regulations and related outcomes. For those concerned
with costs, it eased the recommended child-staff ratios
and instead stressed group size. Moreover, the Abt study
endorsed regulations that most day care providers could
meet at little or no additional expense. Its scientific
methodology was at least credible to most social
scientists. Thus, the influence of the National Day Care
Study on policy stemmed not only from its scientific
validity but also from its accord with the dominant,
opposing political positions. The Abt study in a sense
provided the catalyst for a compromise that met the
demands of both child development interests and proprietary day care providers. As with other components of the
policy process, it was more than the inherent scientific
worth of the research that determined its influence in
the policy process. Its interactions with other
components—constituency pressure, prevailing values, and
so forth—altered its influence, in this instance
enhancing it.

By and large the only type of research that was
consistently influential on tax policy were studies of
the revenue loss and the distributional effects of
specific tax initiatives. Since the basic conflict in
tax policy making is between the integrity of the tax
structure and the equitable distribution of the tax
burden—i.e., costs in revenue and costs to constituents—

relevant research usually focuses on the costs of a proposed tax policy provision. Analyses of revenue loss, however, even when the tax burden is distributed across income classes, may not adequately measure the benefits of an initiative. In the case of the job development deduction, for example, the research, both prospective and retrospective, did not assess the impact of the provision on domestic employment or on employment incentives in general. It examined only potential and actual revenue losses. In this respect it seems that tax initiatives are seldom evaluated in terms of their efficacy in achieving their stated goals. We did not encounter analyses at any stage in the formation of the child care tax deduction/credit that examined the impact of various child care tax benefits on work incentives, types of care selected, employment, or similar variables. Decision makers made consideration of the broader impact of particular individual income tax provisions less relevent to their deliberations than potential revenue loss.

In sum, we note that research of all types--knowledge-building, problem-exploring, policy-forming, and program-directing--can influence federal decision making. The more specifically focused a study is on a particular program or decision, the more crucial its timing becomes. Often the same study can be used by opponents in a policy debate; just as often opposing research results can be equally influential. Moreover, as with other components of the federal policy-making process, the interaction of research with other factors and forces significantly affects its impact.

INTERACTIONS AMONG COMPONENTS
IN FEDERAL POLICY FORMATION

Interactions among components are the most complex and therefore the most difficult aspect of the policy formation process to analyze systematically. These interactions or relationships among components, rather than the isolated roles of individual actors, media presentations, research studies, or instances of constituency pressure, explain policy outcomes, although each of these appears to have an identifiable impact.

To some extent the narrative of the case studies is an account of relevant interactions that are, in effect, the story line of each case. In the 1968 origins of WIC, for example, prevailing social values and beliefs held that

pregnant women and infants are a target population
deserving special benefits. Popular media dissemination
of information concerning the special needs of this group
focused attention on their condition. Because the
sentiment of media presentations agreed with the dominant
social values, it helped define malnutrition among this
group as a serious problem requiring federal government
action. Popular expositions of hunger in America and the
salutary effects of proper nutrition and feeding habits
on fetal and infant development focused public attention
on undernourished pregnant women and young children and
placed them on the political agenda. Consonantly, the
high visibility of this group made it an attractive target
for the Nixon administration's response to criticisms of
its existing food assistance programs, particularly WIC.
This process illustrates the interaction of constituency
pressure (the Poor People's March), media attention
(CBS's "Hunger in America"), and social values (feed
hungry babies). Moreover, ongoing research on nutrition
and infant development reinforced the inclination of
proponents to provide food assistance to this target
group.

Complex interactions of this type are evident in an
examination of any one of the contributing decisions
presented in the case studies. Yet, as we suggested
earlier, policies of the sort represented in the case
studies are not the result of individual decisions such
as the passage of the 1968 Supplemental Food Program.
They are instead the product of numerous decisions made
over a prolonged period of time, involving a large number
of participants with different agendas and intentions.
Policy represents a cumulative product. Understanding
the dynamics of policy making involves understanding not
only the process leading to individual decisions but also
how such decisions create patterns affecting future
events in the process and, ultimately, determine policy
formation.

The creation of the WIC program, for example, resulted
from a confluence of several decisions from two relatively
independent levels in the policy-making process. At one
level were decisions contributing to the expansion of the
child nutrition complex--a multibillion-dollar collection
of politically invulnerable programs. Inclusion in this
legislative phalanx protected a fledgling WIC program
from a veto. The relatively small group of WIC advocates
was strengthened by the broad array of interests that had
long supported the School Lunch Program and related

programs. It was not until 1978 that WIC faced congressional and executive scrutiny as a separate legislative
act. By then there was an administration more favorable
to it, an annualized budget of $440 million, and a million
participants in the program.

WIC's early linkage to the child nutrition complex
ensured its passage before the full Congress. The key
legislative action was its inclusion as a provision of
this bill. Very few legislators, mostly senators, needed
to be convinced of its worth to effect this addition.
One Senate staff member and one advocate convinced a
single senator (admittedly of great stature) of the
program's value. Although narrowly defeated in the
conservative Senate Committee on Agriculture, Herbert
Humphrey successfully waged a floor fight. The powerful
sympathy for feeding infants and pregnant women combined
with the relatively small size of the initiative to
produce a lopsided vote favoring WIC's inclusion. On the
House side, the approval of a single committee's chair
ensured WIC's acceptance in the conference report on the
child nutrition bill. Proponents needed to convince very
few decision makers to effect passage. Its association
with the complex of child nutrition programs made it
veto-proof.

Once enacted, the locus of policy making shifted to
another level. The conflict then involved a recalcitrant
USDA and a public interest law firm. The arena of
decision making shifted from the Congress to the courts.
A court ruling favoring the implementation of the program
changed both the size and purpose of WIC. The court
essentially transformed any decision about WIC's future
from one based on scientific evaluation to one based on
specific legal issues. Program expansion became a
function of judicial interpretation of congressional
intent and not a function of its efficacy as adjudged by
science.

WIC's rapid expansion can be attributed to the interplay of organizational behavior patterns with the court
decisions, the power of the appeal of feeding hungry
infants, the interest groups supporting the overall child
nutrition bills, and evaluations that could be interpreted
as favorable. The nexus for all these components was the
deliberate efforts of a handful of proponents. Although
one would be hard-pressed to demonstrate that vision
created and sustained the overall food assistance
programs, WIC appears to be chiefly a product of the
ideas and efforts of few actors. It is distinctive for

its sensitivity to both interests and ethos. Circumstances created a window for change; human ingenuity opened it.

Without going into similar detail, we observe that the case of the Federal Interagency Day Care Requirements also reflects this movement over time and in and out of different levels of policy making. The requirements themselves were largely a product of intradepartmental debates. Although constituency pressure was evident in these debates, it did not reach a broad, intensive level until enforcement appeared imminent. Yet when consideration of the requirements became integral to the larger policy issues surrounding the FAP and Title XX, the terms of the debate and the key actors changed. Children's advocacy groups and federal agency heads found themselves facing large labor unions, major state lobbies, leaders of Congress, and the President.

The role of individual components of policy formation shifted as the level of the policy debate changed. What had been determined by a few bureaucrats and advocates abruptly became a struggle among leaders in Congress and the executive branch. Indeed, presidential primary politics became relevant at one point. Once these larger issues were resolved, the debate again became an intradepartmental matter involving a few advocacy groups. These shifts over time in the character and stakes of decision making, which are evident both in the WIC and the Federal Interagency Day Care Requirements case studies, are of crucial significance in understanding the policy formation process. In the case of the child care tax deduction/credit we note that the policy debate never quite rose to the level of the child nutrition program complex, FAP, or Title XX, nor did it sink to the intradepartmental level at which much of the day care requirements were played out.

From our analysis of the interactions among components of policy making, we conclude that they create identifiable patterns suggesting a framework for understanding the process of policy formation. We detail this approach in the next chapter.

4 A Policy Framework: Three Levels of Decision Making

Policy making affecting families and children is, as we anticipated when we initiated the case studies, time-consuming, polycentric, and complex; this much is obvious to participants and observers alike. The panel sought to go beyond these observations to create an analytic account of the policy formation process that would draw on existing scientific understanding of policy determination, resonate with the panel's experience and expertise, and be capable of yielding prescriptions for practitioners.

The panel's search for explanatory frameworks was guided by certain predilections. First, policy making is not only time-consuming but is also sequential, specific events being significantly shaped by what has occurred before and virtually never ending. Second, policy making seems to occur at several distinct hierarchical levels of government--from the top political leadership to middle-level program officials--with horizontal interactions among participants at each level and with policy-making activity at the different levels taking place concurrently. Third, the character of policy making differs depending on the kind of government action being contemplated--for example, whether the issue involves the tax code and the tax-writing committees of Congress or whether it involves direct expenditure programs and, consequently, authorizing committees of Congress.

A large, rapidly growing, and richly diverse body of research exists on public policy formation. We judged it to be beyond the scope of this report to present a comprehensive survey of this literature. We reached the conclusion, however, that no single model or approach presented in existing literature adequately captures the cumulative "feel" of the cases and the types of policy making they represent. Thus we were led to use the information in

the cases to derive an analytic framework, the application
of which would fulfill the criteria outlined at the
beginning of this chapter.

From our examination of the case studies we observed
distinguishable patterns of interactions among components
of the policy formation process. These patterns reflect
the dynamic relationships among the nature of the policy
issue, the participants who are involved in the policy
debate, and the types of resulting government action. We
describe these relationships according to an analytic
framework involving levels of decision making that are
distinguished by what issues are to be resolved, who is
typically involved in resolving them, and how they are
resolved.

This framework may be usefully expressed in terms of a
game metaphor. Its analytic appeal derives largely from
its capacity to depict complex problem-solving phenomena
involving participants who employ strategies to maximize
their positions in contexts constrained by agreed-on
rules, laws, and conditions.

We believe the framework presented below provides a
useful basis for formulating conjectures about the complex
relationships among observable elements of the policy
formation process. We stress that this presentation is
designed to be suggestive in interpreting complex policy
developments; it is not a definitive statement of testable
or tested propositions. Considerable further work is
needed before such a statement is possible.

THE POLICY FRAMEWORK

We believe that policy making in the federal government
can be described as occurring at different levels, and,
for purposes of analysis, we postulate three levels:
high, middle, and low. They differ along three major
dimensions: the nature of the issues in question, the
participants who are involved, and the types of government
action that can result. The nature of policy issues can
vary from highly value laden—for example, whether government should mandate and support preschool education for
all children—to essentially technical—for example, how
to most effectively and efficiently immunize children
against polio once a decision to immunize has been made.
In addition, the degree of consensus among participants
in the decision-making process over a policy issue may
vary. At each level, decision making involves a large

number of participants who can be distinguished by their goals and the resources available to them. These resources include their position or office, expertise, information, and time. Moreover, the types of resulting government action may also vary. Some may involve major alterations in the existing social order--for example, mandatory employment of all welfare mothers. Others may involve less dramatic initiatives, such as expanding the Head Start budget. At each level of decision making the role of various components of policy formation--contextual factors, constituency pressure, media presentations, and research--and their interactions change. The high level essentially involves deciding whether government action is warranted and appropriate. The middle level involves deciding more concretely what the government's role should be. The low level involves the precise design of that role and selecting the details of its execution.

These three levels of decision making represent distinct arenas in which certain actors in the process have greater control and advantage. Depending on the level of activity, different strategies are more or less appropriate for different actors. In addition, the levels of decision making presented in this schema do not represent a hierarchy. Policy making at the high level, although more visible, is not necessarily more significant or more essential than policy making at the middle or the low level. The stakes may be equally great at all levels. The three levels of decision making suggest a logical priority for determining the nature of a social problem, agreeing on a programmatic response, and finally establishing the legal regulations and guidelines to implement it.

The High Level

At the high level, decision making involves the definition of social conditions as social problems, the formulation of solutions to those problems, and the resolution of major conflicts in societal values. The high level represents the contest to make an issue political--that is, a legitimate object for government action. Policy making at this level addresses major questions concerning the nature of social goals. Does society have a problem that requires government action? What is the nature of that problem? Is more or less government intervention warranted? Why? The debate is about philosophies of

government, the fundamental responsibilities of institutions, and basic principles of social justice. Intense
controversy is likely, often fueled by the actions of
single-issue constituencies or powerful elites. Policy
proposals generally involve significant alterations of
the existing social order--for example, the nature and
extent of government involvement in the lives of American
children and their families. The principal governmental
actors are the President, the congressional leadership,
and the Supreme Court. Powerful private interests are
also significant participants. Among the components of
policy formation, media presentations, influential
leaders, and large coalitions of interests are predomin-
ant. Often, new visions wrought by economic, demographic,
or cultural changes are principal components at the high
level. Research is less significant. Although it may
serve to illuminate high-level issues, it rarely settles
them.

The original School Lunch Act of 1947 represents a
classic example of decision making at the high level.
The major issue was whether the federal government had a
responsibility to ensure that children are adequately
nourished. It entailed defining a role for the federal
government in "ordinary" times--no war and no depression--
that it had never had previously. Large coalitions of
education and farm interests supported the measure. The
President and leaders of Congress made it a legislative
goal. Though television was not yet a major force, other
media presentations examined and editorialized the issue.
Research on the medical etiology of men rejected from
military service illuminated the problem.

Similarly, the hunger crisis of 1967-1968 also involved
decision making at the high level. A mass media exposé
on malnourished children and adults ignited widespread
public response and focused presidential attention on the
problem. It helped define a new goal for the federal
government--the elimination of hunger in America.
Research illuminated the issues. Large coalitions of
interest groups and the public at large, led by influential individuals in the Senate, pressed for congressional action. The decision-making process at the high
level ended when the elimination of hunger became an
accepted national goal and a federal responsibility.

The Middle Level

The middle level of decision making involves the choice
of means to achieve high-level goals. It is a contest
over the allocation of authority and resources to attain
an agreed-on objective. Since government must act, what
type of action should it take? How should responsibility
be assigned among levels of government and government
agencies? How much should be spent on what types of
benefits and services? Policy proposals generally
represent programmatic responses to acknowledged social
problems--for example, the establishment of the Child
Abuse and Neglect Program to help deal with the problems
of physical and psychological abuse of children by family
members. The debate is about the results of alternative
government actions--i.e., their effectiveness and
efficiency, their fairness, costs, and distributional
effects, and the administrative competence of alternative
agencies. The principal participants are presidential
appointees, members of Congress, and the designees of
either group. Among policy components, the media are
less prominent than in the high arena. Interests are
more parochial and coalitions smaller. Ideas and visions
are more technocratic and focused; they deal in probabili-
ties, not possibilities. The choices made are among
existing options and structures of values. Research
frequently can help resolve middle-level issues. Although
it is in some senses more political than decision making
at the high level, reasoned compromises are frequently
easier to reach.

The policy debate surrounding the child care tax
deduction/credit centered at the middle level of decision
making and concerned the equitable distribution of the
tax burden. It was a contest among members of Congress
and presidential appointees. Media presentations influenced the decision making infrequently. With the exception of the issue of women's equality, which touched many
politically sensitive issues besides the deduction, there
was little presidential involvement. Changes among major
contextual factors--for example, changing patterns of
women's labor force participation, particularly among
those with young children--and visions of equal treatment
for women in the marketplace were high-level issues, but
their ramifications for the tax system were not. Constituency pressure was parochial: unions with women in their
membership, employer organizations with a high percentage
of women workers, and some professional legal associations

concerned with the integrity of the tax code. Research was significant in revealing the effects of various proposals for child care tax benefits and in preventing the passage of some measures that projected significant revenue losses.

The Low Level

The low level of decision making involves the design of means chosen at the middle level to achieve an end determined at the high level. It is a technical contest over how best to implement an agreed-on approach to a problem. Since government must act and the type of action has been determined, how precisely should that action be implemented? How will eligibility, standards, or exceptions and exclusions be defined? How will compliance be determined, monitored, and enforced? How will vendors be selected and funds transferred? The answers to these questions reflect the judgments of specialists and technicians concerning factors such as the feasibility of administration, legal sufficiency, costs, etc. Decision making at the low level involves the fine-grained processes of government and tends to reflect the concerns of those with fiscal (budgeting, enforcement, auditing) or programmatic (administration, staffing, efficacy) responsibilities. The principal participants, therefore, are the staffs of Congress and the executive branch agencies. Media presentations and vision are less significant at the low level. Constituency pressure is very specific and targeted--often involving the use of technical experts in a particular area. Research and evaluation generally loom large in decision making at this level as arbiters of disputes over the effectiveness and efficiency of alternative plans.

Throughout most of the process of regulation writing, the development of the Federal Interagency Day Care Requirements involved decision making at the low level. The issue was technical: how to design requirements to govern federal day care programs. The principal actors were federal agency staff members. Media and contextual factors had no discernible impact. Consitituency pressures by a few advocacy groups were narrowly focused. Research was very important, if only in the form of advice from experts on what was in the best interests of children.

In many respects the nature of an issue is the key to
determining the level of decision making. If the issue
involves the intrinsically value-laden question of what
the role of government is, decision making must take
place at the high level. If it involves the more technical question of how the government shall act, decision
making usually takes place at the middle level. If it
involves the question of how a policy or program shall be
designed, decision making is generally centered at the
low level. In short, an issue involving social values is
resolved at the high level, an issue involving equity at
the middle level, and an issue involving efficiency at
the low level. Although the existence of an issue is the
basis of decision making at each level, it does not
necessarily have to involve conflict. Decision making
takes place regardless of whether there is a dispute
concerning appropriate government action. It is not the
magnitude of agreement or disagreement that distinguishes
the level of policy making, but rather the character of
the agreement or disagreement.

Similarly, although many participants take part in
federal policy making, the level is distinguished by the
actor who is capable of resolving the issue. For example,
an OMB budget examiner participates, as a rule, in
decision making at the low level, but he or she might
prepare an analysis of congressionally approved legislation that significantly influences a presidential veto.
If the legislation involved an issue of social justice,
the budget examiner would in effect have participated at
the high level. The President alone, however, is capable
of resolving the issue by exercising veto power. The
presence of the President in conjunction with other
factors distinguishes the level of decision making as
high.

Certain actors are typical to each decision-making
level. Actors who participate at a level other than
their typical one take greater risks, expend more
resources, cannot participate alone, and often perform
ineffectively. A President, for example, who becomes
involved in regulation writing is participating at the
low level--not the typical level. The President expends
more resources--namely, time--to deal with regulation
writers, who are generally technocrats, and frequently
performs poorly at this level, lacking the technical
expertise and the necessary amount of time to participate
effectively.

The stakes or potential outcomes of policy making vary
according to the level of decision making because possible
types of governmental action at each level differ. Their
significance and ultimate impact are not necessarily
greater at the high level than at the middle or low level.
Congress and the President agreed, for example, that
handicapped children should have equitable access to
educational opportunities and passed a law mandating the
provision of special facilities and services to all handicapped children of public school age (P.L. 94-142). The
crux of the issue and the greatest stakes, however, rested
on the regulations promulgated to effect that high-level
end. Whether federal regulations would mandate states
and localities to spend billions of dollars on special
transportation systems, teachers, and other facilities
for the handicapped was in fact the crucial question and
involved the highest stakes. Decision making at the low
level, therefore, does not necessarily involve low stakes.

As we suggested earlier, no hierarchy is necessarily
implied among the decision-making levels, although there
is a logical priority. A broad social issue is resolved
into a programmatic issue of how to execute the decision
made at the high level; the resolution of a programmatic
issue requires a decision of how best to implement an
agreed-on initiative. Policy making, however, rarely
reflects this smooth linear flow. The policy process is
often characterized by solutions looking for problems,
rather than problems looking for solutions. Policy makers
do not always reach agreement first on broad goals, then
on programs, and finally on details of implementation.
Policy making is a dynamic, convoluted process of conflict
resolution, in which consensus at the high level can
easily be destroyed at the middle or low levels, where
programmatic and implementation issues are addressed. In
addition, because policy making is a fluid and dynamic
process, events and participants can shift the level of
decision making. And a given policy issue may involve
decision making at more than one level simultaneously.

In the WIC case we observed that once the elimination
of hunger became a national goal, the policy debate
shifted from the high level to the middle level. There
the contest involved choosing among available programmatic means: direct distribution, food stamps, the
provision of supplemental food, and other possible
programs to reach the goal. More parochial interests
surfaced over which vehicle would most benefit particular
constituencies, including farmers, the schools, and the

poor. Members of the cabinet, the subcabinet, and congressional committees debated the size of appropriations and the expansion of specific programs. Targeting food assistance to pregnant women, infants, and young children appeared as an attractive strategy in part because of the findings of several research studies that explored the physical and developmental effects of malnutrition on infants and young children. After the issue of means was resolved, the debate shifted again to the low level, where the major concern was for the precise design of a targeted supplemental food program. New issues arose over the purchase price of food stamps, the contents of a supplemental food package, and the requirements governing program participation. Staffs dealt with these questions; middle-level participants approved their answers. An expert from a nongovernmental antipoverty group advised on a regulation. A research study of the nutritional needs of pregnant women was influential in determining the contents of the food packages. The program was implemented and over time expanded. The media accorded little or no attention to issues and decisions at this level.

Decision making at the low level in the development of the Federal Interagency Day Care Requirements was disrupted continually by the middle- and even high-level issues that embroiled it. It is worth noting that when the requirements were moved into the middle or high level, the interests, ideas, and actors changed substantially. Child-staff ratios that agency heads and their staffs could agree on became one of untenable once threats of their enforcement created new, unresolved conflicts at the middle or high level. The issue became one of whether the federal government should regulate and standardize care for preschool children and, if so, by what measure and to what extent. The interests, ideas, and research that had sustained the requirements at the low level simply could not carry it at the middle level.

In vetoing the Mondale-Brademus bill, President Nixon transformed a middle-level issue of program design to a high-level issue of government interference in the family. Whether Nixon actually believed that the Comprehensive Child Development Act threatened the sanctity of family life and promoted communal approaches to childrearing, the administration was dissatisfied with the legislation, particularly its administrative provision--reauthorizing the Office of Economic Opportunity and establishing a network of community-based prime sponsors. Philosophical

issues concerning the child development program were in
fact never raised during the congressional debate over
the legislation. Nixon's use of inflammatory language in
his veto message suggests that the administration realized
its only hope of defeating the legislation was to elevate
it from a middle-level debate over programmatic means to
a high-level debate over social values. The political
costs of trying to override the veto were too great for
most members of Congress to risk, and the bill died.

The case studies provide numerous instances of decision
making at all three levels of the policy schema. In each
situation the nature of the issue, the goals and resources
of the involved actors, and the objectives of the policy
proposal determined the level of decision making. Yet in
some cases--for example, the drafting of the day care
requirements and the negotiations surrounding the Comprehensive Child Development Act, we observe that the level
of decision making shifted in response to events in the
policy process and the specific and conscious actions of
key participants to achieve their goals. These actions
and their consequences for policy outcomes suggest that
not only is our analytic framework helpful in explaining
past events but also that it has operational significance
for participants in future federal policy making as well.

OPERATIONAL IMPLICATIONS

The analytic framework provides a means of bringing order
to complex phenomena and of drawing lessons about effective participation in the policy formation process. At
each level of decision making, a number of conditions
exist that affect the potential roles of the components
of policy making, the options available to different
actors in the process, and the possible policy outputs.
Understanding the nature of these conditions and their
influence on policy making suggests certain strategic
opportunities or levers that are available at each level
to aid participants.

As previously noted, certain actors are typical, even
necessary, to decision making at each level and therefore
have positional advantage. At the high level, issues can
be resolved only by the President, selected members of
the congressional leadership, and the Supreme Court. At
the middle level, decision making requires the participation of members of Congress, cabinet members, and other
presidential appointees or their designees, but not

necessarily the President. At the low level the principal actors are congressional staffs and officials in the executive branch agencies. Nongovernmental interests can participate at all levels of decision making, but to be most effective they must involve strong and visible coalitions at the high level and more specific political advantage and technical expertise at the middle and low levels. Although all of these actors operate to some extent at each level, they are most effective at their typical level. For all participants there are costs associated with participation at levels other than their typical ones. They must build effective ties, develop relationships, and often trade favors, all of which require the expenditure of resources, especially time. Without such ties and relationships, a participant is less likely to succeed.

One important aspect of effective participation at any level of decision making is access to the key participants who are necessary to the resolution of the issue in question. The high level is most difficult to penetrate for the average participant in federal policy making because he or she must enlist the support of a few, largely inaccessible key actors. Strategic opportunities are principally a matter of access: to the most visible, high-level policy makers in government; to powerful non-governmental interests; to the mass media, which are integral tools for mobilizing the public and interest groups; and to institutional controls, such as high-level appointments, legislative vetoes, and the authority to rule existing laws and statutes unconstitutional. Because there are more actors who typically participate at the middle and low levels, these arenas are more easily entered by outsiders.

Another important aspect of effective participation is recognizing how and when changing social, economic, demographic, and political factors create conditions that are favorable to new policy initiatives. The changing socioeconomic status of women and their rapid entry into the labor force stimulated the establishment of the child care tax deduction/credit. Similarly, the civil rights movement contributed to the social awareness that created a favorable climate for nutrition programs, compensatory education programs, and other initiatives designed to overcome poverty. Contextual factors frequently present windows for change. At each level of decision making, actors who recognize these opportunities and act on them can significantly advance their causes.

Power at the high level, it has been noted, is largely
the power to persuade and to dramatize. It is the power
to shape public opinion and define or redefine social
goals. To achieve success at the high level requires an
understanding of broad currents of public opinion, of the
larger strategic issues of national politics, and of the
large strategic power blocs. It also requires greater
political support or consensus than at other levels.
Therefore, participants seeking access to policy making
at this level usually do so through coalitions and
alliances. Although necessary to effect change, such
alliances generally involve compromises among interests
and often result in the distortion of an idea or policy
initiative from its original form. They frequently
require a significant commitment of time to build and a
great deal of energy to maintain. Because of its
visibility, decision making at the high level is very
seductive, yet it can also be very costly for participants who lack the essential strategic opportunities and
resources. Many short-term political appointees and
elected officials, for example, find it difficult and
impractical to enter the high level of decision making.
Because of their generally brief tenure of office (just
over two years on the average), they can accomplish more
on behalf of a particular constituency and have greater
influence over federal policy initiatives at the middle
and low levels, which are their typical arenas. Under
normal circumstances, only when especially favorable
opportunities present themselves can such actors effectively participate in decision making at the high level.

At the middle level of decision making, strategic
opportunities are more concrete. They involve access to
individuals and institutions with the power to initiate
and enact legislation affecting the authorization of
programs and agency structures and the appropriation of
funds. Power at the middle level is the power to control
programs, personnel, and budgets. It is not the power to
shape public opinion or define public goals, but rather
to design and initiate programmatic means to achieve them.

To achieve success at the middle level requires a
different type of political support than at the high
level. It requires continuous political interaction with
other participants and frequently creates problems of
divided loyalties. In contrast to the high level,
effective participation at the middle level is a matter
of establishing effective working relationships with
committee and subcommittee chairmen, program officials,

and the executive staffs of interest groups with high stakes in specific outcomes. Coalitions of interests may be smaller than at the high level and have more specific goals—for example, the enactment of a program or the expansion of an appropriation that does not involve issues or conflicts concerning fundamental social values. Decision making at the middle level is less visible and therefore participants are less concerned with access to the media than access to researchers and other professional communities having knowledge and strong interests in program content and size. Information about programmatic content, effects, and political feasibility as well as organizational control over the structure of programs and administering agencies are far more essential levers to decision making at this level than visibility. Effective participation requires a sense of timing, maneuver, opportunism, and an instinct for identifying trade-offs and fashioning compromises. Though middle-level decision making is frequently a prolonged process, it is generally less time-consuming than decision making at the high level. For that reason, many elected officials and political appointees find they can be more productive by participating at this level. They can frequently wield significant influence by introducing a bill, adding an item to the President's budget, or instituting an agency reorganization.

At the low level, the primary strategic opportunity or lever is expertise. Power at the low level resides in regulation writing and project management—the implementation of policies and programs established at the high and middle levels. Technical knowledge is essential to achieving success. Research results, especially those of evaluation studies, are frequently influential in the design of delivery systems, the establishment of eligibility requirements, or the drafting of specific regulations and guidelines. Effective participation at the low level is a matter of communicating with experts and technicians. It requires a sense of how specialists work, of how long it takes for them to produce answers to questions, and of the limitations on their perspectives. Political support is also significant in decision making at the low level, though generally it is much more specifically targeted than at the high or middle levels and does not usually require the establishment of large coalitions among interests. Public visibility generally offers no advantage. In fact, participants at this level generally believe their position is enhanced by <u>not</u>

attracting broad attention. When attention is drawn to low-level decision making, unresolved middle- and high-level issues are likely to surface and shift the policy-making arena as well as introduce new key actors.

As we have noted, the level of decision making is generally determined by the nature of the issue in question, the goals and resources of the participants, and the objectives of the policy proposal. From time to time, however, actors may decide to shift the level of decision making in order to advance their cause, particularly as a means of blocking a particular policy initiative. By shifting the level of decision making a participant not only introduces new issues into the debate but opens the process to new participants. Resolution depends on the strength and support of a new group of key actors. In the defeat of the Mondale-Brademus bill, this strategy was successful. The President vetoed the bill, and congressional proponents could not muster the votes to override. Nevertheless, without assured support and control at a higher or lower level, a move to shift the level of decision making can be risky. In general, it is a less effective strategy for initiating a new policy proposal than for blocking one already under consideration.

In summary, a major lesson emerges from our application of the analytic framework to the concrete instances presented in the case studies: To enhance one's position in the policy formation process, a participant must understand the conditions and constraints of decision making at each level. He or she must recognize the typical level at which different types of issues can feasibly be resolved and with what possible policy outcomes. Similarly, a participant must recognize the level of decision making at which he or she has the greatest positional advantage and concentrate his or her energies there. When there is cause to shift the level of decision making, a participant must carefully assess the costs and the risks associated with operating at a different level. If one can gain access to key actors and can attract the necessary political support, visibility, administrative control, and expertise to participate effectively, the change may produce a desired outcome; if not, it is likely to result in failure.

In the next chapter we apply these general principles to participation in federal policy formation affecting children and families.

5 Future Federal Policy Formation Affecting Children and Their Families

As stated at the beginning of this report, the panel undertook its study of federal decision making affecting children and their families as a basis for creating a more sophisticated understanding of how federal policy toward this target group is formulated; identifying conditions and constraints that characterize the federal policy formation process and that are likely to influence the content of new proposals in the near future; and exploring how future participants on behalf of children and their families might more effectively influence federal decision making.

The panel's analysis of the case studies produced some interesting insights concerning the dynamics of federal policy making in the context of the Special Supplemental Food Program for Women, Infants, and Children (WIC), the Federal Interagency Day Care Requirements, and the child care tax deduction/credit. Two major questions remain:

1. What have we learned from our study about the conditions and constraints inherent in federal policy making toward children and families that is likely to influence the content of policy proposals in the near future?

2. What have we learned about how participants in federal decision making in general can most effectively influence the process on behalf of children and families?

In the 1980s, Congress and the Reagan administration will face the problems of high inflation, increasing unemployment, declining productivity, uncertain energy supplies at predictably higher prices, and severe international tensions. Most of the domestic policy alternatives under discussion propose to constrain program

72

growth, to limit government expenditures, to substitute
categorical programs with block grants to the states, and
to improve the productivity or effectiveness of government
involvement where it already exists. With the possible
exception of youth employment and training initiatives,
few if any new proposals are directly focused on improving
the well-being of children and families, either through
the establishment of new programs or the refocusing of
existing ones, despite the continued calls of children's
representatives both within and outside government.

What, then, are the prospects for children's policy in
the 1980s? To a significant extent they are shaped by
the existing federal response to children's needs and the
process that has produced these programs.

As in other areas of social policy, policies and
programs for children have evolved piecemeal over time.
As the case studies presented here suggest, they have
involved a number of decision points and intermediary
actions. They are not the result of any coherent process
of contemplation, debate, and choice.

Responsibility for policies and programs for children
and families remains widely distributed among many congressional committees and administrative agencies. As
the case studies demonstrate, the House Education and
Labor Committee, the House Ways and Means Committee, the
Senate Agriculture Committee, the Senate Finance Committee, and the Senate Committee on Labor and Public Welfare
are just a few of the diverse groups in Congress responsible for the interests and well-being of children and
families. Similarly, in the executive branch, many
agencies in the departments of Agriculture, Labor,
Justice, the Interior, Health and Human Services, and
Education operate programs for this target group, all
with little coordination or even communication. Indeed,
the recent establishment of the new U.S. Department of
Education represents a further splintering of executive
branch responsibility for children's policies and
programs. Although the panel does not suggest that this
widely decentralized structure of control and responsibility for children's policies and programs is undesirable, we do suggest that there is no central high-level
agent charged with coordinating federal initiatives on
behalf of this target group.

Policy making for children and families is generally
influenced by a large number of organized interests
representing service providers, professional groups,
labor unions, parents, researchers, the poor, blacks,

Hispanics, women, and even selected groups of children themselves. As we have observed, these groups promote a variety of interests and perspectives that sometimes agree, but more often than not disagree, over policy objectives. On the occasions when they have worked together they have enhanced their positions--for example, the alliance between farm interests and antipoverty groups in the WIC case. When they have worked at cross-purposes, these organized interests have frequently diminished the political strength of all.

As a result of this process, children's policies and programs, unlike the universal programs that have emerged for older Americans, veterans, and the unemployed, have tended to be selective responses to selective needs. Federal attention has focused on the problems of child abuse, inadequate nutrition, learning disabilities, sudden infant death syndrome, juvenile delinquency, teenage pregnancy, foster care, and the special needs of handicapped children, to name just a few. Similarly, programs such as Aid to Families with Dependent Children, the Supplemental Security Income Program, and the Work Incentives Program have helped address the income and unemployment problems of families with children. Nevertheless, more comprehensive policy proposals--the Family Assistance Plan and the Comprehensive Child Development Act, for example--have consistently failed.

As Steiner points out, "the children's cause can boast of few absolute successes" (Steiner, 1976:240). The reason is probably not that America is not a child-loving nation, and it goes beyond the fact that children cannot vote, lobby, or be elected to Congress. The reasons are far more complex. First, there is no fundamental agreement concerning the appropriate responsibility of government to intervene in the privacy of the family to ensure that children are adequately cared for and that their physical, emotional, and developmental needs are met. In a democratic society that places a high priority on the integrity of family life and that worries about the possibility of state control over childrearing, disagreement over the appropriate limits of public intervention in parent-child relations is inevitable and appropriate. As we observed time and again in the case studies, this ambivalence, although understandable, leaves no basis for legitimizing child development and family relationships as an item on the public rather than the private agenda-- except in clear cases in which children are orphaned, abandoned, physically or mentally handicapped, or abused.

Moreover, it discourages far-reaching designs, such as the proposal for the Family Assistance Plan or the Comprehensive Child Development Act.

Second, there is no focal point within government on either the legislative or administrative side to unify and strengthen federal responsibility for children's policies and programs. The Subcommittee on Aging, Family and Human Services of the Senate Committee on Labor and Human Resources would seem a logical body within Congress to provide leadership in matters of children's policy. Yet because children are a part of every congressional constituency and because the responsibility for nutrition, welfare, education, health, and human development is distributed across several standing committees, the subcommittee has never managed to establish itself as a legislative focal point. In addition, because neither it nor its predecessor, the Subcommittee on Children and Youth, has ever achieved any important legislative victories, it has failed to develop a strong identity and reputation.

Similarly, the establishment of the Children's Bureau in 1912, the Office of Child Development in 1969, and the Administration for Children, Youth, and Families in 1976 were all intended to provide executive branch leadership. They have each failed to do so. This failure is in part due to the wide distribution of responsibility for children's programs and research across the federal bureaucracy and in part to the inability of this long line of child-focused agencies to attract and hold key personnel and programs--with the exception of Head Start. Of all the major federal program initiatives on behalf of children and families--Aid to Families with Dependent Children; the Early and Periodic Screening, Diagnosis, and Treatment Program; the School Lunch Program or any of the child nutrition programs; and Title I of the Elementary and Secondary Education Act or any of the major education programs, to name just a few--none is housed in the Administration for Children, Youth, and Families or was in its predecessor, the Office of Child Development. These agencies have seldom taken the initiative in proposing major new programs for the federal agenda or in restructurizing existing policies and programs to improve their effectiveness and efficiency. As we observed, the Office of Child Development's drive for the Comprehensive Child Development Act was vetoed by Nixon. Subsequently, the agency suffered from a lack of credibility and respect among decision makers and children's advocates. The Administration for Children, Youth, and Families has yet to recover.

A major consequence is that no mechanism currently exists for formulating federal policy toward children and families at the high level. In fact, since the failure of the Mondale-Brademus bill, there has been almost no high-level federal policy making toward this target group. Activity has centered at the middle and low levels, primarily the latter. The vast majority of governmental actors interested in the well-being of children participate at the low level. Their primary responsibility is to implement and monitor programs that have been designed and established by others. Indeed, even if the President were to propose a dramatic new comprehensive family policy approach—as Carter did in 1976—no vehicle exists for translating that directive into operating programs. The result is that such proposals further energize the existing unorganized scramble of governmental and nongovernmental representatives for children and families.

Third, children's representatives inside and outside government have too often lacked an adequate understanding of the dynamics of the policy formation process and how most effectively to influence decision making on behalf of children and their families. The disarray characteristic of federal activity is inevitable in light of the fragmented approach traditionally taken by legislators, bureaucrats, and nongovernmental interests alike. They continually call for more programs and larger appropriations, when in fact more may not mean better. In so doing they not only compete for scarce resources with advocates for the aging, the handicapped, farmers, and the unemployed, but they also compete among themselves. Lack of coordination among children's advocates and their failure to establish priorities are not the only hindrances to the children's cause. Participants in federal policy formation have frequently failed to comprehend the governmental decision-making process itself. Specifically, they have not recognized that policy outcomes depend to a large extent on the mechanisms by which they are formulated, that there are few governmental actors well-positioned to enhance the children's cause, and that strategic opportunities and levers for change vary according to the nature of the policy issue and the participants involved. Moreover, few participants, regardless of their ideological or political affiliations,

recognize their position in the decision-making process
and understand how they can most effectively exert
influence.

In sum, the forecast for federal policies affecting
children and their families does not look radically
different from that of the past decade. Short of a major
upheaval in social values, no theory or ideology is
likely to emerge that will clarify the appropriate place
for children's policy and programs on the public agenda.
Short of a major reorganization of the congressional
committee system and the agency structure in the
Department of Education and the Department of Health and
Human Services, coherent federal leadership on matters of
children's policy is unlikely very soon--and probably not
desirable. Hence, the primary means available for
improving (without necessarily expanding) public policies
toward children and their families is for concerned
governmental and nongovernmental participants to improve
their understanding of the policy formation process and
to develop better strategies for participation. To this
end the Panel for the Study of the Policy Formation
Process has directed its efforts.

References and Bibliography

Bane, M. J. (1977) Here To Stay: American Families in
the Twentieth Century. New York: Basic Books.

Banfield, E. C. (1961) Political Influence. New York:
The Free Press.

Bardach, J. (1977) The Implementation Game: What
Happens After A Bill Becomes a Law. Cambridge,
Mass.: The MIT Press.

Berne, E. (1964) Games People Play. New York: Grove
Press.

Cobb, R. W., and Elder, C. D. (1972) Participation in
American Politics. Boston, Mass.: Allyn & Bacon.

Dahl, R. (1963) Modern Political Analysis. Englewood
Cliffs, N.J.: Prentice-Hall.

deLone, R. H. (1979) Small Futures: Children,
Inequality, and the Limits of Liberal Reform. New
York: Harcourt Brace Jovanovich.

Downs, A. (1972) Up and down with ecology--"the
issue-attention cycle." Public Interest
28(Summer):38-50.

Dye, T. R. (1972) Understanding Public Policy.
Englewood Cliffs, N.J.: Prentice-Hall.

Easton, D. (1971) The Political System. New York:
Knopf.

Easton, D. (1979) A Framework for Political Analysis.
Chicago: University of Chicago Press.

Family Impact Seminar (1978) Toward an Inventory of
Federal Programs with Direct Impact on Family.
Washington, D.C.: Family Impact Seminar.

Freud, S. (1964) An Outline of Psychoanalysis. In
Standard Edition, Vol. 23. London: Hogarth Press.

Froman, L. A., Jr. (1967) An analysis of public policy
in cities. Journal of Politics 29(February):94-108.

78

Gamson, W. A. (1968) Power and Discontent. Homewood, Ill.: Dorsey Publishers.

George, A. L. (1979) Case studies and theory development: the method of structured, focussed comparison. Pp. 43-68 in P. G. Lauren, ed., Diplomacy: New Approaches in History, Theory and Policy. New York: The Free Press.

Greenberg, G. D., Miller, J. A., Mohr, L. B., and Vladeck, B. (1977) Developing public policy theory: perspectives from empirical research. The American Political Science Review 71:1532-1543.

Hage, J., and Hollingsworth, J. R. (1977) The first steps toward the integration of social theory and social policy. Annals of the American Academy of Political and Social Sciences 434(November):1-23.

Heclo, H. H. (1972) Review article: policy analysis. British Journal of Political Science 2:83-108.

House, E. R. (1977) The Logic of Evaluative Argument. Los Angeles, Calif.: UCLA Center for the Study of Evaluation.

Keniston, K., and the Carnegie Council on Children (1977) All Our Children: The American Family Under Pressure. New York: Harcourt Brace Jovanovich.

Lash, T., and Sigal, H. (1975) The State of the Child: New York City. New York: Foundation for Child Development.

Lasswell, H. D., and Kaplan, A. (1970) Power and Society. New Haven, Conn.: Yale University Press.

Lowi, T. J. (1968) Public Policy Making Reexamined. San Francisco, Calif.: Chandler.

Lowi, T. J. (1972) Four systems of policy, politics, and choice. Public Administration Review 32(July/August):298-310.

Lynn, L. E., Jr. (1978) Fiscal and Organizational Constraints on Family Policy. Unpublished paper prepared for the International Seminar on Family Policy, March 16-17, University of Notre Dame.

Lynn, L. E., Jr. (1980) The State and Human Services: Organizational Change in a Political Context. Cambridge, Mass.: The MIT Press.

Mills, C. W. (1956) The Power Elite. New York: Oxford University Press.

Mundel, D. S. (1980) The Apparent Lack of Connection Between Congressional Concerns and Those of Parent Program Proponents. Unpublished paper presented to Parent Education and Public Policy Conference, Bush Institute for Child and Family Policy, University of North Carolina, Chapel Hill.

National Research Council (1976) Toward a National Policy for Children and Families. Advisory Committee on Child Development, Assembly of Behavioral and Social Sciences. Washington, D.C.: National Academy of Sciences.

National Research Council (1978) The Federal Investment in Knowledge of Social Problems. Volume 1: Study Project Report. Study Project on Social Research and Development, Assembly of Behavioral and Social Sciences. Washington, D.C.: National Academy of Sciences.

Ranney, A. (1968) Political Science and Public Policy. Chicago: Markheim Publishers.

Rose, R. (1976) Government Programs Affecting Children: The Federal Budget FY 1974-1976. Unpublished paper prepared for the Study of Research and Development Needs for the Making of Social Policy Toward Young Children. J.F.K. School of Government, Harvard University.

Schelling, T. (1960) The Strategy of Conflict. Cambridge, Mass.: Harvard University Press.

Snapper, K. J., Barriga, H. H., Baumgarner, F. H., and Wagner, C. S. (1975) The Status of Children 1975. Washington, D.C.: Social Research Group, The George Washington University.

Stake, R. E. (1978) The case study method in social research. Educational Researcher 7(2):5-8.

Steinbruner, J. D. (1974) The Cybernetic Theory of Decision. Princeton, N.J.: Princeton University Press.

Steiner, G. (1976) The Children's Cause. Washington, D.C.: The Brookings Institution.

Sundquist, J. L. (1968) Politics and Policy. Washington, D.C.: The Brookings Institution.

U.S. Department of Health, Education, and Welfare (1979) Federal Programs That Relate to Children. GPO Document No. 017-091-00227-4. Washington, D.C.: U.S. Department of Health, Education, and Welfare.

Von Neumann, J., and Morgenstern, O. (1953) Theory of Games and Economic Behavior. Princeton, N.J.: Princeton University Press.

Wakefield, R., and Wakefield D., eds. (1978) American Family. Special Report No. 1. Washington, D.C.: Wakefield Washington Assocoates., Inc.

Wakefield, R., and Wakefield, D., eds. (1979) American Family. Special Report No. 2. Washington, D.C.: Wakefield Washington Associates., Inc.

White House Conference on Children   (1970)   Profiles of
  Children. Washington, D.C.:   U.S. Government Printing
  Office.
Wilson, J. Q.   (1973)   Political Organizations.   New
  York: Basic Books.
Wilson, J. Q.   (1975)   The Rise of the Bureaucratic
  State.   The Public Interest 41(Fall):77-103.

Part 2:
Case Studies

The Special Supplemental
Food Program for Women,
Infants, and Children
John R. Nelson, Jr.

INTRODUCTION

By any measure, the Special Supplemental Food Program for Women, Infants, and Children (WIC) makes an intriguing study of the policy-making process. Enacted by Congress in 1972, it was a $20-million pilot program designed to provide specified food supplements to a few thousand pregnant women, lactating mothers, infants, and preschool children determined by health clinics to be nutritionally "at risk." Plagued over its 7-year history by litigation, impoundments, a presidential veto, controversial evaluations, and fiscal austerity, WIC nonetheless reached 2.5 million people at an annual cost of $750 million by the close of fiscal 1980. It is touted by administrators at the U.S. Department of Agriculture (USDA), congressional supporters, and public advocates as the most successful health or welfare program in the federal government. Congress has reenacted it three times with near unanimity. It represents one of the very few major programs greatly expanded under the Carter administration.

This chapter traces the evolution of federal policy toward pregnant women, infants, and children in the areas of health care and nutrition. It pursues the historical strands that led to the creation of WIC, from the New Deal to the Great Society programs of the 1960s. This chapter then focuses on WIC's direct antecedent, the Commodity Supplemental Food Program, which was initiated in 1968. In sequential sections, WIC's origins in Congress, its difficulties with the USDA and the Office of Management and Budget (OMB), its days in federal court, and the evaluations of its efficacy are examined. Throughout the case study, particular attention is accorded to the role of research and evaluation in policy making.

85

CHILD NUTRITION: THE NEW DEAL TO THE GREAT SOCIETY

Direct federal financial support for feeding children
began with a conversation between Harry Hopkins, administrator for the Federal Emergency Relief Administration,
and Frederick I. Daniels, director of New York's Emergency
Relief Administration. The first 100 days of the Roosevelt administration had just ended. Hopkins had been
made czar of the federal relief and employment programs.
Daniels had asked him if some of the $200 million appro-
priated for relief could subsidize New York's financially
strapped school lunch program. Hopkins agreed to match
every two state dollars with one federal dollar. Concomitantly, the Reconstruction Finance Corporation agreed to
loan money to support lunch programs in Mississippi. The
Work Projects Administration (WPA) subsequently supported
local lunch programs with their personnel. The crucial
metamorphosis, however, which carried the nascent programs
beyond the demise of these New Deal agencies into the
1960s, came with the linkage of school lunches to the
disposal of farm surpluses.[1]

Section 32 of the Agricultural Adjustment Act of 1935
provided a compensatory fund from tariff revenues to
increase farm incomes. The theory was that industrial
tariffs compelled farmers to spend more money on their
equipment than they would have to in a situation of free
international trade. The law instructed the USDA to
spend these revenues to increase the price levels of farm
commodities by encouraging "the domestic consumption of
such commodities." Backed by Section 32 funds, the number
of schools serving lunches grew to over 3,800, serving
342,000 children in 1937.[2] The Surplus Marketing
Corporation provided not only lunches but also food for
relief agencies, institutions, and, in 1939, a food stamp
program. Piloted in Rochester, New York, food stamps
spread quickly throughout the country, reaching 4 million
people by 1941. The USDA also began to provide lunch
milk to school children for a penny or free of charge in
mid-1940 and expanded their distribution to 417,000
children in 18 months.[3]

The great expansion of federally supported school
lunches did not occur until late 1940. In August of that
year, the WPA and the Surplus Marketing Administration of
the USDA issued a directive to all regional, state, and
local personnel involved in federal food programs. It
began rather succinctly: "Recent violent disruptions in
world distribution of American farm products and the

prospects of added losses of markets make imperative the development of new outlets for American surplus food-stuffs." The directive specified three areas of expansion: food stamps, direct distribution of commodities, and school lunch programs. They sought to increase the coverage of the lunch program "to not less than six million children during the 1940-41 school term"--fully half of the school population.' It was a goal that they came within 800,000 children of achieving. By fiscal 1943 the USDA was spending over $18 million annually on school lunches and the commodities that local distribution centers received. (For funding, participation, and legislative data, see Appendixes B and C.)

Well before the USDA distributed food for lunches, or for any other purposes, it had published numerous pamphlets on nutrition and diet, e.g., Food for Children (1931), Milk for the Family (1933), and Meals and Recipes for Lunches (1936). When it entered the food distribution business, the stream of booklets became a torrent. The Bureau of Home Economics (later the Bureau of Human Nutrition and Home Economics) published over 50 pamphlets in the 1940s dealing specifically with school lunches. The USDA also provided nutrition and production data to the military for diet planning during the World War II. In 1933 the Programs Planning Division of the USDA began coordinating crop production with human nutritional requirements. The onset of World War II brought the first serious and extensive application of nutritional needs to crop production: If crops were planted according to their nutritional value, then any potential tension between what was distributed as surplus and what was nutritious would dissipate.[5]

World War II stimulated a flurry of nutrition-related activities. At President Roosevelt's request, the National Research Council established the Food and Nutrition Board in May 1941. The board drew together existing research, previous standards, and USDA data to develop recommended dietary allowances (RDA) for persons by age, sex, and level of activity. The original RDA covered calories, protein, calcium, iron, and some vitamins; it specified, in a preliminary manner, the nutritional needs of pregnant women, infants, and lactating mothers. Subsequent reports described the "staggering" extent of malnutrition in antebellum America. "It is obvious," one report concluded, "that an appalling proportion of families were receiving what might with considerable understatement be called an unsatisfactory diet." Guided by these recommendations, the USDA launched a nationwide campaign to improve the diets of Americans. To abet this effort, it expanded the Bureau of Home Economics into the Bureau of Human Nutrition and Home Economics, and created a Nutrition and Food Conservation Branch of the Food Distribution Administration to incorporate all food-related activities in the federal government. Internationally, USDA officials organized the United Nation's Interim Commission on Food and Agriculture, which issued, among other things, worldwide standards for human nutrition.[6]

The lunch program in particular, and the feeding of children in general, did not come under congressional scrutiny until 1943, when the USDA requested a $50-million appropriation for the program's continuance. The war had absorbed the agricultural surplus and rendered direct commodity distribution impossible. Only commercial purchases could maintain the program. Secretary of Agriculture Claude Wichard proposed legislation to the White House through the Bureau of the Budget to create a permanent lunch program. He stressed the necessity of adequate food distribution to children in the face of wartime rationing/and working mothers. He suggested the President convene a national committee on child nutrition. Other USDA officials contacted the Bureau of the Budget to support Wichard. War Food Administrator Marvin Jones explained that the lunch program ensured "proper distribution of the civilian food supply during the war" and "expanded markets for agricultural products and . . . farm surplus during peacetime." A USDA memorandum stressed malnutrition as evidenced by the high rates of draft rejections. In sum, Wichard and the USDA had, by 1943, not only presented all the arguments that would be offered subsequently to support the program but had also identified in their choice of a child nutrition committee all the important elements of what came to be the political coalition for feeding children.[7]

The complex preparation for maintaining a lunch program developed out of a postwar planning commission on agriculture that met in July 1943. The commission anticipated strong economic growth after the war and made four assumptions about agricultural policy: first, that large postwar incomes could maintain a strong market for farm products and adequate diets for Americans; second, that farmers should anticipate expanding their output of commodities to meet this demand; third, the food stamp and school lunch programs would compensate for any slack

in normal market outlets; and fourth, as a result of
these factors, little production restriction would be
necessary. Though by no means the principal instrument
of farm policy, agricultural policy makers considered the
lunch program an integral tool of price stabilization.[8]

While the administration prepared permanent legislation, the congressional agriculture committees permitted
a temporary appropriation to continue the program.
Congress approved of the appropriation as a wartime
exigency to ensure food distribution to children.
Congressional concerns about funding the program beyond
the end of the war resulted in the House rejection of an
appropriation to extend it pending hearings on formal
legislation. A peacetime program awaited the full
legislative process and consideration of the whole issue
of agricultural stabilization and the feeding of
children.[9]

Within the administration a disagreement erupted
between the War Food Administration (representing the
USDA) and the Federal Security Agency (representing the
Office of Education) over administrative jurisdiction of
the proposed School Lunch Program (SLP). The Federal
Security Agency argued that as a program functioning
within the school system for an educational purpose, the
SLP should come under the Office of Education. War Food
Administrator Marvin Jones disagreed. "I cannot too
strongly emphasize," he wrote, "that, although the
educational aspects of this are very significant, the
operational meaning of the program is that it is providing
food. It is a food program in wartime providing proper
distribution of food, and in peacetime expanding markets
for agricultural products and providing orderly removal
of farm surplus."[10] That the USDA prevailed indicates
to some degree that the administration assigned a higher
priority to the farm disposal aspect of the program than
to the educational aspect. With regard to nutrition-
related activities, however, the USDA was the logical
choice: It was by far the preeminent federal agency
involved in nutritional research and information
dissemination. Inertia and the relative clout of the
executive and congressional entities involved in the SLP
also contributed to the USDA's victory.

With the onset of congressional hearings in late 1944
through 1945, a nascent children's feeding coalition
became evident. Various farm organizations and their
representatives served as the bulwark of continued federal
funds for lunches. School lunches, the National Farmers

Union argued, were "a big market farmers cannot afford to lose. . . ." USDA officials also stressed the need to maintain outlets for surplus farm products, which were again becoming a problem in May 1945. Indeed, the program, as Senator Richard Russell noted, "grew up out of the disposition of surplus agricultural commodities, and no one had ever seriously discussed any bill providing for a federal school-lunch program prior to that time."[11] In a brief House Agriculture Committee exchange the "main objective" of the program could not be clarified. Representative Harold Cooley believed that the primary objective was the disposal of surplus agricultural commodities and feeding school children was "just collateral." The majority, however, stressed it as a "two point" program: surplus disposal and children's feeding.[12] The dual stress enabled program promoters to draw a broad range of support outside agriculture.

The children's feeding coalition encompassed nonfarm groups that included school administrators, who had a direct financial stake in continued federal funding, organized labor, PTAs, social organizations, professional nutritionists, and medical experts. In their testimony before the House Agriculture Committee, many nutritionists pleaded for a flat national commitment to children's nutrition regardless of agricultural surpluses. The surgeon general made an extraordinary plea, in terms of need, for a national policy to combat malnutrition when he described Americans as "poorly fed." Another official of the U.S. Public Health Service noted that pregnant women and infants would be an excellent target population for nutritional aid. The committee ignored his comment and all other suggestions to modify or expand federal aid based on nutritional need beyond the lunch program. Such innovations from the depression era as food stamps and the school milk program were not revitalized. The ideologically conservative Congress of 1946 authorized only a limited federal role in nutritional welfare.[13]

Support for the program, particularly among southern members of Congress, stemmed from several factors other than farm incomes. The primary basis was the enormous popularity of the lunch program among constituents throughout the nation. Second, feeding school children was an inherently appealing activity. Even those few members of Congress opposed to federal support praised school lunches as an eminent state or local endeavor. In addition, there was the problem, conceived in terms of national security rather than social welfare, of malnutrition in America, demonstrated by selective service rejection. General Lewis Hershey, the Selective Service director, testified that 40 to 60 percent of those rejected for military service had defects related to nutritional deficiencies. Overall, this meant that roughly 1 of every 10 draft-age males was sufficiently malnourished to preclude induction. Nutrition-related rejections were concentrated in poor southern states and were much higher among blacks, though this revelation evoked little congressional comment. The South, too, faced the problem of newly consolidated rural schools that required busing children, making it impossible for them to return home for lunch. Regardless of the school's distance from home, the absence from home of working mothers during the war made a home lunch difficult in all parts of the nation.[14]

The School Lunch Act of 1946 set the basic terms under which the lunch program operated into the early 1960s. Funding for the first decade remained around $80 million per year. In light of the explosion of the school population and inflation, this constant funding level represented a continuous decline in federal participation. Federal funds were paid as matching grants in a ration declining from 1:1 to 1:4 over a 5-year period. This ratio was adjusted according to the extent to which a state's per capita income varied from the national average--an advantage to the South. Finally, the legislation provided for nutritional standards, nondiscriminating discounts or free meals to poor children, nonprofit programs, and priority purchases of commodities in surplus. The preamble of the act "declared [it] to be the policy of Congress, as a measure of national security, to safeguard the health and well-being of the nation's children and to encourage the domestic consumption of nutritious agricultural commodities. . . ." The policy statement struck a balance between the two major interests of the children's feeding coalition.[15]

In 1946 the USDA issued detailed nutritional requirements for school lunches. They divided the lunches into three types and provided a declining scale of reimbursement dependent on the lunch's nutritional adequecy. Type A supplied one third to one half of the daily nutrient needs of a child. Type B supplied roughly one third of a child's daily needs. Type C was one half a pint of milk. A more complete lunch yielded a higher federal subsidy. The local school or district chose the exact composition of the meal with an eye to what commodities were in surplus. Although this practice often precipitated a jejune diet, the nutritional regulations did limit abuse of the mandate that required the use of commodities in surplus.[16]

Prior to the 1960s, Congress enacted only one other federal program related to feeding children: the Special Milk Program (SMP). As the Korean War ended, the USDA's Commodity Credit Corporation found itself accumulating milk at an increasing rate. In 1954 its price support operations absorbed 10 percent of the total milk supply—more than triple its acquisitions of the year before. Milk prices declined, and national farm incomes suffered from this weakness of its largest single component. Not only production increases wrought from mechanization, but also a decade-long decline in per capita milk consumption had created a crisis for the dairy industry. Their organizations turned to Congress and the USDA. The result was a revival of the depression era school milk program, renamed the Special Milk Program, a $50-million "domestic disposal program" to ease dairy surplus by providing subsidized milk to school children in addition to lunch milk.

When the SMP came up for a supplementary appropriation and renewal in January 1956, the USDA proposed a 20 percent increase in the appropriation and an expansion of the program into nonschool areas devoted to children. As in the initial legislation, the burden of congressional testimony came from USDA officials and dairy organizations.

The passage of the new law increased SMP funding by 20 percent in fiscal 1956 and by 25 percent more in fiscal 1957. More significantly, the new law extended the SMP to nursery schools, day care centers, summer camps, settlement houses, and "similar non-profit institutions devoted to the care and training of under-privileged children on a public welfare or charitable basis."[17] By 1959, gross federal spending exceeded $210 million on the lunch and milk programs operating in a wide variety of settings.

Although both programs were administration initiatives, their maintenance and expansion became the hobbyhorse of Congress. In the final two years of the Eisenhower administration, the huge surplus of the Commodity Credit Corporation, which had directly stimulated the SMP, began to ease. Coupled with a general fiscal conservatism, these circumstances led the administration, through the USDA, to oppose any increases in the SLP and seek a retrenchment of the SMP. The issue involved more than a change in farm surplus or fiscal policy. An important reason for the stagnation of nutrition programs for children in the 1950s was the decision to use that surplus abroad as an instrument of foreign policy (P.L. 480 and the Food for Peace Program). This decision reflected the exigencies of international relations and the impact domestic disposal was purported to have on prices. "The commodities contemplated to be set aside," Agriculture Secretary Benson explained, "are so large that it is not anticipated any substantial portion can be disposed of through domestic channels without disrupting markets and our future price support programs. The only solution to the problem," he concluded, "lies in recourse to distribution abroad." The nature of the agricultural market and foreign policy combined to prevent the expansion of the programs. Indeed, had it not been for Congress, the programs would have been curtailed.[18]

Against the administration's proposed cuts assembled the now familiar agricultural lobbies, school administrators, PTAs, and newly formed food service organizations. At their prompting, citizens inundated Congress with protest letters over the cuts. Farmers did not want subsidized markets reduced nor did parents, educators, or service workers want reduced federal aid or increased costs. The SMP alone accounted for 2 percent of the aggregate fluid milk consumption and probably much more in terms of establishing the habit of drinking milk among children. One of every two school children drank SMP milk. The lunch program purchased $750 million in agricultural products. One of every three school children ate SLP lunches. Overall, approximately one third of the lunch costs were born by the federal government. When the administration attempted to retrench and restrain appropriations for these programs on the grounds of the improved farm situation, it was overwhelmingly defeated in Congress. There was simply no support for the cuts and a phalanx opposed to them.[19]

The administration's challenge did lead supporters of these programs to begin to rethink their heavy reliance on the farm surplus situation for justification. The surplus tended to have an amorphous quality, given form only in terms of the relationship of price to parity. The separation of children's feeding programs from the "surplus" could well mean even higher prices for farmers without the usual criticisms of price support programs. To the various agricultural interests and their representatives, stressing nutritional need in these programs or allowing more input to educators and health specialists would not hamper the programs in their role as a market. Indeed, if need and nutrition were given sway, perhaps the programs might expand beyond the constraints of surplus and parity. No farmer would turn down a price higher than parity. Moreover, the support of members of Congress from nonfarm states would come more easily for food assistance than for price support. As long as it was not used to curtail any price support programs, nutritional need was a method of disposing of surplus agricultural products that was acceptable to the agricultural interests.

The reorientation of federal feeding from surplus disposal toward nutritional need occurred slowly during the 1960s. The farm interests receded in preeminence and the educators, nutritionists, physicians, social workers, and service organizations moved into the forefront of federal policy for feeding children. Although federal policy leaned more toward nutrition than agriculture, the programs still drew political strength from their impact as a subsidy to American agriculture. For this reason they received a great deal of congressional support that would otherwise have been hostile to social welfare measures. On the other hand, a great deal of support that otherwise would have opposed farm subsidies found no objection to feeding needy children and adults. In public opinion polls, food stamp programs (and by inference other feeding programs) enjoyed much greater popular approbation than either cash subsidies for the poor or price supports for farmers (see Appendix A).

The Eisenhower administration was the last to argue for alterations in children's feeding programs based exclusively on changes in farm prices. When Kennedy assumed office, the USDA ceased its opposition to extension of the SMP and expansion of the SLP. Instead, the USDA became an advocate of reform and larger appropriations. Expansionist fiscal policies and an effort to restructure program allocations to reflect better participation rates and nutritional needs led the administration to propose increasing the funding of the SLP and changing the 1946 allocation formula. The old formula used per capita income and the school-age population as the bases for apportionment of federal funds, regardless of the actual participation rate. States therefore found it more financially advantageous to keep participation rates down. Congress revised this formula to reflect participation rates and followed an administration initiative to include a specific appropriation for needy children and schools. By 1962 the SLP and the SMP had been expanded to over $260 million and directed more toward need. This subtle shift in emphasis alienated no one, for funding was adjusted

upward based on need. No middle-class children were
dropped. Aggregate program expenditures on farm products
rose. An expanding economic pie would bring the "other
America" into the affluent society.[20]

Under the auspices of the Johnson administration,
political recognition of America's poor people reached a
level unattained since the prewar depression. The new
administration's stress on need coupled with the burgeoning
financial drain of the war in Vietnam spawned a White House
drive to reorder the priorities in children's feeding
programs and cut back the SMP by 80 percent in fiscal
1967. The drive commenced with Bureau of the Budget's
directives to the USDA to withhold $3 million of the SMP
appropriation for fiscal 1966. The reaction from the
dairy and education interests was swift and predictable.
Bureau of the Budget Director Charles Schultze wrote to
outraged representatives and senators of "the increased
Vietnam defense requirements" and the subsequent decision
to hold SMP expenditures down to $100 million in fiscal
1966. Schultze felt compelled to inform the President of
the vehement opposition to this slight cut and the inevitable outcry against the $79 million cut proposed for fiscal
1967. In defense of this cut he added, "Why subsidize
milk for wealthy Montgomery County school children!" He
sought to restrict the SMP to needy children and schools
without any lunch program. Aside from the losses to the
dairy industry, the only problem the Bureau of the Budget
foresaw was that schools with few needy children might
drop the SMP if federal reimbursement were available only
for the needy. The net savings of $65 million and the war
demands on the budget outweighed these concerns. Whatever
the merits of the arguments, Congress was not impressed.[21]

The thrust of the argument before Congress was that
"the dairy situation is greatly improved now from what it
was in 1954 . . . [and] the diversion of milk to avoid
adding to surplus inventories is no longer a compelling
objective." The only remaining justification for a milk
subsidy was financial need. The remaining $21 million
provided adequately for needy children in the program.[22]
Congress parried with the argument that need, though
significant, could not be used to curtail a subsidy
program. "This is," Representative Sisk told Agriculture
Secretary Freeman, "no way to cure the ills of our dairy
industry. . . ." SMP defenders added that middle-class
children could be malnourished as well as poor ones.
Finally, to the administration's exigencies-of-war plea,

Senator Gruening retorted "perhaps today we should be talking about having both milk and napalm."[23] The mangled cliché had made the point; Congress would allow no $80-million cutback in the SMP.[24]

Although retrenchment of these programs was all but impossible, expansion on the basis of need was relatively easy. The Johnson administration's Great Society programs geared toward needy children drew support from agricultural interests, educators, nutritionists, food service organizations, and social welfare groups. The first comprehensive legislation related to the feeding of children, the Child Nutrition Act of 1966, allocated funds for reduced-price and free lunches, construction of lunch facilities, and a pilot program for needy children. Revived in 1960 and made permanent in 1964, the Food Stamp Program (FSP) joined the SMP as the only program that provided food for poor children and their families outside the school context. Although direct distribution of commodities did precede and continue as a noninstitutional, in-kind nutritional aid to children and poor families in general, the FSP was the only federal program that provided non-commodity nutritional assistance to children outside an institutional context.[25]

In 1967, the year following passage of the Child Nutrition Act, Agriculture Secretary Freeman testified before the House Agriculture Committee for expansion of the FSP and extension of the SLP into preschool and nonschool child care institutions serving needy children. He spoke of the "dual objectives" of the programs: "(1) To get food to people who need it, . . . and (2) to build up the demand for the [farm] production that we are capable of making." The National Welfare Rights Organization joined agricultural interests in support of these changes. The hearing also marked the first time that an agricultural committee of either the House or the Senate had allowed an organization representing needy recipients to testify. There was, however, open hostility between the National Welfare Rights Organization and Senate committee members. Despite this uneasy connection, an avenue had been cleared for feeding the poor and subsidizing the farmers. When the media, the public, and the federal government "discovered" the extent of hunger in America, food aid to the needy supplanted the Commodity Credit Corporation and overshadowed the middle-class subsidies endemic to the SLP and the SMP as the principal domestic outlet for surplus farm products.[26]

Programmatic Antecedents

The Johnson administration's highly orchestrated commitment
to feeding America's hungry children and adults rendered
it particularly vulnerable to the public and congressional
pressures brought to bear in 1967 and 1968. Senate hearings on hunger in Mississippi, chaired by Iowa Senator
Clark and presided over by several presidential aspirants,
revealed severe malnutrition. Charges of allowing blacks
to be starved out of the South and choosing guns over food
cut deeply into the administration's credibility in its
war on hunger and undermined its already hard-pressed
military policy in Vietnam. The approach of an election
year fueled administration fears that Republican leaders
might "take advantage of the issue to embarrass the
administration and present the [Republican] Party in a new
humanitarian image."[27] One blow followed another as
private research groups issued publications such as
Hunger, U.S.A. and Your Daily Bread and CBS televised its
"Hunger in America" documentary, all of which alleged
widespread incompetence and callousness in administration
food programs, especially by the USDA. Public pressure
culminated in the Poor People's Campaign.[28]

Confronted by this political pressure as well as the
November election, the administration attempted to strike
a balance between wartime fiscal constraints and the now
ineluctable demands for action. Freeman viewed the
demands as partisan attacks on the administration--
calculated to discount all its achievements of recent
years. Still, in direct response to this pressure, he
expanded the FSP and improved the quality of the food
available to the poor. Finally, he proposed $15 million
"supplementary commodity packages to improve the diets of
150,000 mothers, 100,000 infants, and 200,000 young
children."[29] This final proposal became the centerpiece
of the administration's response.[30]

Why the Supplemental Food Program (SFP) emerged as the
central response is complex. In the 1967 Senate nutrition
hearings, Harvard University's Robert Coles, among others,
raised the issue of the potential for permanent physical
damage to malnourished infants and small children.
Physicians working in the Maternal and Child Health Service
of the U.S. Department of Health, Education, and Welfare
testified to the health problems attributable to malnutrition. The Children's Bureau, as noted above, had also
been advocating a supplemental food package for high-risk
groups. In early 1968 a "citizens" board of inquiry into

hunger and malnutrition specifically recommended supplements to the diets of pregnant women and infants. All of these finds were reinforced by the subsequent House and Senate hearings on malnutrition.[31] The seriousness of the problem cannot alone explain the administration's choice; hunger among adults was an equally serious problem.

Food aid to pregnant women, infants, and very young children had a clearly delimited target group, a group that had a strong emotional appeal. There was a strong health rationale as well as a social welfare imperative. Existing health clinics and direct distribution outlets could handle the food packages. Since it was aid in kind, there was little basis for charges of "chiseling." Moreover, the administrator of USDA's Consumer and Marketing Service, Rodney E. Leonard, had a strong interest in nutritional aid for pregnant women and infants.[32] His interest, as well as the concern for the target group in the secretary's office, had been fostered in large part by research detailing permanent damage as a result of malnutrition in infants.[33] Above all, such aid was cheap relative to other proposals for federal offensives against hunger. To feed over half of the target population of 2.1 million would cost only $42 million--a fraction of the costs of other food aid proposals. It possessed a dramatic hue in the same sense that initial expectations for Head Start envisaged taking the "ghetto" out of the child. Supplemental food for pregnant women and infants offered the future as a salve for the present. As one official noted, "ballooning" aid to pregnant women and infants was not a real solution to the problem of widespread hunger. Nonetheless, the administration chose it as a politically viable and fiscally sound response to public and congressional pressure.

In the closing months of the Johnson administration, Leonard and his staff implemented the SFP. Physicians, nurses, or "other competent personnel" would prescribe nutritious food packages for pregnant women, infants, and preschool children who qualified for family food assistance. Initial plans called for an annual expenditure of $7.3 million to reach 250,000 people in fiscal 1969. The package would include foods rich in protein, vitamins, minerals, and iron to meet the nutritional deficiencies cited most often in hearings and studies of the target group.[34] Even with the change in administrations, prospects for the SFP remained good. In his first month of office, Nixon had been struck by a news summary of the congressional hearings into hunger. What particularly interested the President was that "unborn children and infants are said to suffer permanent brain damage from malnutrition. . . ." He asked HEW Secretary Robert Finch and USDA Secretary Clifford Hardin for recommendations to deal with the problem. Nixon suggested "a strong statement . . . followed by some symbolic action now and a long-range program later."[35]

His interest in infant nutrition continued at least into March. In a memorandum to Nixon, domestic adviser Daniel P. Moynihan summarized the research into mental retardation and malnutrition. Although Moynihan noted that there was still some question about the severity of malnutrition required to produce retardation, he strongly affirmed the seriousness of the problem, adding, "once again, your concern for the first five years of life is turning out to be critical."[36] The Urban Affairs Council, including Moynihan, Hardin, and Finch, issued a statement calling for the expansion of the SFP. The President's concerns translated into several other actions: an interagency task force on food programs for the poor, rapid inauguration of local supplemental food programs, and announcement of a December White House Conference on Food, Nutrition, and Health—the "symbolic action now." In July the task force issued a report, which recommended among other things ending the exclusive right of health clinic personnel to certify SFP eligibility. Although they acknowledged that this reform might lessen incentives for visiting clinics, they reasoned that the extent of health care facilities for the poor would limit the SFP and prevent needy recipients from receiving benefits.[37]

By spring 1969, Hardin and Richard Lyng, the assistant secretary of marketing and consumer affairs, who presided over the food programs, had begun a strong campaign to expand the SFP. Lyng wrote Moynihan that the research evidence linking infant and prenatal malnutrition to retardation "fully justifies our proposals to give highest priority to eliminating serious malnutrition among expectant mothers, infants, and small children." Moynihan enthusiastically concurred.[38] In testimony before the Senate Select Committee on Nutrition and Human Needs, Hardin requested additional funds for the SFP. He proposed expansion of the FSPs into every American county, consolidation of the USDA's food programs into a new Food and Nutrition Service, and a pilot voucher program within the SFP "to eliminate some of the logistical problems involved in providing the supplemental food packages by taking full advantage of the private food marketing system."[39]

Hardin's proposed pilot voucher program developed from discussions among Lyng, Howard Davis of the Food Distribution Division, and other USDA personnel. As a commodity program, the SFP presented several problems to the USDA in terms of policy and logistics. The decision to make food stamps the primary federal food assistance program committed the USDA to replacing its direct distribution apparatus within normal commercial channels. It was incongruous to retrench direct distribution in general while expanding one relatively small in-kind distribution program. Moreover, wherever direct distribution was changed over to food stamps, the costs of storing, transporting, and distributing supplemental food packages became prohibitively expensive--increasing in some areas to 50 percent of the total food costs. Finally, a successful voucher SFP could be integrated into the FSP as bonus stamps for pregnant and lactating women, infants, and small children.[40] One other, less prominent consideration was a White House idea to consolidate all welfare programs, including food assistance, within one administrative agency. Incorporating the SFP into food stamps would accord well with any transfer of the Food and Nutrition Service to another department.[41]

The SFP received a serious setback when a study of the District of Columbia's program, commissioned by the Food and Nutrition Service, appeared in April 1970. In the study, the USDA's Economic Research Service found that distribution costs averaged 35 percent of parcel costs and that the transportation problems of participants reduced package pick-up to 60 percent of the certified population. Most damaging of all, the study revealed that the foods were used by all members of the household. Since the food was not consumed by the target group, it represented a food subsidy to the entire family that food stamps could provide. These findings reinforced the resolve of Lyng and Food and Nutrition Service Director Edward Hekman to consolidate the SFP with food stamps or, at the very least, make it into a voucher program.[42] Thus, between February and May 1970, the USDA announced the start of pilot food certificate programs in five different areas. It also commissioned a study of the pilot program by David Call of Cornell University's Graduate School of Nutrition.[43]

In April 1970 the USDA prohibited any expansion of supplemental food programs into counties in which the newer FSP operated. They dropped children who were one to five years old from the SFP and eliminated powdered eggs, potatoes, and peanut butter from the packages. Four months

later the USDA impounded a $20-million appropriation for
fiscal 1972; enrollment fell 20 percent. Indeed, all the
child nutrition programs experienced financial constraint
in fiscal 1971 and fiscal 1972. Employing its regulatory
powers, the USDA slowed the expansion of these programs in
an effort to fulfill the administration's goal of fiscal
restraint.[44] The FSP would, Lyng wrote, "eliminate the
need for specialized programs" and pare the government's
welfare outlays.[45]

By 1971 the future of any federal program targeted to
indigent pregnant women and infants rested on the pilot
certificate programs, which were straightforward enough.
Local welfare and health offices issued free booklets of
25-cent coupons, which could be spent for milk, infant
formula, and baby cereal. Pregnant women received $5 per
month through one year postpartum, and those with infants
received $10 per month for one year. All food stamp or
public assistance recipients were eligible, as were those
referred to the program by local health clinics. Others
were required to apply through local welfare offices. The
program underwent evaluation between August and December
1970.[46]

Call's evaluation employed a 24-hour recall method to
obtain information on the daily food intake of
participants. Cross-sectional data were collected for
five sample groups: food stamp and certificate
recipients, food stamp recipients alone, certificate
recipients alone, certificate recipients referred by
clinics, and persons receiving no food aid. The sample
size included one quarter of the Chicago program's
participants and one half of the participants in Bibbs
County, Georgia--roughly 500 women and infants. The
findings devastated the program:

> The pilot program did not significantly
> increase the quantity of milk and formula intakes
> of infants . . . nor did it increase their
> nutrient intakes.
> The program did not successfully increase the
> milk intakes of either pregnant women or mothers
> of infants in a consistent fashion.
> By implication, the income elasticity for
> program foods of the target families is very
> small, i.e., near zero.

From the study the Food and Nutrition Service concluded
that the pilot program "significantly influenced neither

the qualitative nor the quantitative aspects of the diets
of the recipients." They prepared to abandon the
specialized food programs.[47]

Hekman and Lyng believed that the Economic Research
Service study and Call's evaluation had demonstrated the
ineffectiveness of the SFP and the voucher program. They
were expensive to operate, of dubious nutritional value,
and not target-specific. Both science and fiscal
restraint dictated retrenchment of the program; politics,
however, did not. Every regulatory step the USDA took to
curb the SFP evoked numerous protest letters from local
health and welfare organizations and particularly
vitriolic attacks by Senator Phillip Hart and Senator
George McGovern. In the 1972 election year, jobs and
economic growth replaced fiscal austerity in administration policy. Slack purse strings and a desire not to
alienate potential voters reversed some of USDA's
reductions in the SFP. The Food and Nutrition Service
expanded a few supplemental food programs and, employing
a regulatory nuance, ceased to close programs in food
stamp counties of key Southern states. A few foods
previously removed from the packages were restored. That
these reprieves were only temporary was nevertheless
evident to nutritional aid advocates--if for no other
reason, because an avowed opponent of all food assistance
programs, Earl Butz, had recently been designated
secretary of the USDA.[48]

The Beginnings of WIC

Although the USDA had concluded that targeting programs
to pregnant women and infants was ineffective, physicians
in community clinics, children's lobbyists, state social
services departments, and other supporters of such a
program believed that the problem lay in the design and
implementation of existing programs. The idea, they
argued, remained medically and programmatically sound.
To sustain their claim, advocates cited two successful
local programs: one in St. Jude's Hospital in Memphis,
Tennessee, and another in Baltimore associated with Johns
Hopkins University. Maryland's Department of Employment
and Social Services had applied in June 1972 for USDA
funding of statewide infant formula programs based on the
Baltimore project. Lyng rejected the application on the
basis of Call's findings. In an appeal, Rita Davidson,
secretary of Maryland's Department of Employment and

Social Services, criticized the pilot certificate program
on several grounds. She attacked the program's failure
"to determine the biological effects on the target group"
and the nutritional status of participants. Davidson
also cited the pilot program's lack of an educational
component directed toward altering the buying patterns of
participants and its failure to encourage the use of iron-
enriched formulas for infants. Finally, she circulated
copies of her letter and Lyng's response to Maryland's
congressional delegation.[49]

Constituent concerns had created the proper ambience
in Congress for support of a program targeted to pregnant
women and infants. It was, however, the growing body of
research into the relationship of malnutrition to mental
development that inspired the WIC program. The role of
nutrition in pregnancy had been a matter of controversy
since World War II. Wartime studies of pregnant women
receiving a prescribed diet had revealed a decline in
stillbirths and infant mortality. A 1950 review by the
National Research Council of maternal and child health
had noted the high correlation among race, low income,
and high infant mortality, which was attributed to malnutrition and poor health care. During the 1950s, further
research had questioned the strength of the connection
between prenatal nutrition and infant health, particularly
assertions that wartime diet alone led to lower infant
mortality. During the 1960s, better laboratory techniques
and more sophisticated theories enabled scientists to
develop a clearer idea of the relationship between prenatal nutrition and infant health. In November 1963 a
seminal article by Dr. Joaquin Cravito appeared in the
American Journal of Public Health, suggesting that nutrition had a direct and significant impact on mental
development in young children. His thesis provoked
additional research into the relationship of nutrition
and mental development.[50]

Cumulative findings grew throughout the late 1960s and
early 1970s; they affirmed with animal and human studies
that nutrition was indeed critical to brain development
in the fetus and infant at least until the age of two.
HEW provided research funds to the Committee on Maternal
Nutrition of the National Research Council's Food and
Nutrition Board for a series of studies on prenatal
nutrition. In 1970 the Food and Nutrition Board
published a major report, Maternal Nutrition and the
Course of Pregnancy, making seven major recommendations:
(1) provide better-quality maternal care, including

nutrition; (2) accord infants, adolescents (as potential
pregnancies), and pregnant women a higher priority in
low-income family supplements; (3) strengthen nutritional
curricula in medical schools; (4) add more nutritionists
to community health facilities; (5) provide more education
on nutrition; (6) disseminate more information on nutrition; and (7) provide for the special needs of adolescent
pregnancies in schools. Popular dissemination of research
findings on the effects of malnutrition on brain development became so dramatic in presentation that the National
Research Council's Food and Nutrition Board felt obligated
to issue a position paper on the "Relationship of Nutrition to Brain Development and Behavior" in June 1973.
The board warned that "popularized summaries of results
of research . . . frequently tend to misinterpret the
effects or are overly simplistic in interpretation of
cause and effect." Although the paper reaffirmed the
crucial role of nutrition in mental development, it also
stressed that environmental factors were equally if not
more important to mental development.[51]

By early 1970s the research on nutrition and mental
development had reached all those concerned with food
assistance programs. In August 1970 the Office of Child
Development (OCD) of HEW proposed a 3-year, $2.5-million
demonstration project on prenatal nutrition. Similar in
design to the USDA's voucher project, the demonstration
was never funded, due to cuts in OCD's research and
demonstration budget. Continuing research into prenatal
nutrition did impress two men, James Thornton, a staff
member of the Senate Agriculture Committee, and Rodney
Leonard, president of the Community Nutrition Institute.
Since his tenure at USDA's Consumer and Marketing Service,
Leonard had evinced a strong interest in nutrition aid to
pregnant women and infants. Thornton had been struck by
the research and the results that St. Jude's Hospital and
the small Baltimore project obtained with selected food
assistance to malnourished infants. In July 1972 they
went to Senator Hubert Humphrey with a summary of the
problem and a proposal for a federal program to aid
pregnant women and infants. Humphrey's involvement as
vice president in foreign food aid and his general
humanitarian concerns for hungry children made him
receptive to the proposed program, and he agreed to
introduce it.[52]

During hearings before the Senate Subcommittee on
Agricultural Research and General Legislation on H.R.
14896, the child nutrition bill, Humphrey submitted an

amended bill, S 3691, which included provision for a
Special Supplemental Food Program for Women, Infants, and
Children (WIC). Testifying on behalf of this bill,
Humphrey cited the supplemental food program in Detroit
and the Baltimore project as examples of maternal and
infant feeding. He noted the repeated efforts of the
Food and Nutrition Service to cut the programs and the
need for a new congressional mandate. Though targeted to
similar groups, WIC aid would be in the form of vouchers
for specified foods known to be essential to proper
nutrition. Medical examination and certification would
supplant the income standard as the chief criterion of
eligibility. Finally, the bill provided $20 million
annually over two years. This funding level was
guaranteed by Section 32 tariff revenues regardless of
congressional appropriations.[53]

To support WIC, Humphrey brought in David Paige of
Johns Hopkins University to testify on the effects in
infant malnutrition on mental development. Paige noted
the substantial improvements in infants who were fed
iron-enriched formulas in a Baltimore project. Several
local administrators of supplemental food programs added
their support to the WIC amendment. Thornton and Leonard
displayed photographs and X rays dramatizing brain damage
from severe infant malnutrition and showed a film about
the infant nutrition program at St. Jude's Hospital. They
presented this visual evidence to committee members and
key staff.[54] The USDA also became aware of Humphrey's
WIC amendment.

Deputy Assistant Secretary Phillip Olsson wrote to
Senator Robert Dole, a Republican committee member, about
the feasibility study of the pilot program and the evaluation of the Washington, D.C., supplemental food program--
ostensibly to provide materials "relevant . . . in your
consideration of the various child feeding bills," but in
reality to block WIC's report out of committee.[55]
Senator James Allen, the subcommittee chairman, requested
an official USDA response to the WIC amendment. Assistant
Secretary Lyng responded with three principal objections
to WIC: the target groups included children up to age
four, not just infants in the critical year of need; the
ambiguity of the low-income, nutritionally at-risk
criteria for eligibility; and the similarity of the
program to the pilot certificate project discredited by
Call's study.[56]

Questions raised by the USDA, the lack of more thorough
hearings, and the conservative nature of its members led

the committee to bring the child nutrition legislation to the full Senate without the WIC amendment. Aided by a vivid photographic display of emaciated infants and their underdeveloped brains, Humphrey engaged in a floor fight to pass the amendment. In the full Senate, Senator Allen and Senator Miller led the battle against the WIC amendment. Miller read the damning conclusions of Call's evaluation of the pilot program. Humphrey responded that Call's evaluation did not extend to medical data and faulted his methodology. Allen noted that WIC duplicated the SFP and had not been subjected to adequate committee hearings. Humphrey countered that the use of medically prescribed foods in WIC was unique to the program. In the midst of the exchange, Senator Carl Curtis offered an amendment to the program that specified a medical evaluation by the USDA and the U.S. General Accounting Office (GAO). With Curtis's provision, WIC passed the Senate by a 67-16 vote.[57]

Failing in the Senate, Lyng wrote to Representative Albert Quie, a House Republican on the Education and Labor Committee to urge that WIC be deleted in conference. He again cited ineffectiveness, duplication, and the lack of adequate congressional consideration as reasons to reject the Senate version. Humphrey, however, had already convinced Carl Perkins, the chairman of Quie's committee, to support his amendment. The conference committee retained the program, and both chambers approved the amended child nutrition bill. WIC survived, but only as a two-year experimental program subject to a rigorous evaluation prior to any extension or expansion.[58]

In many respects the WIC legislation was unique among children's feeding programs. It specified the protein and vitamin content of the foods to be made available to participants and outlined the target population in terms of medical requirements for eligibility. These technical requirements also strongly suggest the significant role that nutritional research played in the design of the program. Medical monitoring and general health care were integral elements. The bill mandated annual evaluation reports to Congress by the USDA and the GAO to determine the benefits of nutritional assistance and make recommendations with regard to its continuation. Finally, unlike all other feeding programs, results were to be measured, not only by the number of participants or the quantity of foods distributed, but also by the improvement in the health of the target population. Since the problem, the solution, and the evaluation that delimited the WIC program were scientifically based, WIC held out a concrete promise of being either a demonstrable success or an incontestable failure.[59] The legislation reached the President's desk in mid-September 1972. WIC represented only a small fraction of the overall child nutrition programs. The bill contained the unassailable SLP and passed without dissent in Congress. With the election only six weeks away, a veto would have been not only politically damaging but also futile. When Lyng wrote to OMB Director Casper Weinberger, he recommended that Nixon sign the bill. Turning to WIC, Lyng noted that "while this is a provision to which we initially indicated our opposition, we believe that subsequent modifications and an opportunity to fully evaluate the program make the provision acceptable." Lyng was confident that a scientific evaluation would prove WIC as ineffective as the pilot certificate and the supplemental food programs. Weinberger concurred in Lyng's recommendation. Research, he noted, had demonstrated the need for adequate nutrition at early stages in an infant's development, though Weinberger doubted the efficiency of programs in this area. The bill, however, possessed a veto-proof majority and touched the emotional issue of hungry children. There were, he concluded, no alternatives to presidential concurrence. Nixon signed the measure, praising the programs it authorized.[60]

WIC's enactment presented two problems to Lyng: how to obey the law without spending more money on special food programs he considered ineffective and how to deal with the mandate for a medical evaluation. He proposed to resolve the first problem by directing WIC programs into SFP areas, thus balancing WIC expenditures with SFP reductions.[61] With regard to the medical problem, Lyng decided to attempt a transfer of the program to the U.S. Department of Health, Education, and Welfare (HEW). Explaining to HEW Undersecretary John G. Veneman that the medical orientation and the need for medical evaluation were "far beyond the abilities or resources of the Department of Agriculture," he offered the WIC program to HEW as part of its maternal and child health programs.[62] Although enthusiastic in their support of the WIC program, HEW concluded that no legal basis for the transfer existed, and the appropriate congressional committees were unwilling to provide one. Health personnel from HEW did offer to help the Food and Nutrition Service design the program and its evaluation.[63]

The evaluation was of critical importance, for, according to the law, it would determine the future of WIC. Several relevant actors had different conceptions of precisely what the program and its evaluation should contain. Once the President signed the bill, Humphrey, Thornton, and Leonard assembled a group of nutritionists and physicians to prepare a set of guidelines for the USDA in implementing the program. Humphrey and Carl Perkins jointly forwarded these guidelines to Agriculture Secretary Butz in late December 1972. "The committee stresses," their memorandum concluded, "the need for this program for at least 5 years to enable a vertical study to gather neurointegrative data."[64] Butz, of course, ignored the five-year suggestion. William Morrill, OMB's assistant director, reminded Butz that the proven ineffectiveness of existing programs of this kind and "the potential cost of reaching all the people in this target group gives great importance to the required evaluation."[65] Beyond these concerns, Hekman and Clayton Yeitter, Lyng's successor, had to consider the postelection budgetary retrenchment that the administration had mandated.[66] Above all, there was the distaste of the Food and Nutrition Service, on whose shoulders fell the administration of what they conceived to be a health program. Other actors, however, soon upstaged the lot.

The Advocates and the Courts

Two events in spring 1973 drew WIC out of the depths of the Food and Nutrition Service and into the light of the federal courts. The first was a Redbook magazine article by Virginia M. Hardman, titled "How to Save Babies for Two Dimes a Day." Her piece detailed the St. Jude's Hospital project of feeding malnourished infants. Punctuated by a series of before-and-after photographs of a malnourished infant undergoing treatment, the article pointed toward a 75 percent decrease in infant mortality among project participants. Hardman recounted the relationship of malnutrition to brain cell deficiency and the relative costs of preventive nutrition and hospital care. She quoted physicians attacking the USDA's reductions in supplemental food packages and limitations on food stamp allotments. Finally, the article urged all readers to write Secretary Butz or their congressional representatives to demand that the USDA implement P.L.

92-433 and "end delays in feeding hungry children."
Redbook's circulation approached 5 million. Butz himself
received over 200 letters.[67]

A more significant event occurred in spring 1973, when
the delay in implementing WIC came to the attention of
Ronald Pollack, director of the Food Research and Action
Center, which was then a public interest law firm based
in New York and Pollack its founding attorney. As far as
he could ascertain, the USDA planned to implement WIC as
a $5- or $6-million pilot health program sometime in
fiscal 1974. Even this limited program would be executed
only grudgingly. Pollack, for his part, envisioned WIC
as the inception of a major federal feeding effort
directed at pregnant women and infants. Only litigation
could bring such an effort to fruition.[68]

Pollack and a colleague, Roger Schwartz, decided on a
strategy to use the USDA's recalcitrance to maximize WIC's
expansion. The key to their strategy was obtaining a
federal court order mandating expenditure of all WIC
appropriations on a cumulative basis. If they could
legally compel the USDA to spend all $40 million author-
ized for fiscal 1973 and fiscal 1974, the annualized
expenditures of the final month of fiscal 1974 would at
the very least effectively double the program's size.
Moreover, every departmental delay would compress further
the time available for the expenditure. Thus, if the
USDA failed to begin funding WIC projects until January
1974, it would have to spend the $40 million in the six
months remaining in the fiscal year. The annualized
expenditure would be $80 million by the end of fiscal
1974, and a $20 million program would be quadrupled in
size.[69]

In June 1973, Pollack and Schwartz filed a class action
suit on behalf of potential WIC beneficiaries in the
District of Columbia federal court. Submitting affidavits
from Humphrey and other members, they sought to prove that
Congress intended to feed needy pregnant women and infants
with the authorized funds, not to sponsor a small, complex
medical experiment. They asked Judge Oliver Gasch to
order the USDA to promulgate WIC regulations immediately,
accept local applications for funding programs, and carry
over the unspent $20 million to fiscal 1974. Since
Humphrey and Thornton had anticipated resistance on the
part of the USDA in implementing WIC, in drafting their
bill they had deliberately included mandatory language
and secured the appropriation through Section 32 funds.
They did this to ensure that if WIC fell victim to

impoundment and administrative delays, litigation over
its implementation would be successful. It was, and on
June 20, Gasch granted the injunction and ordered the
USDA to publish regulations for WIC by July 6, 1973. In
a final hearing he ordered the unspent $20 million carried
over and added to the fiscal 1974 authorization.[70]

Complying with the court order, the Food and Nutrition
Service issued final regulations in July, but due to time
constraints took the extraordinary step of refusing prior
public comment on them. Though they fulfilled the court
order and incorporated the nutritional requirements of
the legislation, critics believed the regulations to be a
form of impoundment through obfuscation. Lack of public
comment and the requirement of extensive demographic data
made the application process very cumbersome. The Food
and Nutrition Service also planned to designate pilot
areas by September 1, 1973, and begin feeding operations
one month later. The October date was crucial to conducting an adequate medical evaluation by the end of
fiscal 1974.[71] Despite these plans, which the USDA had
prepared for Gasch's scrutiny, Food and Nutrition Service
Director Edward Hekman still resisted implementing the
program. He wrote Yeutter that "it is clear to us that
Agruculture is not the appropriate administrator of this
program--and that the effort to administer here can only
harm both the Department and the program." Yeutter
responded that WIC was probably here to stay and that the
Food and Nutrition Service should "make this program work
as smoothly as possible." Although political considerations precluded him from saying so at the time, Yeutter
supported WIC.[72]

Hekman recognized that the court decision had transformed WIC radically. From "a small pilot program
designed only to provide medical evaluation of food
intervention" to a feeding program, WIC would double in
size between fiscal 1974 and fiscal 1975, if the court
did not modify its injunction. Hekman requested that the
U.S. Department of Justice ask Gasch to stay the carryover
mandate. The Food Research and Action Center, too, was
preparing to return to court--this time to obtain a civil
contempt citation against Secretary Butz for failing to
name any WIC grantees. In the ensuing legal confrontation
in October, Pollack argued that regardless of annualized
program level, Congress had intended all $40 million to
be spent and the USDA had failed to obey the law and the
court. Noting that the jails were overcrowded and that
Butz was probably incorrigible anyway, Gasch declined to

cite Butz for contempt. He did, however, reaffirm his order that the USDA spend all $40 million authorized for WIC in fiscal 1974. In the remaining months of 1973 the Food and Nutrition Service named 143 grantees, and it began funding the program in January 1974.[73]

WIC's operation was relatively simple. The Food and Nutrition Service provided cash grants through a U.S. Department of Treasury letter of credit to approved state health departments and Indian tribes for distribution to approved local clinics. Participants included pregnant women to six weeks postpartum, lactating women to one-year postpartum, and infants and children to four years of age. Eligibility rested on three criteria: residence in the approved project area; qualification for a clinic's free or reduced health services; and determination by a competent professional to be at nutritional risk due to anemia, inadequate growth or nutritional pattern, or a history of high-risk pregnancies. A woman and her children would come to the clinic to be certified as eligible and would be placed in the program's delivery system. Food could be delivered through vouchers, home delivery, direct distribution, or any combination of the three. The types of foods were restricted to iron-fortified infant formula or cereal, fruit juice, milk, cheese, eggs, and vegetable juices. WIC allowed 10 percent of the program costs for local administrative expenses. Finally, the Food and Nutrition Service contracted with Joseph Endozien of the University of North Carolina's School of Public Health for a detailed medical evaluation.[74]

By the close of fiscal 1974, WIC was operating at an annualized level approaching $100 million. Due to expire in June, congressional supporters proposed an extension of WIC through fiscal 1975 with a $100-million authorization level. To their original arguments about the critical role of nutritional aid to the target groups, supporters added the USDA's attempts to scuttle the program and the need to allow sufficient time for a proper evaluation. To the program's benefit, Congress was waging a major battle with the administration over impoundments; WIC had been a significant legal victory in this confrontation. Finally, to fund the program at any lower level would involve expunging some pregnant women and infants--a politically unwise move in any contingency. As McGovern noted, this authorization level "represents little more than maintenance of the status quo." In conference the Senate funding level, $131 million, and that of the House, $70 million, were reconciled. Congress

voted overwhelmingly to renew WIC and mandated expenditure of the $100 million plus any carryover funds in
fiscal 1975.[75]   Richard L.
Feltner, Yeutter's replace-
ment as assistant secretary for marketing and consumer
affairs, wrote OMB Director Roy Ash that USDA favored
signing the child nutrition bill, including WIC. He
explained that WIC's annualized level was approximately
$100 million and that the almost unanimous support of
Congress made a veto pointless.[76]

   OMB's budget examiners vigorously opposed WIC's expansion "to a level of unsubstantiated perpetuation." The
150 percent increase in funding "would eliminate any
vestiges of the original demonstration character . . .
[and] lock the Food and Nutrition Service into a program
whose effectiveness is highly questionable." In his
recommendation to the President, OMB's assistant director
noted the staff's objections, but acquiesced to a higher
political reality. "On the merits, and in terms of its
effects on the budget, HR 14354 [the WIC authorization]
is clearly undesirable. However, in view of the widespread support for 'programs to feed hungry children,' as
evidenced by the congressional votes, a veto of this
legislation would most likely be overridden and would
therefore be counterproductive."[77]   The President signed
the bill into law. To ensure that the USDA spent the
entire authorization and any unused fiscal 1974 funds,
the Food Research and Action Center returned to court in
July and obtained Gasch's order stipulating these expenditures. Defeated in court and in Congress, Feltner and
Hekman, working with OMB, began to rethink their approach.

   Several policy imperatives were still operative in the
USDA: elimination of direct commodity distribution,
avoidance of any federal responsibility for delivery
systems, and, above all, reduction of food assistance
costs. Feltner and Hekman had resigned themselves to the
fact that WIC was no longer a pilot but a permanent
program. Their problem was that Congress had mandated
the maintenance of the SFP in any area that chose to
retain it, despite the replacement of direct distribution
programs with food stamps. Local SFP administrators were
bringing pressure on the USDA through Congress to provide
additional federal funds to support the increased delivery
costs, once direct distribution programs ended. Faced
with further increases in what was already an enormously
expensive program to administer, Feltner believed that
the only way to reduce outlays and avoid involvement in
commodity delivery systems was to replace the SFP with

113

WIC. He hoped to facilitate this replacement by quickly
approving Georgia's applications for WIC programs in
order to solicit the aid of Senate Agriculture Committee
Chairman Herman Talmadge of Georgia in removing congressional constraints on the USDA's elimination of SFP.[78]

Whatever savings the changeover from the SFP to WIC
might achieve represented a small fraction of the $2-
billion child nutrition programs. Only a wholesale
reorganization of these programs would yield any substantial savings. Toward this goal the OMB prevailed on
Feltner to accept a block grant proposal similar to Title
XX of the Social Security Act. Each state would receive
sufficient funds to provide one third of the recommended
dietary allowance for all its needy children. State
officials could then decide how to allocate those funds.
Overlapping programs and some federal administrative
costs would be eliminated. The proposal would reduce
outlays by $500 million. Moreover, it would take the
USDA to a large extent out of the food assistance
business--something Secretary Butz ardently desired.
There were, however, serious difficulties in any
legislative realization of the proposal.[79]

A grand reorganization, such as block grants, risked
opening the child nutrition programs to an equally grand
expansion by congressional supporters. Without concrete
proposals for each nutrition program, committee advocates
could discard the administration's proposal outright and
substitute legislation antithetical to budget restraint.
Practically all relevant interests groups, particularly
educators, food service organizations, health administrators, PTAs, and agricultural lobbies, would resist
any decentralization that might vitiate their influence
on programs and policy. Terminating these federal
programs would subject the administration to the political
onus of abandoning the nation's children. Moreover, the
Watergate scandal, which resulted in a Republican debacle
in the midterm election, had brought a new infusion of
liberal Democrats into a Congress already weighted against
the administration. Finally, the legislation would have
to pass through the House Education and Labor Committee,
whose chairman, Carl Perkins, considered the SLP his
special child. In retrospect it is not difficult to
understand why Feltner had second thoughts about introducing the block grant proposal in 1975. OMB, however,
decided to go ahead.[80]

The 94th Congress ignored the administration's proposal; no bill containing it was introduced. Instead,

Feltner's worst fears were realized. The House and the
Senate produced child nutrition bills that exceeded
administration requests by $1 billion. In the House,
Representative Perkins offered a child nutrition bill,
which included a 3-year, $200-million WIC authorization;
the Senate version provided a $300-million authorization.
Both bills had been written in large part by the Food
Research and Action Coalition. Since the Endozien
evaluation had not been completed, advocates within and
outside Congress relied on a program survey of WIC clinics
by the Senate Select Committee on Nutrition and Human
Needs. Local clinics reported substantial birth-weight
gains and declines in anemia, stillbirths, and infant
mortality among participants. Their written reports,
supplemented by testimony at committee hearings, were
convincing. Indeed, Congress revised the language of law
establishing WIC. Its preamble now read: "The Congress
finds that substantial numbers of pregnant women, infants,
and young children are at special risk in respect to their
physical and mental health by reason of poor or inadequate
nutrition or health care, or both. . . . [T]he purpose
of this program . . . is to provide supplemental
nutritious food as an adjunct to good health care during
such critical times. . . ." The tentative tone of the
earlier legislation was gone.[81]

After the first floor debate over WIC in 1972, no real
congressional controversy surfaced over subsequent
expansions of the program. Evidence of WIC's success,
the political appeal of feeding infants and pregnant
women, and the attention focused on funding levels for
the huge SLP combined to facilitate WIC's unmolested
passage through Congress. The single issue the program
raised was the funding authorization. Though not an
entitlement program in the strict sense due to its
spending ceiling, the WIC legislation did guarantee the
entire authorization with Section 32 funds. Regardless
of House Appropriation Committee action, WIC would receive
all the funds authorized and the USDA would be compelled
to spend them. Some members of Congress had problems
with this method of appropriation. It circumvented the
House Subcommittee on Agricultural Appropriations. It
also violated provisions of the Budget Control Act, which
sought to replace executive impoundment with congressional
spending ceilings. Finally, mandated spending might cause
unwise expansion of the program merely to obey the law.
Supporters responded that such a worthwhile program
required guaranteed funding in the face of the USDA's

continuing resistance to implement WIC according to the wishes of Congress. Entitlement supporters triumphed; the USDA's recalcitrance had again resulted in expansion of the program.[82]

Once disagreements over the lunch subsidy were resolved, Congress passed the child nutrition legislation by large majorities. As it had all along, the USDA opposed passage due to the high costs. In their view the lunch subsidy increase was inflationary. They wanted WIC extended only one year, pending Endozien's evaluation report. Butz advised the President to veto the bill. OMB concurred; the legislation cost too much, aided children who were not in need, and expanded WIC prematurely. On October 3, 1972, Ford vetoed it, citing inflationary pressures and the concomitant dangers of recession. WIC itself went unmentioned in his veto message. Within four days, Congress overrode the veto and the $250-million WIC program became law.[83]

The administration's whole approach to child nutrition programs was in shambles. The USDA complained to OMB that "had the Department been in a position to discuss specific amendments on their merits, nothing of this magnitude [of budget increase] would have occurred, but, of course, the Department was in no such position, having been compelled to argue against all existing programs for a block grant." Republicans in Congress were also incensed by OMB's approach. Minority leader John Rhodes wrote the President a letter criticizing the tactics of OMB and the administration. "It is difficult," he railed, "for Republicans to sustain a veto or become enthusiastic under these kinds of circumstances. Late transmittals of the proposal, lack of proper groundwork, and the absence of congressional input accounted for the dismal vote of 397 to 18 overriding the veto."[84]

The revised WIC legislation expanded the program in several respects. WIC now included children up to five years of age. Congress ordered the secretary of agriculture to "take affirmative action to insure that programs begin in areas most in need of special supplemental food." The law required him to convene an advisory committee of representatives from the Maternal and Child Health Service, the Center for Disease Control, the U.S. Public Health Service, the American Academy of Pediatrics, the National Research Council, the American Dietetic Association, the American Public Health Association, and others "as the secretary deems appropriate," to suggest the best methodology for evaluating

the health benefits of WIC. The law also established the
National Advisory Council on Maternal, Infant, and Fetal
Nutrition, consisting of six state, local, and federal
WIC administrators from various geographic regions, two
parent recipients, two physicians, one retail food distri-
butor, and two HEW and two USDA employees experienced in
maternal and child nutrition. The council would study
WIC and any related program and report annually to Con-
gress and the President its findings and recommendations.
Finally, the legislation authorized a funding level of
$250 million from fiscal 1976 through fiscal 1978.

Defeated in Congress, OMB formulated a scheme to
decelerate WIC's expansion and reduce costs in fiscal
1977. They suggested to the USDA a continuation of the
now familiar tactic of replacing the SFP and pilot
certificate programs with WIC to offset expenditures and
cuts. Their new idea, however, rested on a fiscal quirk:
the transition quarter. In 1976 the federal government
changed its fiscal year from July through June to October
through September. Due to the transition, there would be
a three-month hiatus during July, August, and September
1976. Instead of prorating the appropriation for WIC
(the standard procedure), OMB required that the USDA
spread the $250-million authorization over five quarters--
a procedure that cut the program by 20 percent. After
discussions with Feltner and Hekman, Butz informed OMB
Director James Lynn that the USDA could not legally compel
an SFP area to switch to WIC. Moreover, the aggregate
caseload of the SFP, the pilot certificate program, and
WIC would exceed the $250-million level and invite a
funding increase. Butz suggested instead elimination of
the pilot certificate program and a 25 percent reduction
in the SFP; he did agree to spread the authorization over
five quarters.[85]

The consequent slowdown in WIC's expansion did not go
undetected. The program's growth had spawned an informal
network of health clinics and clients participating in
the program. Coordinated in Washington by Stefan Harvey
of the Children's Foundation, letters, phone calls, and
meetings could be employed to make key members of Congress
aware of problems in the program. The American Academy
of Pediatrics had also lent its prestige to WIC. When
the five-quarter spread of WIC's funds became known,
supporters complained to Congress and obtained a House
resolution ordering the Food and Nutrition Service to
spend $250 million in fiscal 1976. In Senate committees,
McGovern and Kennedy attributed this impoundment to

election-year politics. The President, they argued, was merely responding to Reagan's conservative challenge in the primaries. As evidence they compared Ford's loudly trumpeted fiscal conservatism regarding programs to aid children with his well-publicized, avid support of the largest peacetime military budget in history. Despite this resolution and congressional committee badgering of USDA officials, the pace of expansion remained measured.[86]

Confronted by the USDA's intransigence, the Food Research and Action Coalition, in consultation with other advocates, brought another class action suit in federal court, Durham et al. v. Butz et al. Pollack again argued that the USDA had failed to execute the law. He asked Judge Gasch to enjoin the USDA from withholding WIC funds and order them to spend all the authorized money plus any previously impounded funds. The transition quarter, he insisted, should be included on a pro rata basis. Gasch concurred and ordered the USDA to spend $562.5 million plus any carryover funds from fiscal 1974 and fiscal 1975 before September 1978. The judge further required the Food and Nutrition Service to submit quarterly reports to the bench and to the Food Research and Action Coalition detailing WIC's progress. In signing the consent decree, the USDA agreed to distribute funds using the Title V formula of the Social Security Act and to recover all unspent funds each quarter for redistribution to states capable of increasing their WIC caseloads further.[87]

Program Evaluations

Delayed for over a year, the long-awaited University of North Carolina medical evaluation of WIC appeared in July 1976. Under the direction of Joseph Endozien, 100 clinics in 14 states provided data from periodic examinations of WIC participants between February 1974 and May 1975. They examined pregnant women every trimester and infants at birth, 6 months, and 11 months. Clinics measured weight gain, birth weight, height, head circumference, anemia, infant mortality, and prematurity. Dietary intake was recorded through 24-hour recall. In all, the study included 6,300 infants and 5,400 women. The data were collected and analyzed at the university. Endozien concluded that infants in WIC evinced increases in weight, height, head circumference, and mean hemoglobin concentration; anemia decreased. With the exception of eggs, intake of foods provided through the WIC program

rose for participants.[88] According to the evaluation,
the program was an unmitigated success.

Despite its scope, the evaluation had begun and
remained under a cloud. As early as September 1973, the
GAO issued a report to Congress questioning the practicality of any medical evaluation of WIC. Again in
December 1974, the GAO restated their concerns over the
value of any evaluation. There were four salient problems
"inherent in human nutrition evaluations": (1) lack of
precise definitions of good health and adequate nutrition
by which to measure deviations, (2) lack of precise determination of the types or quantities of nutrients necessary
to improve nutrition status and assess the impact of
supplemental foods, (3) lack of control groups to allow
accurate attribution of the causes of improvement in test
groups, and (4) lack of adequate indicators of mental
development to ascertain improvement in infant development
due to the program. The GAO concluded that these problems
"cannot practically be overcome and must be recognized as
precluding a conclusive determination of the program's
benefits."[89]

An earlier draft of the report had recommended cancel-
lation of the evaluation contract. It found Endozien's
data unreliable due to variations in the clinic personnel
taking participants' measurements. To forestall this
recommendation the USDA went to staff of the Senate Select
Committee on Nutrition and Human Needs and convinced them
to pressure the GAO into dropping it. It was deleted,
but a subsequent report did proffer such a recommendation.
Continuing criticism of the evaluation led Feltner to
contact President William C. Friday of the University of
North Carolina, complaining that reviewers had found that
the evaluation "lacks scientific credibility in some
essential areas of the study." Endozien, he continued,
had not been sufficiently responsive to these criticisms.
The money, time, and importance of the evaluation demanded
a better product. Friday responded that changes would be
forthcoming.[90] Some minor alterations and its multi-
million-dollar investment finally induced the USDA to
release the evaluation to Congress in spring 1976.

Concomitantly, Feltner forwarded to Congress another
USDA-commissioned study of WIC's delivery system. Conducted by the Urban Institute in April 1975, the study
evaluated the efficacy of WIC's operation as a service
provider to its target group. The institute sampled 96
clinic administrators and 3,600 participants in a nationwide survey of WIC. Rich in detail, the study found 80

percent of the participant households used WIC foods for
family meals. Although 63 percent of the clinics provided nutritional counseling, only 12 percent of the
participants indicated they had learned anything about
better nutrition. The study noted increases in clinic
visits for participants: 14 percent for women, 27 percent
for infants, and 77 percent for children. These increases
resulted from the requirement of most local clinics that
all WIC participants enroll in health programs. The
average monthly cost per participant was $20 for food and
$4.92 for administration. The study observed that people
with the lowest incomes tended to have difficulties in
visiting clinics and thus often failed to participate.
However, it also found that 96 percent of the participants were satisfied with the program.[91]

Ostensibly, these two evaluations armed Feltner and
the USDA with powerful weapons to retard WIC's expansion.
The GAO and some members of the scientific community had
repudiated Endozien's medical evaluation. The Urban
Institute study had reaffirmed Call's basic findings that
targeting food to specific family members was ineffective
and nutritional instruction had failed to alter sharing
among family members. Yet Feltner declined to make any
recommendation based on the evaluations. The USDA was
committed to the administration's grant proposal for child
nutrition programs. Although privately Feltner discussed
the possibility of incorporating WIC into food stamps, he
made no public comment on specific programmatic changes
for fear of undermining the administration's proposal.
The USDA's refusal to relent on the block grant position
allowed the advocates and the courts to dictate the
course of WIC.[92]

The third and most recent nationwide study of WIC
became available in late 1977. Produced for the Food and
Nutrition Service by the Center for Disease Control in
HEW, the work analyzed medical data submitted by WIC
clinics throughout the country on 5,692 children. In
many respects the study replicated Endozien's evaluation.
In the wake of the flap over the Endozien evaluation, the
Center for Disease Control carefully qualified its conclusions by noting the strong possibility of sampling and
measurement errors. States submitting data, the study
noted, "represent some of the better WIC programs." The
study warned that "these data must not in any way be
considered representative of the WIC Program as a whole."
Having made these qualifications, the study found that
children entering WIC evinced a high prevalence of anemia,

linear growth retardation, and excessive weight. One year
of program participation improved hemoglobin and hemato-
crit values, increased weight-to-length ratios and linear
growth, decreased proportion of infants with low birth
weights, and curbed some overeating. The study suggested
that more stress be given to nutritional education as a
necessary adjunct to food assistance in combating malnutrition. The researchers were very cautious in presenting their findings, but it was their conclusions, not
their reservations, that received all the attention.[93]

To supporters of WIC the study by the Center for
Disease Control and the Endozien evaluation simply reinforced their convictions about the program's effectiveness. They attributed questions concerning the scientific
credibility of these studies to the nitpicking to which
any evaluation of this size and complexity was vulnerable.
From the Urban Institute's work they pointed to the sharp
rise in clinic visits as further evidence of WIC's value.
Supporters pushed for more nutritional education to curb
the sharing of WIC foods among family members. With much
the same perspective they reinterpreted Call's evaluation
of the pilot program. In passing, Call's study had noted
the prevalence of anemia among program participants; WIC
advocates forgot Call's evaluation and instead seized on
the anemia findings to bolster their case. An evaluation
that had questioned a program's efficacy was thus transformed into a nutritional survey that affirmed its need.
From the advocates' perspective it was just as difficult
to disprove WIC's benefits as to prove them. As long as
the need remained uncontestable, which indeed it did, a
programmatic response directed at pregnant women and
infants could not be proven by science to be a political
mistake.[94]

The Carter Years

In the year of Proposition 13, perhaps the Democratic
presidential victory can be best viewed as a change of
men rather than of measures. The new men and women in
the USDA, however, presaged significant changes in
nutrition policy. Bob Bergland, the new USDA secretary,
noted at the outset that he was "firmly committed to a
broad-constituency department which includes a comprehensive food and nutrition policy." He created a new
assistant secretary for food and consumer affairs—a
position filled by Carol Tucker Foreman, former president

of the Consumer Federation of America. Lewis Straus, director of the National Child Nutrition Project in New Jersey, became administrator of the Food and Nutrition Service. Two of Foreman's principal staff members, Robert Greenstein and Jody Epstein, worked in the Community Nutrition Institute and the Children's Foundation, respectively, before joining USDA. These people represented very different backgrounds from such agricultural economists as Lyng, Yeutter, and Feltner, who had presided over nutrition and food assistance programs in prior years.[95]

Many of these personnel changes were made possible by the new assistant secretary's office. Bergland had separated the Food and Nutrition Service from its former place under the assistant secretary for marketing and consumer affairs. This move allowed the assistant secretary presiding over the Food and Nutrition Service to concentrate on food assistance and nutrition instead of on marketing soy beans or cotton. The Ford administration's block grant proposal was dropped as was any thought of incorporating WIC into the FSP. Indeed, now that the advocates who had been fighting for food assistance and nutrition programs were in power, the USDA accorded WIC a new status as its leading initiative against malnutrition. Despite an auspicious beginning, three serious challenges threatened WIC in the first years of the Carter administration.

The first came in the form of a short article on WIC by Joel Solkoff in the New Republic. Based loosely on his brief work with the congressional Joint Economic Committee, Solkoff presented a sketch of WIC's development and impact that in attempting to be iconoclastic, sounded sophomoric. His attitude toward the problem was ambivalent; he at once ridiculed an effort to deal with a problem he admitted to be serious. Moreover, he seemed to conclude, though his ambiguous prose precludes definitive judgment, that WIC was a necessary and useful program after all. Ordinarily such an analysis would be rewarded by obscurity. That issue of the New Republic, however, was devoted entirely to the Carter administration's first months in office. Solkoff's piece also found its way into the Washington Star. Consequently, a synopsis of his article reached the President's desk. Carter, White House aide Lynn Daft told Foreman, was "upset" by it.[96]

Immediately after its publication, Deborah Norelli, the leader of the Joint Economic Committee project on WIC in which Solkoff had participated, wrote to Bergland to repudiate the article and its connection to committee findings. "Mr. Solkoff's article," she told the secretary, "misrepresented our research findings in both its substance and tone." Project findings "did not suggest that WIC was either a wasteful or ineffective program." It "has been a valiant effort to achieve a monumental objective." The implication of Norelli's letter was clear: Solkoff had been more interested in selling a manuscript than in analyzing a program. At Foreman's suggestion, Bergland forwarded Norelli's letter to the White House. The matter was laid to rest.[97]

The second challenge to WIC surfaced in a HEW reorganization memorandum submitted to OMB in 1977. Prepared by the Office of the Assistant Secretary for Planning and Evaluation and the Bureau of Community Health Services, the memorandum stated that "in HEW's view, it is essential that the Special Supplemental Food Program for Women, Infants, and Children be administered directly by HEW. . . ." Beginning with a historical sketch of nutritional aid to pregnant women and infants, which heavily stressed HEW's role, the memorandum focused on four reasons why the program should be transferred: it is basically a health program; interdepartmental administration caused duplication and confusion at the local level; monies from the Bureau of Community Health Services supported much of WIC's administrative costs; and the USDA had not demonstrated, until recently, any great concern for WIC.[98]

At stake were several things, primarily the question of who should spearhead the expansion of community health services. WIC regulations mandated that each program area provide health services to participants. Rapid extension of WIC programs had seized the initiative, to some extent, from the Bureau of Community Health Services in extending clinical services throughout the country. WIC's popularity in Congress and among health advocates made it a compelling acquisition; it would add more than $500 million to the budget of the Bureau of Community Health Services. There was also, according to staff of the Food and Nutrition Service, some jealousy among the professionals of the Bureau of Community Health Services at the success of the preventive and self-care orientation of WIC's nonprofessional administration under the Food and Nutrition Service. Finally, there was great appeal to health care providers in a program that contained health costs through prophylactic feeding.[99]

These plans of the Bureau of Community Health Services
for WIC went nowhere. The USDA wanted to retain WIC as
its showpiece of food assistance programs. Its administrators were enthusiastic supporters of the program.
Key members of Congress and the relevant committee staffs
opposed transferring a successful, politically popular
program for any reason not divinely ordained. Advocates
in the Children's Foundation and the Food Research and
Action Center also opposed turning WIC over to HEW, since
their brethren now occupied the chairs of authority at
the USDA. Everyone involved in WIC, outside the Bureau
of Community Health Services, was reluctant to see it
assimilated into the health services leviathan at HEW.
The program survived its second challenge.[100]

The final challenge was the legislative authorization
of WIC due to expire at the close of fiscal 1978. The
process of renewing the program and its budget was less a
battle than an interaction among USDA administrators,
advocates, and members of Congress to reach a consensus
on the shape of WIC over the next few years. At the
outset there was unanimity on more than doubling the
program's funding level in fiscal 1979. In large part
the Durham decision dictated this increase. By September
1978, WIC's annualized expenditure reached $440 million.
There were other issues involved in the funding level,
the most important of which was WIC's authorization for
fiscal 1980. Fiscal 1980 would be the first year in
which the provisions of a court order would not determine
the annualized expenditure level. Without this impetus,
Congress would have to decide the extent of WIC's expansion on the program's merits and not simply to avoid
cutting participants. Since the USDA took the budget one
year at a time, this question devolved largely on
Congress.

The USDA did have a significant role in WIC's fiscal
1979 budget. Foreman originally proposed $614.5 million,
but in response to Bergland's concerns about spending
scaled it down to a $600-million request with a $550-
million "minimum line." She explained to Bergland that
WIC was critical and expansion was necessary. In an
attachment, probably prepared by program personnel, WIC
was described as "perhaps the most effective nutrition
and health program operated by the federal government
today." The attachment cited the evaluations by
Endozien, the Center for Disease Control, and the Urban
Institute (for clinic visit increases) to support the
budget request. It also noted two recent state health

department studies in Arizona and Oregon that reported
improvements in birth weight, anemia, and infant mortality. Although Foreman's plea convinced Bergland, OMB
reduced WIC's funding to the minimum figure of $550
million and, subsequently, to $535.5 million.[101]

Perhaps the more controversial departmental decision
was to drop entitlement language from their proposed
bill. Generally speaking, entitlement legislation
requires the dispensation of benefits to any person or
institution meeting the prescribed legal requirements.
The authorization itself creates a legally enforceable
claim to benefits and preempts the appropriations process.
Both the court decisions and the language of the 1975
legislation had accorded WIC entitlement status up to the
authorization ceiling. The principal justification of
this language was the Ford administration's relentless
efforts to eliminate the program. Since the USDA had
turned completely about on WIC, there was little reason
to continue entitlements to protect the program from
administrative recalcitrance. Still, WIC's strongest
supporters, the Children's Foundation and the Food
Research and Action Coalition, convinced Senator Muriel
Humphrey, Senator George McGovern, and Senator Robert
Dole to preserve the entitlement language in the bill
they introduced. Entitlement, they believed, would
maximize the recipient population.[102]

Humphrey's bill differed from that of the administration in two other respects. It specified authorizations
of $650 million in fiscal 1979 and $850 million in fiscal
1980 and provided for the maintenance of three- and
four-year-olds in the program. To deal with OMB budget
reductions the USDA proposed to exclude children over two
from participation. Foreman attributed this revision in
part to an effort to reduce program redundancy, though
only half of the children to be eliminated from WIC
received any other federal food assistance. More important, she approved the revision to make the best use of
limited resources. She pointed out that research on
malnutrition and brain development had demonstrated that
critical cellular growth occurred prior to a child's
third birthday. Children under three were therefore the
most vulnerable to permanent neurological damage from
malnutrition.[103]

Foreman explained her reasoning to the Senate Select
Subcommittee on Nutrition and Human Needs in testimony on
the administration bill. Senator Dole and Senator Bellmon
emphasized that this change would leave most needy three-

and four-year-olds without any food assistance. It would
cause older preschool children to share food with their
younger siblings still in WIC and result in less food for
the most critical age groups. "I tend to be kind of a
tightfisted budgeteer," Bellmon admitted, but "not to the
point of letting a 4-year-old go hungry, if they are
needing food." Foreman expressed her empathy with his
point of view but added, "if you have a limited number of
dollars, you have to make choices." "I am not," Bellmon
responded, "going to be the one who stands up on the
Senate floor and says that we are letting 4-year-olds go
hungry. . . . [We] will have an amendment to feed these
kids." Congress retained children up to age five in
WIC.[104]

The funding question was not resolved so easily. It
soon became evident that program supporters would not
settle for less than a four-year authorization to secure
WIC's future. Without entitlement language, however, the
authorization would act only as a ceiling; actual funding
levels would be subject to appropriations. Enthusiasm
for WIC was much greater in the House Education and Labor
Committee and the Senate Subcommittee on Nutrition than
in their respective appropriations committees. In terms
of both principle and power, the appropriations committees
disliked any legislation that circumvented their purview.
Consequently, the House Appropriations Committee proposed
to amend the WIC bill reported out of the Education and
Labor Committee to disclaim specifically any entitlement
provision. In the Senate Appropriations Committee,
Senator Thomas Eagleton amended the Senate bill to reduce
the fiscal 1979 authorization to $550 million and the
entitlement provision to two years, fiscal 1979 and
fiscal 1980. Despite "seriously consider[ing] deleting
entitlement altogether," Eagleton's committee concluded
that the unusual history of WIC--impoundments, litigation,
and court decisions--constituted "good and compelling
reasons to retain a 2-year entitlement."[105]

The two amended bills passed their chambers without
opposition and went into conference in the preadjournment
pandemonium of October 1978. Basically, the bills
differed in the entitlement provision and in the authorization levels. The House provided $650, $850, $900, and
$950 million from fiscal 1979 through fiscal 1982; the
Senate provided $550, $800, $900, and $950 million over
the same years. In conference the negotiations were not
so much between the Senate and House as among House
members. Carl Perkins, chairman of the House Education

and Labor Committee, agreed to rescind a provision in the
child nutrition bill, of which WIC was a part, mandating
expansion of school breakfast programs within the states.
In return, House Appropriations Committee representatives
acceded to the entitlement language and the Senate's
authorization levels. The bill passed both houses by
voice vote.[106]

Congress's confidence in WIC is reflected not in the
fiscal 1979 authorization, which the annualized participation level of fiscal 1978 had largely determined, but
in the fiscal 1980 authorization of $800 million. In
effect they elected to double the program over current
levels with the fiscal 1980 authorization and guarantee
that increase by entitlement. The effective organizational work of the Children's Foundation rallied constituent support for WIC. Its link to the SLP legislation
undoubtedly helped ensure passage. Though the infant
formula companies and milk producers supported the
program, their impact was minimal. WIC's political
success was due to the Mom-and-apple-pie appeal of
feeding medically and financially needy infants, children,
and pregnant women as well as the persuasive scientific
evidence that it reduced mortality, prematurity, anemia,
and the possibility of neurological damage. Moreover,
the program promised to reduce future health care costs.
"For every day," one physician testified, "that I can
keep a baby inside a well-functioning uterus, I can save
somebody $600, because that is the cost in my hospital to
maintain a premature infant in our intensive care
nursery." A potential savings of $30 billion per year,
it was argued, could be realized with the elimination of
nutrition-related illnesses.[107]

The purported evidence of WIC's salutary impact on
health care cannot be overemphasized in explaining the
program's backing in Congress and the USDA. Suggestions
from some local WIC administrators to drop the medical
requirements for participation were rejected. Congressional supporters wanted to maintain WIC under the medical
penumbra to avoid any welfare stigma. Though all agreed
that low income was the surest criterion of medical need
for nutritional aid, very few WIC advocates wanted to
forsake the politically persuasive scientific data on its
efficacy that the medical requirement yielded. Writing
to Secretary Bergland, McGovern and Humphrey summed up
the source of the program's appeal to policy makers: "We
believe WIC is the best conceived of all the food delivery
programs. It is the most target specific and health

oriented of all the programs, its effects can be specifically evaluated, and its participants have made available
to them a full range of preventive health services."[108]
Toward the end of October 1978 the child nutrition
legislation went to the White House for signature.
Although it was only a small portion of overall expenditures for child nutrition in past years, WIC would account
for one quarter of those outlays within two years. The
program's fiscal 1979 authorization level, which exceeded
the administration budget by $15 million, presented little
difficulty. In fiscal 1980, however, the authorization
rose another $250 million—a level guaranteed by entitle-
ment. The fiscal 1980 figure exceeded OMB allowances by
$200 million. OMB recommended that the President veto
the WIC extension. Since Carter had publicly committed
himself to severe budget reductions in social welfare
programs to curb inflation, following this advice became
a real possibility.

Robert Greenstein, of Assistant Secretary Foreman's
staff, prepared two letters for Bergland's signature, one
for OMB Director James McIntyre and another for Domestic
Affairs Advisor Stuart Eizenstat, recommending that the
President sign the bill. Though following similar lines
of argument, the letter to Eizenstat was more comprehensive and politically astute. Expanding WIC, Greenstein
argued, had resulted from a major policy decision within
the USDA to concentrate resources on the most effective
nutritional programs. Medical evidence of WIC's effects
attested to striking reductions in anemia, mortality, and
low birth weight. To counterbalance this budget increase,
the USDA was determined to reduce expenditures for the
nonneedy or the less effective SLP by $130 million.
Greenstein cited an upcoming Congressional Budget Office
study that demonstrated that lunches did not improve the
nutritional status of children from households with
incomes more than twice the poverty level. "The findings
should in the current atmosphere of concern over government spending, make it possible to secure strong and
influential support on Capitol Hill" for this reduction,
he noted. He concluded that this savings and a $50-
million cut in the fiscal 1980 WIC authorization would
compensate for the increase mandated in the legislation.
In closing, Greenstein noted that after fiscal 1980, all
WIC authorizations were subject to regular appropriations
procedures and therefore more open to fiscal
management.[109]

128

The letter to Eizenstat pointed out the political
realities of the situation. WIC possessed broad
congressional support spanning the ideological spectrum.
A veto would only invite criticisms that the President
was insensitive to human suffering, inept at choosing
where to cut spending, and shortsighted in ignoring the
potential savings in health care costs afforded by a
prophylactic nutritional program. Moreover, a veto would
be challenged as the first order of business in the 96th
Congress; it would poison the administration's efforts,
as it had destroyed the Ford administration's efforts, to
reduce costs in less effective child nutrition programs.
"In Congress, even in the current political atmosphere,
the WIC program is a 'motherhood and apple pie' issue
. . . [because it] has one of the most remarkable records
of achievement of any domestic social program." A veto,
Greenstein's letter concluded, was foolhardy.[110] After
obtaining McGovern's assurance that WIC's fiscal 1980
authorization would be pared by $50 million, Carter
signed the child nutrition bill into law in November 1978.

NOTES

[1] Bruce McClure, Secretary, Federal Emergency Relief
Administration to Frederick Daniels, July 7, 1933,
"Policy," Old General Subject Series, 69, NA; Children
and Youth, III, 1437.
[2] P.L. 74-320; Hearings before the Senate Committee
on Agriculture and Forestry, 78:2 (May 2-5, 1944), 8;
Studies of Human Need, Senate Select Committee on
Nutrition and Human Needs, 92:2 (June 1972), 45-46.
[3] Baker, Century of Service, 182-188. Murry R.
Benedict explains the USDA movement into food
distribution: "The early [pre-1935] emphasis on reduced
production gave rise to much public opposition. . . .
There was a growing feeling both within and outside
government that more attention needed to be given to
supplying adequate food to all groups, instead of
curtailing production when the overall supply was no more
than adequate to provide a good diet for the entire
population." He further notes that nutritional research
reinforced this "feeling." Farm Policies of the United
States, 1790-1950 (New York, 1953), 384-386.
[4] H. R. Tolley, Surplus Marketing Administration,
USDA, to Colonel F. C. Harrington, WPA Commissioner,
March 22, 1940, General Subject Series, RG 69, NA;

129

Florence Kern, Acting WPA Commissioner, and H. C. Albin,
Chief Distribution and Purchase Division of the Surplus
Marketing Administrations, August 1, 1940, ibid.
   [5] These and other booklets are collected in Box 1,
Food and Nutrition Records, RG 462, NA; Baker, Century of
Service, 229, 304, 325.
   [6] The Food and Nutrition of Industrial Workers in
Wartime (Washington, D.C.: Committee on Nutrition in
Industry, NRC-NAS, 1942), 4-11; Food and Nutrition Board,
Recommended Dietary Allowances (Washington, D.C.:
NRC-NAS, 1943), 1-11; Food and Nutrition Board,
Inadequate Diets and Nutritional Deficiencies in the
United States: Their Prevalence and Significance
(Washington, D.C.: NRC-NAS, 1943), 1-7, 35; Baker,
Century of Service, 324-325; Conner, "History of
Standards," 109-111.
   [7] Claude Wichard to Wayne Coy, Assistant Director,
Bureau of the Budget, February 18, 1943, and attachments,
"School Lunch Program: S29," Series 39.1, RG 51, NA;
Marvin Jones, War Food Administrator, to Harold D. Smith,
Director, Bureau of the Budget, November 26, 1943, ibid.
Also see drafts of school lunch legislation in Food and
Nutrition Records, Box 17, RG 462, NA.
   [8] Baker, Century of Service, 321.
   [9] P.L. 78-129.
   [10] Administrator, Federal Security Agency, to F. J.
Bailey, Assistant Director, Legislative Reference, Bureau
of the Budget, October 27, 1943, "School Lunch Program:
S29," Series 39.1, RG 51, NA; Marvin Jones to Harold D.
Smith, November 26, 1943, and February 14, 1944, ibid.
   [11] Hearings before the Senate Committee on
Agriculture and Forestry, 78:2 (May 2-5, 1944), 34, 188.
   [12] Hearing before the House Committee on Agriculture,
79:1 (March 23-May 24, 1945), 232.
   [13] Ibid., passim (especially page 32).
   [14] Ibid., 34-41; Hearings before the Senate Committee
on Agriculture and Forestry, 78:2 (May 2-5, 1944), 12;
also see the summary of the floor debate in the
Congressional Quarterly Almanac: 1946 (Washington, D.C.,
1947), 37-42, and Marvin Jones to the Senate Committee on
Agriculture and Forestry, May 2, 1944, "School Lunch
Program: S29," Series 39.1, RG 51, NA. (Henceforth, the
Congressional Quarterly Almanac is cited as CQA.)
   [15] House of Representatives Report 684, Committee on
Agriculture, 79:1 (June 5, 1945), passim; P.L. 79-396.
   [16] All the lunch regulations are collected in Box 16,
Food and Nutrition Records, RG 462, NA.

[17] Hearing before the Senate Committee on Agriculture and Forestry, 83:2 (March 15-17, 1954), 321-515; Bureau of the Budget Memorandum, Resources and Civil Works Division to the Director, November 16, 1964, "C&MS, SLP, SMP, General," Series 61.1, RG 51, NA; P.L. 83-690; Hearings before the Subcommittee on Dairy Products of the House Committee on Agriculture, 84:2 (January 24, 1956), 1-3; ibid., (June 13, 1956), 15-22; P.L. 84-465; CQA: 1956, 442-443.

[18] Benson to Joseph M. Dodge, Bureau of the Budget Director, February 27, 1954, "T5-11," Series 52.1, RG 51, NA; Dodge to President, November 30, 1953, ibid.; Minutes of the Interagency Committee on Agricultural Surplus Disposal, September 13, 1954, et seq., "75-11/2," ibid. For the early foreign policy question see Edward S. Mason, Deputy Special Assistant to the President, to Frederick J. Lawton, Bureau of the Budget Director, and enclosures, July 12, 1950, and Lawton's response, July 21, 1950, Box 63, Series 47.3, ibid.; Bureau of the Budget Memorandum, Agriculture-Interior Branch to the Director, March 16, 1950, "T5-24/50.1," ibid. In the last memo the author wrote: "The primary reason the Government now holds or will acquire such surplus commodities is 'price support,' not 'welfare, health, or security.'"

[19] Hearings before the Subcommittee on Dairy and Poultry of the House Committee on Agriculture, 86:1 (March 17, 1959), 22-25, 29-35 (May 20, 1959), 30 (January 20, 1960), 9-11, 24-25, 39, 48-51; Hearings before the Subcommittee on General Education of the House Committee on Education and Labor, 86:2 (August 23, 1960), 6-8, 38-41, and passim.

[20] Hearings before the Subcommittee on General Education of the House Committee on Education and Labor, 78:1 (August 31, 1961), 7-14; Hearings before the Subcommittee on Dairy and Poultry of the House Committee on Agriculture, 87:1 (April 11, 1961), 12 ff.; Studies of Human Need, 51-60; CQA: 1962, 222-223.

[21] Bureau of the Budget Memorandum, Resources and Civil Works Division to the Director, November 16, 1964, "C&MS, SLP, SMP, General," Series 61.1, RG 51, New Executive Office Buildings Records (henceforth, NEOB); Bureau of the Budget Memorandum, Resources and Civil Works Division to the Director, November 24, 1964, ibid.; Elmer B. Staats, Deputy Director of Bureau of the Budget, to Senator Winston L. Prouty, January 14, 1966, ibid.; Charles Schultze, Bureau of the Budget Director to

President Johnson, January 15, 1966, ibid.; White House
Memorandum, Henry Wilson to Charles Schultze, February
19, 1966, ibid.; Bureau of the Budget Memorandum,
Resources and Civil Works Division to Mr. Hughes,
February 17, 1966, "Nutrition Programs--Legislation,"
ibid. The executive branch memoranda on this issue are
voluminous.

[22] Hearings before the Subcommittee on Dairy and
Poultry of the House Committee on Agriculture, 89:2
(February 18, 1966), 1-51.

[23] Ibid. (June 24, 1966), 29.

[24] Hearings before the Subcommittee on Agricultural
Production, Marketing and Stabilization of Prices of the
Senate Committee on Agriculture and Forestry, 89:2 (May
12, 1966), 2-42; P.L. 87-823.

[25] Wilbur J. Cohen, Undersecretary of HEW to Joseph
Califano, February 2, 1966, "Nutrition
Programs--Legislation," Series 61.1, RG 51, NEOB;
Hearings before the Select Subcommittee on Education of
the House Committee on Education and Labor, 89:2 (March
9, 1966), 6-17, 50; CQA: 1966, 328-333.

[26] Hearings before the House Committee on
Agriculture, 90:1 (March 15, 1967), 7-13, 27-36, 62-70,
96.

[27] Bureau of the Budget Memorandum, Resources and
Civil Works Division to the Director, July 14, 1967,
"Nutrition Programs--Legislation," Series 61.1, RG 51,
NEOB.

[28] Orville L. Freeman to President Johnson, June 29,
1968, ibid.; Bureau of the Budget Memoranda, Resources
and Civil Works Division to the Director, July 19, 1967,
and August 4, 1967, ibid.; Bureau of the Budget
Memorandum for Ivan Bennett, February 12, 1968, ibid.;
Bureau of the Budget Memorandum, Natural Resources
Programs Division to the Director, February 20, 1968, and
April 25, 1968, ibid. Bureau of the Budget Memorandum on
White House Meeting, Natural Resources Programs Division
to the Director, May 3, 1968, ibid.

[29] Freeman to the President, June 29, 1968, ibid.;
Bureau of the Budget Memorandum, Peter Lewis to the
Director, June 21, 1968, ibid.; Hearings before the
Subcommittee on Education of the House Committee on
Education and Labor, 90:2 (January 18, 1968), 4-9, 10-21,
100-113.

[30] Bureau of the Budget Memorandum, Director Zwick to
the President through Joseph Califano, July 1, 1968,
"Nutrition Programs--Legislation," Series 61.1, RG 51,

NEOB; Bureau of the Budget Memorandum, Gladieux to Files
(RE: Carlson Memo of September 25, 1968) October 2,
1968, ibid.; Bureau of the Budget Memorandum, Director
Zwick to Joseph Califano and enclosures, November 8,
1968, ibid.

[31] Hearings before the Senate Committee on Labor and
Public Welfare, 90:1 (July 11 and 12, 1967), 1-63;
Hearings before the House Committee on Education and
Labor, 90:2 (May 21-23, 27-29, and June 3, 1968), passim;
Hearings before the Senate Committee on Labor and Public
Welfare, 90:2 (May 23, 29, June 12, 14, 1968), passim.

[32] Reference slip, March 28, 1968, "Nutrition," RG
462, NA.

[33] The pattern of nutritional research is derived
from discussions with Food and Nutrition Board, NRC-NAS,
staff members and a bibliographic review of the dates of
relevant articles.

[34] Enclosures in Freeman to Representative Jamie L.
Whitten, December 6, 1968, "Nutrition," RG 16, NA;
Freeman to John Gardner, August 22, 1968, "Farm Program
8," ibid. See also the memoranda Dr. Aaron M. Altschul,
Special Assistant for International Nutrition
Improvement, to the Secretary, April 30, May 6, and May
17, 1968, "Nutrition," ibid. Altschul's attention to
domestic nutritional problems was a significant indicator
of the shift within the USDA of nutritional expertise
from foreign to domestic food assistance. Experience
with foreign programs was also significant for Hubert
Humphrey's proposal of WIC in 1972 (interview:
Congressional Committee Staff).

[35] Alexander Butterfield, Deputy Assistant to the
President, to Secretary Hardin, January 30, 1969, "Farm
Program 8-1-1," RG 16, NA.

[36] March 17, 1969, "Nutrition," ibid.

[37] Coordination of Federal Food Programs for the
Poor, July, 1969, "Farm Program 8," ibid.

[38] March 21 and 24, 1969, "Nutrition," ibid.

[39] Text of Testimony, May 9, 1969, ibid.

[40] Lyng to Davis, June 26, 1969, "Farm Program 8,"
ibid.

[41] See especially Erhlichman to Hardin, September 2,
1969, and Hardin's response, "Farm Program 8-1," ibid.;
Edward J. Hekman to Lyng, January 13, 1970, "Nutrition,"
ibid.

[42] Food and Nutrition Service: Program Evaluation
Status Report, no date, RG 462, NA; Lyng to Governor John
Dempsey, June 26, 1970, "Farm Program 8," RG 16, NA.

133

[43] USDA news release, March 31, 1970, "Farm Program 8," RG 16, NA.

[44] Senate Select Committee on Nutrition and Human Needs, To Save the Children, 93:2 (Washington, D.C., 1974), 17-29.

[45] Lyng to Susie Hendrix, Detroit SFP Coordinator, May 10, 1971, "Farm Program 8" RG 16, NA.

[46] Robert E. Wunderle and David L. Call, An Evaluation of the Pilot Food Certificate Program (April 1971), 1-2.

[47] Ibid., 2-9; Food and Nutrition Service: Program Evaluation Status Report, no date, RG 462, NA.

[48] This political transformation of the Food and Nutrition Service can be traced through numerous correspondence between congressmen and the secretary's office in "Farm Program 8 [1971 and 1972]," RG 16, NA.

[49] Lyng to Davidson, June 30, 1972, and his reply, July 26, 1972, ibid.

[50] World Health Organization, Nutrition in Pregnancy and Lactation (Geneva WHO Technical Series Report #302, 1965); Committee on Maternal Nutrition, Maternal Nutrition and the Course of Pregnancy: Summary Report (Washington, D.C.: Food and Nutrition Board, NRC-NAS, 1970), 2-16; Joaquin Cravioto, "Application of Newer Knowledge of Nutrition on Physical and Mental Growth and Development," American Journal of Public Health, 53 (November 1963):1803-1812.

[51] Food and Nutrition Board, The Relationship of Nutrition to Brain Development and Behavior (Washington, D.C.: NRC-NAS, 1973).

[52] Carolyn Harmon, OCD Executive Assistant, to Emerson Eliot, OMB, August 13, 1970, "OCD: Early Childhood R & D," RG 51, NEOB; Interview: Congressional Committee Staff.

[53] Hearings before the Senate Agriculture Committee's Subcommittee on Agricultural Research and General Legislation, 92:2 (July 28, 1972), 26-32. In 1961 the Kennedy administration had employed Section 32 funds to circumvent hostile appropriations committees in implementing the authorized, but unfunded, Food Stamp Program.

[54] Ibid., 69-88; Interview: Congressional Committee Staff.

[55] August 1, 1972, "Farm Program 7," RG 16, NA.

[56] August 14, 1972, "Farm Program 8," ibid.

[57] Congressional Record: Senate, August 16, 1972, 28588-28592.

[58] Ibid.; Lyng to Quie, August 31, 1972, "Legislation (S. 3691)," RG 16, NA.

[59] CQA: 1972, 538-542; Hearings before the Subcommittee on Agricultural Research and General Legislation of the Senate Committee on Agriculture and Forestry, 92:2 (July 28, 1972), 5-32, 47-49, 68-76, 81-87; and Public Law 92-433, Section 17.

[60] September 18, 1972, "OMB," RG 16, NA.

[61] Lyng to Weinberger, November 22, 1972, ibid.

[62] November 24, 1972, and enclosures, "HEW," ibid. See also Gerald F. Combs, Nutrition and Food Safety Coordinator, to Ned D. Bayley, Director of Science and Education, HEW, January 5, 1973, "Nutrition," RG 16, Records in the Office of the Secretary, USDA; cited hereafter as OS/DA.

[63] Richard L. Seggel, Assistant Secretary for Health, to Clayton Yeutter, February 2, 1973, "Farm Program 8," RG 16, OS/DA; and Yeutter to Seggel, March 23, 1973, ibid.

[64] December 22, 1972, "Legislation General," RG 462, Supplemental Food Division Records, USDA; cited hereafter as SFD/DA. The emphasis is in the original document.

[65] November 7, 1972, "Farm Program 8," RG 16, OS/DA.

[66] Hekman to Yeutter, Memorandum on Legislation, January 18, 1973, "Nutrition," ibid.

[67] Redbook (April 1973):68-75.

[68] Interview: FRAC. The case was actually filed by the Center on Social Welfare Policy and Law because of doubts concerning FRAC's legal standing.

[69] Interview: FRAC.

[70] Ibid.; and Dotson et al. v. Butz et al. (June 20, 1973).

[71] To Save the Children, 30-31; CQA: 1973, 550-552; CQA: 1974, 503-505; Federal Register, 38 (July 11, 1973), 1847-1851; and James H. Kocher, Acting Deputy Administrator, FNS, to W. F. Moss, Assistant to the Secretary for Intergovernmental Affairs, July 6, 1973, "Farm Program 8," RG 16, OS/DA.

[72] September 6, 1973, and Yeutter's response September 7, 1973, ibid. For Yeutter's unspoken support see his letter to Carol T. Foreman, October 7, 1977, "Farm Program 7," ibid.

[73] Hekman to Yeutter, September 19, 1973, "Farm Program 8," ibid.; P. Royall Shipp, Acting Administrator, FNS, to Yeutter; December 10, 1973, ibid.; and Interview: FRAC.

[74] Federal Register 38:132 (July 11, 1973), 18447-18451.

[75] Congressional Record: Senate, May 21, 1974, 15860-15862; and Congressional Record: House, June 13, 1974, 19064-19065.

[76] June 21, 1974, "Legislation," RG 462, SFD/DA.

[77] OMB: Legislative Reference File T5-10/74.3, RG 51, NEOB.

[78] Notes for OMB Meeting, RE: WIC/SFP, July 14, 1974, "OMB," ibid.; Feltner to Paul O'Neil, Associate Director of Human and Community Affairs, OMB, July 23, 1974, "Farm Program 9," RG 16, OS/DA.

[79] Feltner to O'Neil and enclosure, December 11, 1974, RG 16, OS/DA.

[80] Ibid.; and Interview: FRAC.

[81] Senate Select Committee on Nutrition and Human Needs, WIC Program Survey: A Working Paper (Washington, D.C, 1975); and P.L. 94-105.

[82] CQA: 1975, 669-676; Interview: Congressional Committee Staff.

[83] See the files on "Legislation (S. 882)" and "Legislation (HR 4222)," RG 16, OS/DA; OMB: Legislative Reference File T5-10/75.5, RG 51, NEOB; and Ford's Veto Message: HR 4222, October 3, 1975, Public Papers of the President: Gerald R. Ford (Washington, D.C.: 1977), item 609.

[84] OMB: Legislative Reference File T5-10/75.5, RG 51, NEOB.

[85] Joseph R. Wright, Assistant Secretary for Administration, to Feltner, December 1, 1975, "Farm Program 7," RG 16, OS/DA; and Butz to Lynn, December 19, 1975, ibid.

[86] Interviews: FRAC and the Children's Foundation; Hearings before the Senate Select Committee on Nutrition and Human Needs, 94:2 (March 30, 1976), 1-50; and see note 15.

[87] Interview: FRAC. The consent decrees are appended to Senate Report 95-884, 122-135.

[88] Joseph C. Endozien et al., Medical Evaluation of the Special Supplemental Food Program for Women, Infants and Children (WIC) (July 15, 1976), passim.

[89] GAO, Observations on Evaluation of the Special Supplemental Food Program (December 18, 1974), i-iv.

[90] See September 1974 correspondence in file "GAO," RG 16, OS/DA; Feltner to Friday, March 26, 1976, and Friday's response, "Farm Program 7," ibid.

[91] The Urban Institute, Efficiency and Effectiveness in the W.I.C. Program Delivering System (Washington, D.C.: USDA Misc. Publication #1338, September 1976), passim.

[92] Feltner to Hekman, June 28, 1976, "Legislation General," RG 16, OS/DA; and Feltner to Speaker Carl Albert, April 15, 1976, "Farm Program 7," ibid.

[93] CDC Analysis of Nutritional Indices for Selected WIC Participants (June 1976), passim.

[94] Interviews: USDA, Children's Foundation, and FRAC.

[95] Bergland to OMB Director James McIntyre, February 1, 1978, "Nutrition," RG 16, OS/DA; and Interviews: USDA and Children's Foundation.

[96] "Strictly from Hunger," New Republic (June 11, 1977), 13-15; Foreman to Bergland, July 6, 1977, "Farm Program 7," RG 16, OS/DA.

[97] Norelli to Bergland, June 22, 1977, "Farm Program 7," RG 16, OS/DA; and Bergland to Daft, July 11, 1977, ibid.

[98] Memo on Reorganization, Califano to OMB, 1977 [provided by BCHS-HEW Personnel]; and Interview: BCHS-HEW.

[99] Interviews: USDA and BCHS-HEW.

[100] Interviews: FRAC, Children's Foundation, USDA, and congressional committee staff.

[101] Foreman to Bergland, September 6, 1977, "Appropriations (FNS)," RG 16, OS/DA; and Jerome A. Miles, Acting Director of Budget, Planning and Evaluation, to Bergland et al., December 9, 1977, ibid.

[102] Elmer B. Staats, Comptroller General, to Senator Thomas Eagleton, April 13, 1978, "Legislation General," RG 462, SFD/DA; Interview: Children's Foundation; and Richard D. Lieberman, Senate Committee on Appropriations Staff Member to Foreman, February 28, 1978, "Farm Program 7," RG 16, OS/DA.

[103] Foreman to Representative Bob Traxler, May 15, 1978, "Organization (FSQR)," RG 16, OS/DA.

[104] Hearings before the Senate Agriculture Committee's Subcommittee on Nutrition, 95:2 (April 12, 1978), 330-339.

[105] House Report 95-1153 and Senate Report 95-1020 for H.R. 12511 and S. 3085, respectively.

[106] Interviews: congressional committee staff, Children's Foundation, and USDA.

[107] The prophylactic feeding argument can be traced through Hearings before the Senate Select Committee on Nutrition and Human Needs, 94:2 (March 30, 1976), 1-39, 48-50, 69; Hearings before the Subcommittee on Elementary, Secondary and Vocational Education of the House Committee on Education and Labor, 94:2 (August 30, 1976), 632-701; and Hearings before the Subcommittee on

Nutrition of the Senate Committee on Agriculture,
Nutrition and Forestry, 95:2 (April 6, 1978), 195, from
which physician's comment about the "well-functioning
uterus" is drawn.

[108] Ibid.; Interview: USDA; Senators Hubert Humphrey
and McGovern to Bergland, February 17, 1977, "Farm
Program 7," RG 16, OS/DA; and Hearings before the
Subcommittee on Nutrition of the Senate Committee on
Agriculture, Nutrition and Forestry, 95:2 (April
6,110-12, 1978), passim. The evidence-of-success
argument was dominant in all congressional floor debates.

[109] Bergland to McIntyre, October 30, 1978,
"Legislation (S. 3085)," RG 16, OS/DA.

[110] Bergland to Eizenstat, October 30, 1978,
"Nutrition," RG 16, OS/DA.

Appendix A

GALLUP PUBLIC OPINION POLLS, 1935-1971

I. Relief and Welfare

Month/Year

9/35   Relief expenditures.
        Too little: 9%
        Too great: 60%
        Just right: 31%

12/36   Approve of government's reduction in relief
        expenditures?
        YES   NO
        60%   40%

4/37   Reduce relief expenditures further?
        YES   NO
        56%   44%

4/37   Do away with WPA and give only direct cash
        relief?
        YES   NO
        21%   79%

4/37   Should state/local governments pay greater
        share of relief costs?
        YES   NO
        62%   38%

12/37   Relief for work or just cash?
        Work Relief   Direct Cash
        90%   10%

139

12/37   Is it government's responsibility to pay
        living expenses of those needy out of work?
        YES   NO
        69%   31%

3/38   Reliefers getting as much as they should?
        YES   NO
        71%   29%

3/38   Will U.S. have to continue relief
        appropriations permanently?
        YES   NO
        67%   33%

5/39   How given?
        Work relief   Cash relief
        89%   11%

5/34   Greatest FDR   Worst FDR
        Accomplishments   Accomplishments
        Relief/WPA   28%   Relief/WPA   23%
        Banking reforms   21%   Spending policy   16%
        CCC   11%   Farm policy   12%
        SS   7%   Foreign policy   6%
        Farm program   5%   Labor policy   6%

7/39   Do you favor a law requiring able-bodied
        reliefers to work at any job?
        YES   NO
        81%   19%

        Reliefers only?
        YES   NO
        64%   36%

2/40   FDR proposed cut of 20% in relief
        expenditure.
        Approve   Disapprove
        59%   41%

        20% cut in public work.
        Approve   Disapprove
        62%   38%

        30% cut in farm payments.
        Approve   Disapprove
        52%   48%

8/61   Increase community voice in relief
        regulations: 55%
            Continue federal control as is: 29%
            No opinion: 16%

8/61   Physically able must work somewhere in
        public park, etc. for relief.

	August 1961	November 1964
Favor	85%	82%
Oppose	9%	12%
No opinion	6%	6%

1/69   Equalize welfare payments across the nation.
            Good idea: 77%
            Poor idea: 15%
            No opinion: 8%

6/71   Compel large firms to hire welfare
        recipients and pay three fourths of the
        salary with federal funds.

YES	NO	NO OPINION
67%	27%	6%

II. <u>Food Stamps/Child Health</u>

<u>Month/Year</u>

8/37   Should federal government help state/local
       governments aid mother at childbirth with
       medical care?
              YES   NO
              81%   19%

10/39   Food stamps for reliefers.
              Approve: 62%
              Disapprove: 26%
              No opinion: 12%

        Food stamps for families earning $20 per
        week or less?
              Approve: 57%
              Disapprove: 43%

3/69   Food stamps free to families making less
        than $20 per week?
              Favor: 68%
              Oppose: 25%
              No opinion: 7%

3/69   Food stamps for families earning $20-60 per
        week at reduced cost.
              Favor: 60%
              Oppose: 31%
              No opinion: 9%

III. Farm Aid

Month/Year

9/49   Federal purchase of eggs/potatoes to support prices.

	Eggs	Potatoes
Approve	25%	30%
Disapprove	61%	58%
Neutral	4%	4%
No opinion	10%	8%

2/53   Federal guarantee of price for farmers.
Approve: 49%
Disapprove: 45%
No opinion: 6%

7/53   Federal government should continue to buy and store farm products to keep farm income up?
Should: 72%
Should not: 20%
No opinion: 8%

7/53   Should the President be allowed to send surplus food to famine nations?
Should 72%
Should not: 20%
No opinion: 8%

8/55   What should federal government do with surplus food it has?
Give it away: 76%
Sell it: 14%
Destroy it: 2%

Give it to what country?
U.S.: 50%
Needy country: 14%
Specific country
(India, Korea, etc.): 36%

8/55   Give some to USSR as goodwill gesture?
Good idea: 30%
Poor idea: 60%
Unsure: 6%

Sell at reduced price to USSR?
Good idea: 46%
Poor idea: 44%
Unsure: 10%

12/55   Idea of "soil bank," paying farmer not to grow?
Good idea: 29%
Poor idea: 47%
Unsure: 24%

Farmers only asked.
Good idea: 49%
Poor idea: 32%
Unsure: 19%

8/61   Reliefer must take any job offered at going wage.

	August 1961	November 1964
Favor	84%	85%
Oppose	10%	7%
No opinion	6%	8%

8/61   Persons coming to new area must prove they are not doing so to obtain relief before it is granted.

	August 1961	November 1964
Favor	74%	69%
Oppose	16%	22%
No opinion	10%	9%

8/61   Force mother to name illegitimate child's father in court.

	August 1961	November 1964
Favor	73%	64%
Oppose	16%	24%
No opinion	11%	12%

11/64   Overall feelings on welfare.
Favorable: 43%
Mixed: 45%
Abolish it: 6%
No opinion: 6%

11/64   Amount of money spent in your area on
         welfare.
             Too much: 20%
             Not enough: 18%
             About right: 33%
             No opinion: 29%

Guaranteed annual income.

	9/65	5/68	12/68
Favor	19%	36%	32%
Oppose	67%	58%	62%
No opinion	14%	6%	6%

Guaranteed work to each family wage earner
of certain income.

	May 1968	December 1968
Favor	78%	79%
Oppose	18%	16%
No opinion	4%	5%

Summary of Major Legislative Initiatives Relating to Children's Nutrition and Feeding

Year	Public Law	Programs Involved	House Vote	Senate Vote	President's Position	Summary of Major Provisions/Changes
1946	79-396	School Lunch	276-101	Voice	Pro	Enacted school lunch program, provided for matching state funds.
1954	83-690	Special Milk			Pro	Provided supplemental milk for school children.
1956	84-465	Special Milk	406-0	Voice	Pro	Increased appropriation, extended program to nonschool child care institutions dealing with needy and non-needy children.
1958	XXX	Food Stamp	[Failed to come out of HR rules committee 196-187 (2/3 needed).]	XXX	Opposed, too costly.	Food stamps for needy similar to 1939-43 USDA program, supplements in-kind aid.
1959	86-341	Food Stamp	232-127	44-38	Opposed, too costly.	Authorized pilot food stamp program, gave priority to U.S. needy over food for peace programs.
1962	87-823	School Lunch	370-11 [Ending aid to needy rejected (62-77).]	Voice	Pro	Changed federal funding formula to reflect need and participation more closely, provided special funds for needy children to have free/reduced-price meals, eliminated implicit sanction of segregated schools.
1966	89-642	School Lunch, Breakfast, Special Milk, Non-food Assistance, Summer Food Program	(Voice) Voice [Summer school lunch passed (voice); end breakfast program rejected (52-95).]	(76-0) Voice [Summer school lunch program rejected (37-42); then accepted in conference report (voice).]	Pro, on increases for needy, opposed to continued aid to nonneedy.	Increased programs for malnourished children, expanded aid to construct lunchroom facilities, allowed aid to school-administered preschool programs, consolidated children's feeding in USDA, nutritional meals mandated, increased aid at all levels to programs, initial pilot summer food programs.

Appendix B (continued)

Year	Public Law	Programs Involved	House Vote	Senate Vote	President's Position	Summary of Major Provisions/Changes
1967	90-91	Food Stamps	196-155	voice	Pro	Extended and expanded program appropriations
1968	90-302 (90-463)	School Lunch, Breakfast, Special Milk, Non-food Assistance	398-0	Voice [Agriculture Committee bill deleting aid to nonschool needy and limiting breakfast program rejected (14-38).]	Pro	Extended programs to all child care facilities for needy children, including daycare for working mothers.
1969-1970	91-248	School Lunch, Breakfast, Non-Food Assistance	(384-2) Voice	(84-0) Voice [Expansion for needy amendment passed (38-32).]	Pro	Expanded free and reduced-price lunches, set eligibility standards, set reduced-price meal maximums, increased required state contributions to programs from 2% to 10% over seven years.
1969-1970	91-295 (91-207)	Special Milk	384-2	Voice	Opposed as necessary addition to current aid programs and not helpful to poor.	Extended special milk as permanent program.
1971	92-153	School Lunch	354-0	75-5	Opposed, but later acquiesced in by President and USDA.	Forced USDA to increase proposed ceiling on federal subsidy to reduced-price lunches and blocked elimination of 500,000 to one million children from lunch program.
1971	92-32	School Lunch, Breakfast, Supplemental Food, Special Food	331-0	Voice		Extended programs and increased funds for needy participants; allowed $20 million of Section 32 in-kind supplemental aid for pregnant women, nursing mothers, and infants; provided for special foods for malnourished children; expanded nutritional requirements of programs.

Year	Number	Program	Vote	Administration Position	Description
		School Lunch, Breakfast, Special supplemental food (WIC), Special Food	(Voice) Voice [WIC added (67-16).] [25% requirement dropped (54-30).]	lower spending levels.	expanded all child nutrition program...and extended the rest, increased use of in-kind aid from Section 32 funds, authorized WIC at $20 million for one-year pilot, dropped 25% requirement for low-income area schools contribution to food equipment aid.
1974	93-326	School Lunch, WIC, Non-Food Assistance	(359-38) 345-15	Opposed to any commodity assistance mandate.	Increased WIC funding to $100 million and extended it through FY 75, provided minimum federal commodity contribution to lunches of 10¢ per meal.
1975	94-105	School Lunch, WIC, Breakfast	(335-59) [Maximum lunch price proportion deleted (269-144).] [Blanket 5¢ subsidy for all student passed (213-176).] [Subsidy deleted in conference.] 380-7 (Veto override) 397-18 Voice 79-13	Opposed to expansion & costs. Vetoed as adding "$1.2 billion" to Ford's budget.	Expanded and extended all child nutrition programs in terms of appropriations and eligibility, aid eligibility raised to 195% of poverty level, expanded WIC to $250 million, eliminated pilot aspects of program, mandated expansion into "poorest-state counties."
1977	95-166	School Lunch, Summer Food, Special Milk	(393-19) 386-17 (96-0) Voice	Pro	Extended special milk and summer food programs, increased equipment assistance, provided grants to states for nutrition education, authorized USDA to regulate "junk" food in lunches.
1978	95-627	WIC, School Lunch, Breakfast	(Voice) Voice (82-0) Voice	Pro	Increased WIC to $550, $800, $900, and $950 million between fiscal 1979 and fiscal 1982; reduce breakfast program expansion; eliminate WIC entitlement after fiscal 1980.

Note: Parentheses indicate vote total on initial chamber fill; final votes are on conference reports and are not enclosed in parentheses.

Appendix C

Summary of Expenditures and Participation in Major Children's Nutrition and Feeding Programs

	Expenditures ($ millions)								Participation (millions)		
Fiscal Year	School Lunch Program	Breakfast Program	Non-Food Assistance	Direct Distribution[a]	Special Milk Program	Special Supplemental Food Program (WIC)	Supplemental Food Program	Food Stamp Program[b]	SLP	FSP	WIC[c]
1982						[950.]					
1981						[900.]					
1980						[800.]*					
1979					[49.8]	[550.]*		[2237.5]			[1.8]
1978	[2879.2]---------	----	----		180.3	[297.1]*	[9.6]	1884.5			[1.3]
1977	2827.2----------	----	----		180.3	279.8*	23.2	1884.5			0.95
1976	1479.4	113.0	26.1	380.0	144.2	142.7*	8.1	2128.0	25.9	9.3	0.59
1975	1288.2	86.1	25.4	423.4	123.7	89.2*	6.4	1754.2	25.3	8.6	0.50
1974	1082.7	58.9	27.2	319.2	49.2	10.4*	12.0	1087.3	25.0	6.5	0.21
1973	879.9	34.4	15.3	331.0	90.5		13.2	852.6	25.1	6.1	
1972	738.8	24.9	16.6	314.7	90.3		12.9	718.9	24.9	5.6	
1971	532.2	19.4	36.4	279.2	91.1		12.8	609.1	24.6	4.7	
1970	300.3	10.8	16.7	265.8	101.2		7.8	219.9	23.1	2.2	
1969	203.8	5.4	10.4	272.1	101.3		1.0	91.5	22.1	1.5	
1968	159.8	2.0	0.7	276.0	101.8			69.2	20.6	1.1	
1967	149.7	0.6	0.7	188.3	99.2			42.2	20.2	0.7	

Year					
1966	141.1	174.9	96.5	25.9	19.8	0.4
1965	130.4	272.4	97.4	13.0	18.7	0.2
1964	120.8	195.0	99.3	11.4	17.5	0.2
1963	108.6	179.9	93.6	7.4	16.4	0.1
1962	98.8	182.1	89.2	5.3	15.6	0.1
1961	93.7	132.6	84.2	0.2	14.8	0.02
1960	93.8	132.0	80.0		14.1	
1959	93.9	109.5	80.5		13.3	
1958	83.8	90.8	74.3		12.6	
1957	83.9	148.5	66.3		11.7	
1956	67.1	114.7	60.5		11.6	
1955	69.1	83.1			12.0	
1954	67.3	109.0			11.1	
1953	67.1	66.4			10.7	
1952	66.3	32.2			10.2	
1951	68.2	49.9			9.5	
1950	64.5	55.1			8.6	
1949	58.8	36.1			7.8	
1948	54.0	32.7			7.0	
1947	59.9	8.0			6.0	

Appendix C (continued)

	Expenditures ($ millions)								(millions)		
Fiscal Year	School Lunch Program	Break-fast Program	Non-Food Assistance	Direct Distribution[a]	Special Milk Program	Special Supplemental Food Program (WIC)	Supplemental Food Program	Food Stamp Program[b]	SLP	FSP	WIC[c]
1946	51.3			5.8					5.2		
1945	41.6				5.8				4.6		
1944	26.6			7.8					3.8		
1943	1.0			17.6			4.8		5.3(.8)		
1942				21.9	1.5			49.1	6.2		
1941				13.1	0.6			111.6	4.7		
1940				4.0				82.8	2.5		
1939				1.3				16.4	0.9		
1938				0.6				0.1	0.5		
1937				0.2					0.3		

Note: All figures exclude administrative costs. Fiscal years end on June 30 until 1976; after 1977 they end on September 30. Figures are drawn chiefly from Agricultural Statistics, 1957, 1967, 1972, 1977, USDA publication. Brackets indicate proposed or estimated expenditures.

[a] Direct distribution includes foods purchased with Section 32 (of the Agricultural Adjustment Act, 1935) funds.
[b] Approximately two fifths of Food Stamp Aid accrues to children, who constitute roughly one half of the program's participants.
[c] The USDA estimates that the total eligible WIC population as of August 1977 is 8.39 million including all children under five, pregnant women and infants, at or below 200% of the poverty level. Cost of reaching all exceeds $2.5 billion.

*Funding guaranteed by entitlement.

150

The Federal Interagency Day Care Requirements

John R. Nelson, Jr.

INTRODUCTION

This case study reconstructs the decision-making processes dealing with the Federal Interagency Day Care Requirements (FIDCR), past and present. The first section develops the three traditions of nonparental child care in America: the reformer tradition oriented toward the moral and physical well-being of the children of the poor; the employment tradition directed toward child care that allows the mother to work; and the developmental tradition, concerned with the comprehensive psychological development of the child. All three interacted continuously throughout the history of nonparental child care and are significant in shaping the requirements. The following section details the creation of the FIDCR and the continual subsequent efforts to revise them. The next section examines the crisis of enforcement in 1975-1976 that followed the passage of the Title XX amendment to the Social Security Act. The final two sections of this chapter explore the current debate over the requirements and the most far-reaching scientific examination of their impact, the National Day Care Study carried out by Abt Associates, Inc.

Throughout the paper the issue of child-staff ratios is stressed over the other requirements. This emphasis is due to the care giver's overriding importance both to the cost of child care and to its benefits to the child. In particular, the child-staff ratios for preschool children aged three to five were crucial, since this age group constitutes most of the children receiving nonparental care. Child-staff ratios, although not by any means the only significant aspect of child care touched by the FIDCR, are nonetheless the crux of the politics

and economics surrounding them. In addition to being an
aspect of care easily subject to regulation, the ratios
have been considered by decision makers to be of the
greatest importance.

AMERICAN DAY CARE BEFORE THE FIDCR

Day care and its regulation have no unified past. Depending on the history sought as a prologue, the care of other
people's children finds antecedents in America in one of
three traditions: one directed toward the moral reforma-
tion of the child, another toward the employment of the
mother or care giver, and a third toward comprehensive
development. The earliest day care began in the infant
school of early 19th-century Boston. There, social reformers sought to remove, if only for the day, poor children
from an environment of "want and vice" into a salubrious
milieu of cleanliness and its next-of-kin, godliness.
Similar efforts to care for preschool children followed
the international precedents of Fredrich Froebel's kindergartens and Maria Montessori's work with impoverished
Italian children. In part, these efforts by social
reformers reflected a sincere concern for the well-being
of the children of the poor. In part, too, they were
deliberate attempts at imposing a particular ethos on poor
immigrants who vehemently resented and resisted their
paternalism. The initial peak of the reformer movement
came in the Progressive era of the 20th century with the
professionalization of social work. To uplift the
children of the "deserving poor," social workers opened
settlement houses that provided education, dental and
medical care, and counseling. Day care became part of a
broad social welfare philosophy. After World War I,
rapid turnover of personnel and clientele brought about a
steady decline in these houses.[1]
    A countertrend to day care was the long-standing notion
of keeping women at home to care for their own children.
Labeled the Widows' Pension Movement, this group lobbied
successfully for state financial aid to fatherless
families--fatherless by death, that is. Now paid to care
for their own children, a few "deserving poor" were
channeled away from day care centers and full-time work.
However, the paucity of the pensions often compelled
mothers to continue working, and working women needed some
kind of day care for their children. Despite their
resentment of the social worker and reformer, these women

found day care preferable to giving up their children to orphanages and other institutions. By the 1930s the vestiges of these day care centers surrendered to the depression. Women were thrown out of work and into their homes. Eleemosynary institutions went bankrupt, and the social workers became government bureaucrats. Child care outside the home revived, however, with the Work Projects Administration's nursery schools. Designed to provide jobs for unemployed teachers and food and care for poor children, these schools did not survive the Work Projects Administration.[2]

The second tradition of child care, more central to federal programmatic efforts and in that sense more policy-relevant, is employment-oriented day care. Its history begins in New York City in 1854. Wealthy women created nurseries for indigent and pregnant women. In return for the care afforded them during childbirth, the healthiest of these mothers came to work as wet nurses and maids in the homes of their patrons. The system helped the poor and eased the shortage of domestic servants. The federal role in day care followed more in the employment tradition than that of the reformer, although the employment of mothers was consistently combined with moral and physical care. The nurseries of the Work Projects Administration already mentioned sought to employ teachers, if not mothers. And the Farm Security Administration sponsored a small day care program for the children of migrant workers during the depression to allow both parents to work in the fields.

By far the most massive federal program prior to the 1960s began during World War II, when the massive entry of women into factories placed day care on the national agenda. Reports of children being locked in cars in factory parking lots reached the Children's Bureau, the Office of Education, and Eleanor Roosevelt. Ironically, the children in the locked cars were at least physically safe, unlike others alone at home or on the streets. At the President's behest, in August 1942 the Office of Defense, Health and Welfare began to fund a few local day care centers. In that same month the Federal Works Agency obtained a more liberal interpretation of the Lanham Act for defense housing and public works to allow funding of day care facilities. Under this program the government spent $52 million over three years to care for 109,000 children across the country. Most of the centers were operated by local schools. Others, under the purview of the Children's Bureau, were encouraged to locate away from factories in order not to make working too convenient for mothers. All federal aid for day care ended with the armistice. A handful of states continued funding for a few years to enable families to avoid welfare dependency; most of these, however, faltered in the early 1950s.[3]

Although neglected in most day care chronologies, federal participation in some form revived in the 1950s. Congress passed an authorization for day care grants during the Korean War: the Defense Housing and Community Services Act. Though enacted in September 1951, the day care provision was never funded and the authorization lapsed with the armistice. The most significant federal action to subsidize nonparental child care came in the 1954 revision of the Internal Revenue Act. In it a child care deduction was allowed for low-income working mothers. Working parents with an adjusted gross income under $4,500 could deduct up to $600 in expenses for the care of their children. Widowed, divorced, and separated mothers had no income limit on their eligibility; they merely had to have work-related child care costs. In practice, the measure allowed working parents to deduct over $100 million in child care expenses annually—no mean initiative, considering that the entire budget of the U.S. Department of Health, Education, and Welfare (HEW) was only $1,997 million in 1954. Thus, contrary to general belief, the steady influx of women into the labor force was not unassisted in terms of federal subsidies for child care. The employment tradition of federal aid to day care continued through this deduction, which was justified as a necessary work expense.[4]

The third tradition, that of comprehensive psychological development, originated in the nursery schools of the 1920s—a unique nonparental care effort. Unlike all the other child care efforts, these nurseries catered to middle- and upper-class mothers. They did not keep children while their mothers worked; rather, they cared for children whose mothers were home. These nurseries were products of new psychological theories that proclaimed the dangers to a child of a "smothering" and overprotective mother. The nursery endeavored to enhance the psychological development of the child. Insofar as the child was the object of the nursery, there was a kinship with the goals of the infant schools and other devices of the reformer tradition to uplift children. Nonetheless, there were radical differences in social class, technique, and compulsion between the two. The nursery schools of the 1920s began a tradition that can

be traced through the cooperative nurseries of the 1950s
and ultimately into the Head Start program, in which
centers for comprehensive development finally reached the
children of the poor.

In sum, out-of-home child care entered the 1960s with
three historical purposes: to encourage employment of
the poor, to promote the moral and physical well-being of
their children, and to enhance the psychological development of middle-class children. The latter two traditions
possessed greater appeal to social workers and child
development specialists, while the former held greater
sway over policy makers. Both, however, were ambiguous
regarding the child. Day care for the sake of employment
accorded priority to the cost of services, not their
effects on children. Long-term benefits might accrue to
a child if a family's cycle of welfare dependency were
broken; meanwhile the child might suffer. The reform
tradition was not without its flaws. It was afflicted
with the ambivalence of all public charity: at once
generous and self-serving, caring and condescending,
selfless and arrogant. The developmental tradition had
been narrowly focused in terms of class and psychological
theory. Its theories of development lacked strong empirical bases and had a voguish hue wedded to a popularized
notion of Freudian theory. The legacy of these traditions
to the child care programs of the 1960s was, in a word,
problematic.

Another lineage of out-of-home child care in the 1960s
was government regulation. The first attempt at regulating out-of-home child care dealt mainly with orphanages
and other 24-hour institutions. Their central purpose
was to stem the high infant and child mortality rates in
these institutions. At issue were basic health measures,
sanitation, nutrition, and disease prevention. As
national child advocacy organizations and state licensing
agencies became forces at the turn of the century, their
overriding concern was the prevention of disease and its
transmission among institutionalized children. Similarly,
their licensing codes sought to protect children from
epidemics, fire, severe neglect, and starvation. At the
federal level the Children's Bureau suggested provisions
for state codes and offered goals for better child care.

Licensing laws were by no means comprehensive. Linked
to general fire safety and health codes of cities and
counties, they allowed little room for the variations in
day care. States were loath to enforce their laws against
church-sponsored institutions. Funds were always limited

and often lowest in times of greatest demand for facilities. It was difficult to suspend licenses because the
alternative to poor facilities was frequently no facilities. Finally, the enforcers were drawn from the ranks
of social workers. They lacked experience in administration and found themselves regulating their colleagues.
In sum, over the first half of the 20th-century effective
regulation suffered from poor administration and the
general inadequacy of the regulations themselves.

During World War II the Children's Bureau and the
Office of Education were empowered to approve local and
state day care plans for federal funding. The Office of
Education had jurisdiction over school district plans,
the Children's Bureau over nonschool plans. Since 95
percent of the facilities were school related, the Office
of Education predominated. For the first time the government issued a set of standards for day care. Under the
aegis of the Children's Bureau, the Conference on Day
Care of Children of Working Mothers met in July 1941 to
confront the problem that war mobilization posed for women
and children. A February 1942 report proposed a set of
day care standards based on the experience and expertise
of the conference participants. These standards preceded
approval powers granted in August 1942 and did not have
the force of law. Like all the standards of the Children's Bureau, they were merely recommendations to state
and local authorities.

The standards assumed that school-age children received
adequate education in school and required only supervision
and a safe play area until the end of the work day. They
recommended that children under age three stay with their
mothers and that those women be discouraged from working.
Children aged two to five received the most attention.
The standards suggested a maximum group size of 30 children with a minimum ratio of 10 children to 1 adult. They
discussed the child's need for "warmth and affection" and
opportunities "for music, conversation, poetry, stories,
work with materials, group play, etc." The needs of the
family were also to be considered. Staff directors were
to be trained in a broad range of children's needs,
including education, psychology, family relations, health,
nutrition, and child development. Ideally, a facility
would provide proper nutrition and health training and
would conform to safety codes. Intended only as goals,
these standards were never enforced as a precondition of
federal funding. Federal regulatory authority extended
only to state and local plans, not their operation. As

goals, however, they no doubt exerted some pressure for better day care facilities than otherwise would have developed.[5]

The expiration of direct federal aid to day care did not halt Children's Bureau activities in this area. In 1953 the bureau, in conjunction with the Women's Bureau of the U.S. Department of Labor, held a National Conference on Planning Services for Children of Employed Mothers. The conference stressed the growing number of women with children entering the labor force: They noted that 2 million working women had children under 6, and over 5 million had children under 18. In an effort to promote more state and local aid to day care the conferees pointed to industry's need for labor and the working woman's need for supplemental family income. Forty percent of those working women were the sole supporters of their families. To touch all bases the conferees explained the growth of kindergartens and nursery schools because parents were "eager to profit from the new scientific knowledge of child development. . . ." Their central plea, however, remained the expansion of day care to abet the entry of women into the work force. No federal programs were enacted, but the year following the conference Congress passed the child care deduction.[6]

The issue of day care and its regulation persisted throughout the 1950s. The Children's Bureau conducted a major study of day care in 1958. In October 1960 the Child Welfare League published Standards for Day Care Service. "These standards," Director Joseph H. Reid stressed, "are intended to be goals for continuous improvement of services to children." In many respects the standards recapitulated those issued earlier by the Children's Bureau: health supervision, family counseling, educational experiences, and physical and emotional security. They suggested group sizes according to age: for children age 3, 12-15 per group; for children ages 4-6, 15-20 per group; and for children over 6, 20-25 per group. Each group "should have a full-time teacher and assistant." As Children's Bureau standards emphasized earlier, children under 3 were not recommended for day care. The staff ratios recommended were roughly the same, but the recommended group size was one third smaller in the Child Welfare League standards.[7]

Soon after the publication of these standards the Children's Bureau and Women's Bureau sponsored a day care conference, which noted among other things the continued influx of women into the labor force and their purported demand for day care services. Again the conferees raised the issue of child care in terms of dependency. Day care was touted as a means to escape welfare. President-elect John F. Kennedy wrote approvingly of the conference's recommendations. Once inaugurated, he set his new secretary of HEW, Abraham Ribicoff, to work drafting a welfare reform package for Congress--a package that included a $10-million day care program for welfare clients.

In several respects the legislation was similar to a 1958 day care bill Senator Jacob Javits had proposed to Congress. His bill had gone nowhere, but now packaged with the first of a long line of welfare reforms it became law in 1962. The rationale for the reform measures would become a familiar litany throughout the next two decades. Welfare costs were rising; the present system was an administrative nightmare and a failure; only by breaking the cycle of dependency could the welfare burden be lessened; employment and training were necessary means of breaking that cycle and day care was a requisite support service. The tradition of employment oriented day care reached an apotheosis.

Enacted as P.L. 87-543, the bill authorized $5 million for fiscal 1963 and $10 million for each ensuing year. Although the House report on the bill recounted the latest figures on the numbers of working women with children in its explanation of the day care provision, the promise of lower welfare costs appears more relevant to its passage. After all, women with children had been entering the labor force in significant numbers for well over a decade--a fact of which the Women's Bureau consistently reminded Congress. Even under the welfare reform rubric, the day care program managed only to extract $800,000 of its $5 million authorization from the conservative appropriations committees in fiscal 1963.

From its inception within HEW, the welfare reform legislation contained one specific regulatory provision regarding day care. Federal funding was made conditional on a facility's obtaining a state license. This provision left primary regulatory responsibility to the states, where it had traditionally resided. The promise of federal money encouraged states to modernize their licensing procedures, and 40 percent of that money went in the first years of programs to fund this modernization. The results, however, were less than heartening. Still plagued by the social worker and enforcer, state licensing authorities also suffered from a lack of technical knowledge and funds. Confronted by the choice of closing substandard centers with no prospect of a replacement or allowing them to continue, the regulators chose the latter. To compensate for this bending of the code they intensified their scrutiny of new applications. Thus expansion of day care facilities was curtailed, while older, less satisfactory centers continued to operate. This problem was compounded by the succession of new antipoverty programs, which provided funds for day care to allow mothers on welfare to receive vocational education or other job training. The proliferation of federal programs operated by various agencies and departments precluded any easy centralization of day care regulation, had one been attempted. By default, the states retained regulatory power over the expanding day care industry.

The developmental tradition of child care also had its heyday. In 1964, Congress passed the mainstay of the war on poverty, the Economic Opportunity Act. Head Start, touching on practically every aspect of poverty, became the showpiece of the act and of the Office of Economic Opportunity (OEO). Following in the tradition of middle-class nursery schools, Head Start was designed to enhance the psychological development of poor children. The research of psychologists J. McVicker Hunt and Benjamin Bloom and various local preschool education projects in universities had indicated the positive impact of instruction and a salutory environment on a child's cognitive development. Head Start was more firmly rooted in empirical psychology than its antecedent nursery schools. Although its stated purpose—social uplift—was very similar to the moral uplift sought by the reformers of the early 20th century, there was a significant difference. The poor welcomed Head Start; it was not the kind of hegemonic imposition that the infant schools were. It was also more of an effort to reach the rural than the urban poor. Yet, there was a motif of getting the ghetto out of the child. The prospect of derailing multigenerational poverty had great political appeal. Sargent Shriver, director of OEO, wisely chose to capitalize on it.

Planned as a pilot project involving 100,000 children, Shriver allowed over half a million to enroll. OEO found Congress very willing to increase its budget to fund such a potentially revolutionary approach to poverty. Since employment and the cost of care were less relevant to Head Start's purpose, the issues of smaller groups, more

attention to education, health care, and nutrition became
paramount. Head Start's stress on direct community participation circumvented the traditional federal-state-
local funding chain and escaped the extant licensing
morass. Its priorities were different from employment-
oriented day care, and this difference in priorities was
no better reflected than in their child-staff ratios of 4
and 5 to 1 for preschool children. Based on their own
experience with preschool education and consultations
with outside experts, Head Start's organizers reduced the
traditional day care ratios by one half to two thirds.
Costs, of course, were tripled.

As the federal government expanded its day care funding, a schism in purpose surfaced and slowly widened. In
the developmental area, comprehensive child care grew with
OEO's increase of Head Start. In the employment area,
every new program proposed to replace welfare with "workfare" carried a day care provision. Such provisions
became more integral as the welfare explosion was recognized among unmarried mothers. Work would take them off
the dole and occupy their time with pursuits other than
procreation. Meanwhile the children required care so
that their mothers could find jobs. Ultimately, both
kinds of day care shared the commmon purpose of reducing
poverty and welfare dependency. Nonetheless, their means
were in most respects antithetical. Where minimum costs
were essential to making employment practical, comprehensive services and education were integral to breaking the
poverty cycle. There would obviously be a crisis if the
two were ever compelled to integrate their programs; in
1967 that integration was mandated by law.

The year 1967 was a watershed year for day care. OEO
was coming under heavy criticism from conservatives.
Accused of waste and mismanagement, its programs ran into
the backlash against the urban riots and the economic
pressures of the war in Vietnam. Essentially a creation
of the Johnson administration, few in Congress felt
responsible to defend it. The task fell to Shriver. To
defuse his critics, Shriver formulated a revision to the
Equal Opportunity Act, which promised tighter administrative procedures, expanded OEO's support services for
welfare recipients seeking work, and proposed employing
welfare mothers in child care centers. His revisions
first encountered opposition within the administration.
The Bureau of the Budget feared the administrative
provisions were too constraining and probably unworkable.
Their very complexity ensured that they would not be

followed and would merely invite more congressional
criticism. HEW resented the further erosion of its
policy purview. In particular, they fought OEO's
proposal to administer the day care program. At HEW's
behest, the language was broadened to include HEW. The
change was portentous, since Congress expanded the day
care subsection to include the mandate for the FIDCR.

The legislation encountered more problems in the 90th
Congress. Republicans worked to divest OEO of its more
established programs, such as Head Start, and to restore
more program control to traditional departments. Budget
authorizations were cut and appropriations were reduced.
Finally, the Senate Labor and Public Welfare Committee
sought to bring some administrative order to the plethora
of social welfare initiatives by mandating a set of interagency regulations to govern the numerous federal day care
programs. From the perspective of OEO, HEW, and the
Bureau of the Budget, however, day care regulations were
not the issue. They worried about the potential cost of
the day care programs that were greatly expanded in the
OEO legislation and in the new Work Incentives Program.
Over $1 billion would be needed to care for all children
under six of the working poor affected by these programs.[8]

The new employment thrust of OEO's legislation did not
reduce funds for Head Start nor did it eliminate the
smaller Follow Through Program designed to preserve the
child's early gains. But OEO's suggestion for employment
of welfare mothers echoed loudly in the House Ways and
Means Committee. Confronted by an unanticipated and
politically frightening expansion in the nation's welfare
rolls, the committee and the Congress enacted the AFDC-
Work Incentives Program. The incentive for working was
simplified: get a job or lose all benefits. For the
first time, Congress imposed this requirement on women
with young children. Day care became a necessary support
service and was included in the program. This legislation
as well as the OEO revision complicated the day care
programs further; they required the use of welfare recipients to staff centers. Obviously, employment-oriented
care was overwhelming developmental care in congressional
enactments. The only catch was that those who would
write the regulations governing these day care programs
were from the developmentalist tradition.

The 1968 FIDCR

Although some staff members within the Children's Bureau
and OEO pondered the day care requirements mandate in the
early months of 1968, such interagency coordination could
be achieved only by someone on high. In April, HEW
secretary Wilbur Cohen created the Federal Panel on Early
Childhood to write the requirements. Jule Sugarman,
former director of Head Start, chaired the panel. Cohen
had brought Sugarman to the Children's Bureau as associate
director as part of an overall strategy to ensure Head
Start's transfer into the bureau. Both Cohen and Sugarman
wanted to keep the program out of the Office of Education,
where state school administrators would dominate it.
Cohen also thought it appropriate to include on the panel
representatives from other departments involved in providing day care services. His inclusion created a somewhat diverse group representing OEO, HEW, the U.S. Department of Agriculture, the U.S. Department of Housing and
Urban Development, and the Department of Labor (DOL).
Even the Defense Department participated in very early
panel deliberations. Nonetheless, representatives of the
Children's Bureau and Head Start predominated.

From the outset, panel members divided into two groups:
one favoring comprehensive developmental day care, the
other advocating minimum cost day care to ease the employment of welfare mothers. The former group included the
Children's Bureau, Head Start, and the Women's Bureau of
the DOL. The employment-minimum cost group was cham-
pioned by DOL's Manpower Administration and, always in
the background, the Bureau of the Budget. An agency whose
program was designed principally to employ the poor sought
day care requirements that minimized costs. An agency
that operated a child development and care program pushed
for more comprehensive requirements. Two factors mitigated potential conflict. First, the working committee
consisted of panel and staff members sympathetic to the
developmental comprehensive approach, and it was they who
drafted the requirements. Second, the open-ended entitlement of many of the day care programs made costs of
tertiary concern.

Neither group had a monopoly on the historic function
of day care nor on good intentions. The employment-
oriented group argued that the extent of employment
programs was limited by the availability and cost of day
care. Raising that cost beyond the bare minimum resulted
in fewer jobs for the poor and a less effective employment

program. The developmentalists believed day care to be
the chief means of providing necessary nutrition and
medical services to deprived children. Staff attention
and education would enhance the child's future prospects.
They believed that costs should be secondary to the needs
of deprived children. In a world of limited resources
these two positions were not easily reconciled--if they
could be reconciled at all. Yet 1968 was not a time when
policy makers, at least those drafting the FIDCR, worried
over such limitations.

Sugarman's position was complicated by his administrative post. Coming from the Head Start tradition of comprehensive developmental care, he had just assumed the
number two position in the Children's Bureau. Had he
leaned against the developmentalists, he might have
alienated the personnel in the bureau. His responsibilities to the panel would end with the FIDCR draft; his
relationship to bureau personnel would continue throughout
his tenure there. His solution to these problems was to
draft a set of requirements that, while formally affirming
comprehensive developmental child care, were sufficiently
ambiguous in content and intention to comprehend the
interests of all panel members.

The final version of requirements specified child-staff
ratios and group and family day care. They stated that
the location of facilities must consider the relative need
of the population for federally funded day care, travel
time for users, accessibility to "other resources which
enhance the day care program," and opportunities for
parent and neighborhood involvement. Facilities must
conform to "appropriate" safety and sanitation codes.
"Educational opportunities must be provided every child
. . . under the supervision and direction of a staff
member trained or experienced in child growth and development. Toys, games, and daily activities for each child
"must be designed to influence a positive concept of self
and motivation to enhance his social, cognitive, and
communication skills." Counseling'for child and family
must be available to enable them to choose the best child
care arrangements. Health and dental care must be provided to the child. Facilities must provide "nutritious"
meals and daily checks for any indications of illness in
the child.

The requirements also ordered a periodic assessment of
the "physical and mental competence to care for children"
of staff members. They mandated "continuous in-service
training" and "career progression opportunities" for

staff members. "Parents must have the opportunity to become involved themselves in the making of decisions" concerning center operations. In centers of 40 or more children, parents must be included in a "policy advisory committee" and constitute no less than 50 percent of its membership. Such a committee "must perform productive functions" in program development, funding application, selection of administrators and staff, and channeling complaints. Employment and administration policies must be written out and available to parents and employees. Finally, the facilities "must be periodically evaluated in terms of the Federal Interagency Day Care Standards." The agent for evaluation was left unstated.[9]

Despite their scope and detail, the 1968 FIDCR actually represented a series of rather subtle compromises. The developmentalist group wanted child-staff ratios akin to those of Head Start, which were lower than those suggested for day care by the Child Welfare League. The employment-oriented group objected to the costs these ratios entailed. Sugarman's answer was to allow clerical and housekeeping personnel as well as unpaid volunteers to count as staff for the purposes of the requirement. Such volunteers could include "older children." Moreover, the requirements specified the ratios not "normally" be exceeded. This sort of qualifier was replete throughout the 1968 requirements. Space must be "adequate"; safeguards must be "adequate"; ventilation "adequate"; educational materials "appropriate" to the facility's "type"; and meals "adequate." What constituted adequacy or appropriateness was never specified—and this was crucial.

"The basic responsibility," the FIDCR stated, "for enforcement of the requirements lies with the administering agency." By prefacing the FIDCR with this statement, Sugarman mollified disagreeing panel members. Each agency governed the compliance with the requirements of its funding recipients. The one oversight agency that might have blocked the requirements—the Bureau of the Budget—had no authority to review agency regulations at that time. The developmentalist groups could enforce the requirements according to a strict interpretation; the employment-oriented group could enforce a loose interpretation. To ensure this flexibility, the FIDCR preface also noted that "Noncompliance may be grounds for suspension or termination of federal funds." The funding agency, then, had final determination over the only effective enforcement procedure, a funding suspension.

In her history of the FIDCR, Sara Pope Cooper observes that "discussions were seldom strident and that a strong consensus was reached on most points with remarkable ease."[10] The reason for this ease toward consensus was the tacit recognition among panel members that they were agreeing on an ambiguous, nonbinding set of requirements. In other words, consensus ensued from the common premise that the 1968 FIDCR were a set of goals and, as goals, everyone agreed that they were fine. The panel conducted no cost studies; costs were irrelevant to ideal standards. They relied on their experience with Head Start and their knowledge of child development. Moreover, soon after the promulgation of FIDCR, informal assurances were passed by the Social and Rehabilitation Service through HEW's regional offices to the states that the requirements would not be enforced.[11]

In 1968 a possibility arose that the Children's Bureau would enforce the FIDCR in stages. Although it had no authority over the other day care programs scattered among the bureaucracy, the bureau did control the Title IVA (of the Social Security Act) day care program. Since funding was the only effective means of enforcement, the strongest supporter of the FIDCR--the Children's Bureau-- was in a position to implement them. Moreover, at that time, Title IVA had an open-ended entitlement; money was indeed no object. The bureau's position, however, soon changed. When the Nixon administration reorganized HEW, the Children's Bureau was divided among the Community Services Administration, the Health Services and Mental Health Administration, and the newly created Office of Child Development (OCD). OCD received the enforcement mandate for the FIDCR, but the Community Services Administration received the Title IVA program. Without control of day care funding, OCD was an unarmed police.

In the larger policy conflict of 1967-1968 the FIDCR and its legislative mandate played a symbolic role. Among the slowly shrinking Great Society supporters in Congress, the conservative push to reduce welfare costs through the Work Incentives Program (WIN) portended in the minds of many children's advocates the sacrifice of the children of welfare recipients to shoddy care. On one level, the overriding stress on employment and administration of the WIN program by the DOL indicated that these children could expect the cheapest care supervised by an agency with no interest in them per se. On another level, insofar as Sheila Rothman is correct in arguing that the WIN program's "more fundamental purpose [than employment] was to frighten welfare recipients from applying for relief," the poorer the day care, the more effective the deterrent.[12] Liberals on the Senate Labor and Public Welfare Committee hoped that federal interagency day care requirements might prevent a serious decline in the quality of day care. If it raised the costs of that care, then the requirements might well serve to make welfare payments to mothers at home cheaper than the day care that would allow them to work. Either contingency was more palatable than the WIN program and its day care provisions. The committee vested the FIDCR mandate in OEO/HEW to ensure that the requirements were comprehensive and developmental in orientation.

Events in 1969 recast the political context of the FIDCR. The Westinghouse Study of Head Start questioned the long-term benefits of early invention--a serious setback for developmentalists. In that same year the newly elected Nixon administration advanced a sweeping proposal for welfare reform, the Family Assistance Plan (FAP). Apart from its innovative guaranteed annual income provision, FAP entailed a massive federal day care program as an adjunct to a modified WIN program. HEW estimated that the program would require 400 new day care centers each year for 5 years. Also, HEW Secretary Robert Finch created the OCD and brought in an eminent psychologist from Yale, Edward Zigler, to administer it. Due to their ambiguity and vague criteria for compliance, Zigler believed the FIDCR unworkable in their present form. In light of the proposed FAP day care program, which OCD would administer, he received authorization to revise them.

Zigler aimed for a set of day care requirements that could be enforced and that provided a minimum level of care consistent with the child's health development. Faced with more stringent limitations on social welfare spending under the Republican administration, he worked to strike a compromise between the comprehensive developmentalists and the employment-oriented advocates. Zigler sought the best care for the most children with the fewest dollars. To commence the process of revision, he held a major day care conference in 1970. Over 1,000 parents, child care providers, social scientists, and advocates met to discuss the requirements. The conference produced a manual to guide the revisions. In 1971, OCD began writing a new set of day care requirements.[13]

After the FAP proposal, Congress evinced continued interest in out-of-home child care. Among the employment-oriented group, Wilbur Mills, chairman of the House Ways and Means Committee, requested a HEW report on state licensing procedures. Mills was troubled by reports that inadequate day care facilities limited the expansion of the WIN program. Cumbersome licensing processes delayed the opening of new centers. Moreover, state codes were inconsistent and often inappropriate to child care. Russell Long, chairman of the Senate Finance Committee, also sought to deal with the problems of state licensing. He proposed minimum federal standards to supersede those of the states and accelerate the expansion of day care facilities. Under pressure from these committee chairmen the Nixon administration through OCD initiated a study of state licensing codes. The administration, however, opposed supersedence of any state with federal authority in this matter. OCD did disseminate a guide for day care licensing in 1973 and encouraged states to revise their codes accordingly. Since it was only a guide, its contents reflected Zigler's position that standards must be enforceable and guarantee the minimum needs of the child. He was also sufficiently politic to seek advice during its preparation from all interested parties.[14]

In 1971, congressional advocates of comprehensive developmental child care added a $2-billion program in this area to an OEO extension bill. Sponsored chiefly by Senator Walter Mondale and Representative John Brademas, S 2007 proposed comprehensive services for children in day care. Services would be free of charge for the poor and available on a graduated fee schedule for middle-income families. The bill also provided for new day care requirements to be developed through a complex interaction of government, caretakers, and parents. The innovation in the Mondale-Brademus bill was the extension of federal assistance to day care for nonpoor families. There was no precedent for a categorical federal program to subsidize the day care of middle-class children. The bill bore a large price tag without being linked directly to the employment of welfare clients or other traditional justifications. Among conservatives the program smacked of "sovietizing our [i.e., the nonpoor] children" and undermining the family. Many forgot that the tax law had for 20 years subsidized the nonparental care of middle-class children.

The OEO extension, including the Mondale-Brademus child care program, passed the Congress in December 1971. President Nixon vetoed it, and the Senate sustained the veto. From the administration's perspective, the

legislation contained too many objectionable features,
not the least of which was its cost. The child care
program contained complex administrative procedures
involving hundreds of sponsors working directly with
federal agencies; the administration and several state
governors believed these procedures to be unworkable. It
impinged on the day care provision of the FAP and extended
day care subsidies to the nonpoor. The OEO extension
included an independent governing body for its legal aid
funds. Since cabinet members had complained repeatedly
about OEO-funded litigation against the government, the
lack of presidential discretion regarding the board
controlling these funds became a significant objection to
the bill. Finally, a veto helped to mitigate conservative
criticism of Nixon's foreign policy. No single consideration can explain the veto.[15]

In the wake of the veto, the House Education and Labor
Committee reported another OEO extension bill, H.R. 12350,
without the child care program. (The Mondale child care
program also resurfaced in another bill, which passed the
Senate but died in the House.) To ensure that the administration, which advocates of comprehensive developmentalist child care now clearly perceived as antichild, did
not weaken the 1968 FIDCR, H.R. 12350 included a provision
for comparability, which required any new day care
requirements be "no less comprehensive" than the 1968 set.
The legislation cost $1 billion less than the earlier
vetoed version and modified the objectionable provisions
regarding legal services. There was also an expansion of
Head Start, which the administration opposed, intended to
offset the loss of the comprehensive child care program.

As the bill made its way through Congress in summer
1972, the comparability provision raised problems for
HEW's completed but unapproved revision of the FIDCR.
Secretary Richardson wrote Representative Albert Quie
requesting a clarification of the provision. He explained
the weaknesses of the 1968 FIDCR: They were vague,
ambiguous, and difficult to enforce. The revised version
corrected these problems. Although it increased the
ostensible child-adult ratios, the actual number of
children per care giver was unaffected. Richardson
requested a colloquy between Quie and Education and Labor
Committee chairman Carl Perkins to clarify that the
comparability provision entailed only overall quality,
not "stringent . . . quantative measurement." Quie and
Perkins had the colloquy along the lines Richardson had
requested.[16] In September the legislation, compar-

ability provision included, went to the President for approval.

The alignment of the executive agencies on this bill is significant to the fate of the 1972 revisions to the FIDCR. Both HEW and OEO recommended that Nixon sign the bill. Congress had dropped most of the objectionable provisions of the earlier extension bill. Perkins and Quie had clarified the comparability mandate to allow HEW's revisions. Despite these changes and the other agencies' recommendations, the OMB suggested a presidential veto. The bill in general and the comparability provision in particular "would limit to some extent administrative flexibility in carrying out the program." OMB had always considered the 1968 FIDCR an "unattainable level" of care. Consideration of day care standards, they argued, was relevant only to the still-pending FAP legislation. Despite their recommendation for disapproval, Nixon signed the OEO extension under the probably correct impression that it was the best that he could expect from Congress. Nonetheless, OMB's linkage of any day care requirements to the passage of the FAP would become significant for Zigler's revision of the FIDCR.[17]

In spring 1972, Zigler and his staff completed the new day care requirements. These requirements were much more specific on every aspect of a center's operation. They expanded the regulatory scope to in-home care, detailed age groupings, meals per hour of care, provider responsibilities, and a minimum wage requirement for center employees. In the crucial area of child-staff ratios the requirements increased the child-adult ratios but specified that only care givers, not clerical or janitorial staff, could count in the ratios. Although the 1968 FIDCR mandated lower ratios, it allowed any adult volunteer or older child present in the center to count in that overall ratio. Zigler's revision counted only paid, qualified care givers. Moreover, his revisions included ratios for children under 3 years old: 0-18 months, 3:1 and 19-38 months, 4:1. The 1968 FIDCR had neither requirements for care of children under 3 years old nor any ratios set this low. Zigler had written not only a rigorous set of day care requirements but an enforceable one as well. Due to their content, they encountered OMB's opposition; due to the political context, the advocacy groups opposed them as well.

Secretary Richardson approved the new requirements by June 1972. He proposed to hold a series of congressional and press briefings that summer to describe the admini-

stration's day care policy. The centerpiece would be the
new requirements, their relationship to the FAP, and
modifications in Head Start. Richardson and Zigler
believed the revised FIDCR would affirm the administration's commitment to good-quality day care and to children
in the wake of the child care veto. OMB, however, had
other plans. In a confidential white paper its staff
assessed the HEW proposals. The OMB paper concluded that
the proposed policy would (1) commit the federal government to determining directly the nature of child care,
(2) raise care in the centers to "approximately" the same
quality as that of Head Start, (3) increase FAP's day
care allocation from $750 million to $1.2 billion, (4)
establish a prime sponsor system "similar" to the proposed
system of Mondale and Brademus but with fewer allowable
sponsors, and (5) make an overall policy declaration in
support of developmentalist day care. The staff assessment, in characteristic understatement, concluded that a
policy statement of this sort "would be undesirable."[18]

In their analysis OMB questioned almost every fact of
Richardson's policy proposals. Not only were the staff
ratios challenged, but the very issue of "whether or not
the administration wants to endorse the 'Federal presence'
that these standards and the accompanying enforcement
effort implies [sic]." They questioned the wisdom of the
requirements' application to in-home care, to volunteer
participants in federal programs, and to centers serving
only those persons receiving federal cash subsidies. OMB
pointed out that HEW's proposed child care credit allowance would double FAP outlays and "eliminate parental
incentive to get a 'good bargain,' thus resulting in an
upward cost push." Presumably, the potential cost of the
minimum wage requirement also bothered OMB. In sum, their
central argument was that HEW's proposals "cloud the
difference between child care—a federal responsibility
as part of the workfare provisions of H.R. 1 [FAP]—and
compensatory education, which is primarily a state and
local function." Their alternative was to "leave quality
control to parental discretion under a pure income
strategy or support more limited standards. . . ."[19]

During the first half of 1972 the OMB and HEW were at
loggerheads over a proper day care policy for the administration. OMB wanted a minimum cost employment-oriented
policy; HEW advocated a more comprehensive developmentalist approach. Zigler's revision of the FIDCR was the
linchpin of HEW's approach. Neither Richardson nor
Undersecretary John Veneman would act without OMB's

approbation. As Veneman wrote the secretary in a
confidential memorandum, "I indicated to [OMB] your
desire to reach an agreement on day care [and that] it
would not be your intention to release our position
unless it was mutually determined to be appropriate."
Unable to budge OMB or induce White House intervention,
such a determination never came. The revisions were
quietly buried with the death of the FAP. Soon after, a
frustrated Zigler returned to New Haven.[20]

Ironically, the most vocal opponents of Zigler's
revision outside the executive branch were the staunchest
advocates of comprehensive day care. From the viewpoint
of the Child Welfare League, the Children's Defense Fund,
and others, HEW and the administration had entered an
insidious conspiracy to undermine the quality of federally
funded day care. The revised FIDCR, they believed,
eviscerated the impeccable standards of 1968. Caught in
the middle, Zigler's revisions were soundly condemned by
both sides. Politically the administration had nothing
to gain from promulgating requirements already proscribed
by the very people they were designed to pacify. To the
advocates of comprehensive day care, loyalty to the 1968
FIDCR had become the test of commitment to the proper care
of children. In their minds an ambiguous, unenforceable
icon was preferable to a practical but supposedly weaker
set of Nixon administration requirements. As long as
worship was voluntary, OMB, too, agreed to allow the 1968
idol to stand.[21]

THE FIDCR AND TITLE XX

Two years of relative calm concerning day care regulations
followed the failure of Zigler's revisions. The administration abandoned its FAP proposal and worked toward
keeping down social welfare expenditures; Congress worked
toward increasing them. Not until the passage of the
Title XX amendment to the Social Security Act did the
issue of day care standards arise. Title XX incorporated
an innovation in federal social welfare aid to the states.
In place of categorical programs it broached a less rigid
formula grant approach with fewer restrictions on state
allocations of federal funds. Among the areas to be
funded in this fashion was day care. The administration's
move toward revenue sharing and block grants did not sit
well with many members of Congress and other advocates of
categorical spending. They believed that, uncontrolled,

states and municipalities might spend the grant money in
ways unintended by Congress. Day care advocates also
feared the inevitable competition for funds with more
powerful social service interests. A major issue was the
continued assurance of adequate services to target popula-
tions. In other words, the extent to which service
program grants were earmarked and regulated was central
to the Title XX enactment.

In one respect, the history of Title XX began in 1972.
At that time federal welfare funds were distributed in
categorical fashion to states under an 80 percent matching
formula. Outlays had grown by 450 percent between 1968
and 1972: $350 million to $1.6 billion. To impose some
degree of restraint on this rapid growth, Congress placed
a ceiling of $2.5 billion on federal outlays. This
ceiling, however, would still have allowed a $1-billion
increase in spending--something the administration
strongly opposed. To keep spending well below the congressional ceiling, HEW issued new regulations governing
federal funding in May 1973. Their main purpose was to
tighten eligibility requirements and reduce allowance for
services. Congressional opposition to these regulations
resulted in a postponement of their enforcement until
January 1, 1975.

Congress and the administration had reached an impasse
over social services spending. In meetings with organized
labor, state social service administrators, and other
interested parties, HEW assistant secretary of planning
and evaluation William Morrill devised a strategy to
break the impasse. In return for administration support
of the $2.5-billion ceiling, Congress would enact new
legislation to replace categorical specification of
service programs with block grants. Federal review of
the states' disposition of the funds would cease and only
an independent audit would ensure that the states conform
to the general strictures of the stature.

In support of this approach OMB director Ray Ash
explained to the President that the federal government
could not distinguish as well as state and local authorities the useful from the useless programs. The new
approach promised to reduce federal involvement and
fructify the administration's long-term policy thrust
toward a New Federalism. Ash envisioned no way of
holding outlays below the $2.5-billion ceiling in the
future. Congress's repeated deferrals of HEW's regulations and the various alternative bills boded only more
spending in the traditional categorical vein. He believed

that the administration could at least extract a block grant approach in the process.[22]

With approval from the Social and Rehabilitation Service, HEW's hierarchy, and OMB, Morrill commenced a prolonged series of meetings with all interested parties on the structure and content of what was to become Title XX. Through their meetings he built a consensus for Title XX. Regarding the 1968 FIDCR, the AFL-CIO was particularly insistent that the requirements be retained and enforced. ASPE's draft of Title XX thus included a provision for enforcement of the FIDCR, but, at HEW insistence, the provision also mandated a study of the appropriateness of federal day care regulation. For in-home care they proposed to leave the decision to the states, provided each state granted "all interested individuals and organizations the opportunity to submit recommended standards." Out-of-home care would have to conform to the 1968 FIDCR, except for the requirement mandating educational opportunities for children. Their draft bill gave the secretary authority to prescribe maximum permissible child-staff ratios for children over 5 provided that those ratios did not exceed 13:1 for children ages 5-9 and 20:1 for children over 9. The bill also included a request to the secretary to prepare a report on the overall appropriateness of the day care requirements. Regarding the requirements, OMB made one major change: the clause requiring states to consult "all interested individuals" when setting standards for in-home care became standards set "reasonable in accord with recommended standards of national standard-setting organizations concerned with the home care of children." Popular input was scotched.[23]

The House Ways and Means Committee and Long's Finance Committee dominated congressional action on the bill and other welfare proposals. The Ways and Means Committee concurred in the central thrust of Title XX. They were pleased to be rid of the stalemate over social services spending. The committee lowered the overall recommended staffing ratios and imposed a 2:1 ratio for children under 3. They took this latter step to raise the cost of infant center-based care in hopes of discouraging it. It was, they argued, bad for the young child. The committee also reinstated the educational requirement of the 1968 FIDCR. Finally, as a gesture to those seeking to restrain costs, their report instructed the secretary to consider the cost implications of requirements in an appropriateness report.[24]

On the Senate side, the Finance Committee retained the
principal features of HEW's draft: the higher staff
ratios and the waiver of the educational requirement. In
place of specific staff ratios for children under 3 the
committee gave the secretary discretion in the matter.
Walter Mondale of the Senate and Patricia Schroeder of
the House opposed the relaxation of the FIDCR's staff
ratios as a move toward "warehousing" children.   Despite
this opposition, the House conferees acceded to all the
Senate's provisions regarding standards. The conference
report passed both chambers by voice vote.[25]
HEW approved of the enrolled bill. HEW Secretary
Casper Weinberger wrote Ash that the higher child-staff
ratios were "an improvement over our proposal in this
regard." Apparently they had overestimated the political
muscle of the comprehensive care advocates. The Treasury
Department, however, objected strenuously to the parent
locater provision of the bill. The Internal Revenue
Service, they believed, would be placed in the business
of enforcing child support laws. For the same reason,
OMB joined Treasury in recommending a presidential
veto.[26] President Ford's decision was not made that
easily. As a member of Congress, he had supported
precisely such a parent locater law. The bill incorporated a much-desired revision to existing categorical
programs. Republicans had taken a beating in the fall
elections and the 94th Congress promised to be more
generous than its predecessor in social welfare spending.
Disregarding OMB's and Treasury's advice, Ford signed the
legislation on January 4, 1975.
Title XX did more than change the child-staff ratios;
it altered enforcement precedures for the FIDCR. Before
1975 enforcement rested on a compliance procedure in which
an administrative hearing occurred prior to any federal
suspension of funds. The new method was a "federal
financial participation" procedure in which the government
could suspend funds at the time of the violation and
require the state to reimburse any previously allocated
money. Moreover, Title XX's penalty for noncompliance to
the FIDCR was not the standard 3 percent reduction in
overall funding but a total cutoff of day care payments.
This new procedure was included at the behest of the
AFL-CIO and Child Welfare League as part of the price of
their concurrence in Title XX. Morrill, too, thought a
rigorous enforcement of the 1968 FIDCR could clear up the
question of their practicality. Indeed it would. The
Social and Rehabilitation Service, which administered its

day care programs, estimated that "well in excess of half of the child day care provided under Title XX will not meet the FIDCR." Over $300 million, half of all day care funds, could be withheld for noncompliance. The contrast between the old and new procedures was more striking. Neither the Social and Rehabilitation Service nor any other federal agency had ever held a compliance hearing to enforce the FIDCR within a state.[27]

The first rumbling of the political eruption to follow came in April 1975. That month HEW published for public comment preliminary day care requirements based on Title XX provisions. In the one staffing area in which they had discretion, children under 3, the department based the ratio on Zigler's unenacted revision. Centers were required to have a child-staff ratio of 1:1 for infants under 6 weeks old, 3:1 for children 6 weeks to 18 months, and 4:1 for children 18 to 36 months. All the other ratios, including the most controversial 5:1 and 7:1 for children ages 3-5, were fixed by Title XX or the 1968 FIDCR. Enforcement would begin October 1, 1975. It would include Title XX and the day care authorized under Title IV. As the implications of these requirements became clearer and state enforcement more likely, protest mounted from care givers, state administrators, and members of Congress.

The reasons for the protest were obvious. A 1974 HEW audit of day care centers in nine states indicated that three fourths of them were not in compliance with one or more health or safety requirement. The more serious cost problem was staff ratios. A center's typical child-staff ratio for preschool children was 8:1. To lower that ratio to 5:1 or 4:1 could increase costs by up to 50 percent. In response to this protest, Weinberger changed the final regulations to allow a 4:1 ratio for children between 6 weeks and 3 years old. He recognized, however, that, despite these changes, the FIDCR's enforcement "would significantly reduce the availability of child care in many states." The fracas over the requirements intensified as the October deadline approached.[28]

Congressional protest against the requirements did not divide along ideological lines. Such otherwise diverse politicians as Henry Bellmon, Ronald Dellums, Carl Albert, Peter Rodino, William Brock, and George McGovern petitioned for a postponement. Supporters of the requirements were more of a kind ideologically: Bella Abzug, Walter Mondale, Charles Rangel, and John Brademas, but James Buckley also supported the requirements.

Undoubtedly overwhelmed by ambivalence, Representative
Joshua Eliberg signed letters of protest and of support.
Opponents and supporters argued in surprisingly similar
fashion. The opponents thought that enforcement of the
requirements would price day care centers out of the
market and endanger the well-being of the children.
Supporters felt that failure to enforce the requirements
would allow shoddy, inadequate day care centers to
continue and endanger the well-being of the children.
All were righteous; few were holy.[29]

As the deadline neared, enormous pressures were brought
to bear on HEW. Members of Congress continued to threaten
and cajole. Over 20 bills were introduced to suspend the
requirements. Frantic over the possible loss of $300
million in day care funds, states warned day care operators within their jurisdiction of an impending crackdown.
They responded with calls and letters to Congress. The
AFL-CIO and Child Welfare League threatened to sue HEW if
the requirements were not enforced. In the South, day
care operators did bring suit against HEW to block
enforcement of the requirements. Finally on September
26, four days before they were to have taken effect, a
federal district court judge issued a temporary injunction
against their enforcement pending a hearing October 20.

Within HEW strategies for dealing with the enforcement
problem abounded. No one within the department seriously
considered enforcing the requirements to the extent of
closing down day care centers through a wholesale suspension of federal funding. The Social and Rehabilitation
Services, the administering agency, proposed an imaginative, though probably illegal, extension of Section 1115
of the Social Security Act, the demonstration provision.
Under their plan, HEW would "allow the states to experiment with alternate requirements" and waive the FIDCR for
these "experiments." That these demonstration projects
might include over half the federally funded centers
throughout the nation apparently presented no difficulty
for the agency. The general counsel's office rejected
their approach as unworkable and of dubious legality. An
alternative, simply ignoring the law, was also rejected.[30]

The court injunction and the congressional push for
suspension allowed HEW to adopt a less radical approach.
On October 1, Secretary F. David Matthews sent draft
legislation to the House and Senate. The legislation
would amend the compliance features of Title XX. In
place of total cutoff of funds the secretary would only
reduce funding by 3 percent--the penalty for other Title

XX violations. No penalty would be imposed if the state were "making a good faith effort to upgrade day care facilities" to accord with the FIDCR. If a center was not in compliance with "licensure, health, or safety standards," the secretary could suspend all funding. HEW's proposal dealt with the crux of the issue for all concerned: the staffing requirement for children under 6.[31] A good-faith effort or, at worst, a 3 percent penalty would assuage the fears of the states and their day care centers. Congress, however, chose another route.

The Ways and Means Committee reported out H.R. 9803 on September 29. The bill suspended staffing requirements for 6 months. In deference to supporters of the lower ratios it provided that staffing ratios must conform to state law and be no higher than those in effect prior to September 15, 1975. Overall the bill's manager, James Corman, justified the suspension as a necessary hiatus to allow congressional review of the requirements. The measure easily passed the House and went into Long's Finance Committee.[32]

Long had difficulty with the House suspension. Six months, he argued, would not enlighten congressional decision making. Instead, he envisioned using the requirements to encourage operators to hire welfare mothers for their day care centers. Congress would provide additional funds to enable centers to meet staffing ratios and offer tax credits for employing welfare recipients. Long and Mondale introduced a bill containing these provisions and a $500-million authorization to defray the cost of additional staff. Centers could then meet the requirements without raising fees. Their strategy was simple. Using the threat of FIDCR's immediate enforcement without federal assistance, they hoped to compel members of Congress into passing the aid bill with its welfare provision. Federal funding would assuage the fears of day care operators and states over added costs. The lower child-staff ratios would enlist support from advocates of comprehensive day care. The welfare provisions would attract conservative votes. Finally, anticipating the administration's opposition, they were confident that these combined political forces could ensure presidential acquiescence or, at worst, override his veto. The key was still the impending enforcement of the FIDCR.

With this strategy, Long, a dogged opponent of strict day care regulation, became an advocate of quick implementation, provided his welfare provisions were adopted.

He bottled up the House's 6-month suspension, H.R. 9803,
in his committee. Instead he offered a 1-month suspension
as an amendment to a pending tariff bill. Such a brief
suspension would keep the pressure on Congress and the
administration. In the first week of October the Senate
passed the amended tariff bill and entered into conference
with the House. Still concerned over impending enforcement, the House conferees insisted on a lengthier delay.
Long compromised on 4 months. The report passed the
House by a 383-to-10 vote and the Senate by voice. Since
neither Congress nor the administration was prepared to
enforce the staffing requirement at this time, Ford
signed the suspension pending a more permanent resolution
of the problem.

The hiatus allowed Long to incorporate into H.R. 9803
his and Mondale's provisions for aid to the states in
meeting the requirements and for the employment of welfare
mothers in day care. By a 9-to-9 vote the Finance
Committee defeated a Republican amendment to delete the
staffing requirements entirely. The committee did reduce
the aid authorization from $500 million to $250 million
based on a new estimate of the states' compliance costs.
They waived compliance for centers with fewer than 20
percent of their children receiving federal subsidies.
However, the bill also made the employment tax credit
refundable to encourage nonprofit centers to hire welfare
recipients. This credit, in conjunction with direct
federal funding, would have defrayed up to $5,000 of the
cost of employing a welfare recipient in a day care
center. Finally, implementation of the FIDCR ratios
would be delayed until July 1, 1976. Under these
provisions the employment-oriented advocates and the
comprehensive developmentalists found a common cause in
enforcing the FIDCR. Thus did Mondale and Long stand on
the same ground.

Their bill encountered opposition from both the administration and Senate Republicans. The administration had
decided that the best solution to the staffing problem
was to allow each state to determine its own day care
standards. This accorded with its general block grant,
defederalization approach. Moreover, it would eliminate
the need to augment federal spending to enforce compliance. The administration wanted no new federal "workfare"
programs through the FIDCR. On the floor the issue became
one of federal vs. state regulatory authority. Senate
opponents lost successive amendments to delete the
staffing requirements, to delay them until completion of

HEW's appropriateness study, and to allow states to exempt
more centers from the requirements. At the end of January
1976 the Senate approved the bill 65 to 24. The conference committee made some minor alterations, but the
Senate's provisions effectively remained intact. The
final version passed the House 316 to 72 and the Senate
59 to 30.[33]

A piece of legislation more antithetical to the administration's position could not be easily had. HEW summarized the objectionable provisions to the President.
First, it provided an annualized $250-million increase to
Title XX funds. Second, it imposed the FIDCR without the
appropriateness study or any other evidence that children
needed the services mandated. Third, it earmarked Title
XX funds for day care--a violation of the block grant
intent of the law. Finally, the welfare hiring incentives
disregarded the children's interests by encouraging
employment of unqualified care givers. HEW recommended a
veto and suggested the administration submit legislation
simply to extend the moratorium on FIDCR's enforcement.[34] OMB concurred for many of the same reasons,
but with a significant twist.

HEW's central strategy on the FIDCR was to promote a
prolonged suspension of the ratios pending the appropriateness study. In large part the hierarchy of HEW
believed this approach to be the only politically viable
one in light of Congress's determination to continue
federal enforcement of the day care requirements. It was
not that HEW opposed the administration's position that
requirements were a state responsibility, but that they
recognized the political difficulty of effecting that
position. OMB, on the other hand, wholeheartedly, even
recklessly pursued the state regulatory approach to avoid
additional appropriations. Their cudgel in this matter
was enforcement of the FIDCR without federal funding to
ease compliance. At the very least, OMB believed, the
administration could trade suspension for a further
weakening of federal controls over Title XX funds.

OMB and HEW could agree to veto H.R. 9803 because it
would implement the FIDCR, provide compliance funds, and
enact a new workfare program. Ford, in fact, vetoed the
bill and, in a furious lobbying effort, was sustained in
the Senate by three votes. The post-veto situation,
however, was ripe for the OMB-HEW disagreement to surface.
OMB sought to use the threats of the FIDCR's enforcement
as a stick to force congressional acquiescence in
loosening the strings attached to Title XX money or,

perhaps, the retrocession of regulatory authority over day care to the states. In Congress, Long and Mondale sought to use the promise of increased federal aid as a carrot to marshall state and congressional support for federal enforcement of the FIDCR. The requirements became hostage in this contest. HEW believed OMB's approach would only push Congress into passing another bill like H.R. 9803 and overriding any subsequent veto. While Congress readied new legislation in spring 1976, the OMB-HEW disagreement festered.

In May, Senator Mondale and Senator Robert Packwood, the principal antagonists over H.R. 9803, worked out a compromise on the enforcement of the FIDCR's staff ratios. Enforcement would be suspended until October 1, 1977, when HEW should have completed the appropriateness study. The bill provided $312.5 million over a 15-month period to aid states in complying with the FIDCR's unremitted health and safety requirements. Otherwise the bill mirrored the major features of H.R. 9803. Suspending the staff ratios for 17 months while retaining the additional day care funds, the bill allowed the states and centers to have their carrot while standing more or less still. Although some of those opposing H.R. 9803 had done so to block additional federal spending, the rest had done so to prevent the imposition of federally mandated requirements. In the absence of the FIDCR enforcement provision, the 3-vote margin that had sustained Ford's veto evaporated. Without a genuine threat of veto the administration's stick became a twig.[35]

At the same time whatever leverage the administration had over the revised bill was dissipating, OMB insisted on using the threat of enforcing the staff ratios to prod Congress into amendments more amenable to its position. HEW, however, could clearly see the fatuity of such tactics. William Morrill, assistant secretary for planning and evaluation, bore the brunt of HEW's negotiations with OMB and Congress. In a handwritten memo to Secretary Matthews, Morrill explained that OMB was resisting any prolonged moratorium on the FIDCR. "OMB (O'Neill)," he wrote, "took a strong position that we should extend only to July 1, to keep the pressure on the Congress about the Title XX proposals. With great difficulty, we talked them into October 1." Morrill concluded that OMB "is unlikely to budge."[36]

At OMB's insistence HEW sent letters to House and Senate Republican leaders opposing the additional Title XX funds as illogical in the face of the staff ratio suspension. The required health and safety changes simply did not cost that much money. The letter also objected to earmarking Title XX grants for day care. Despite these objections the bill passed both houses in June and went to conference. In a final attempt to salvage something from the legislation HEW offered to allow a $200-million increase in Title XX funds every year for 4 years in return for incorporating some of the block grant provisions into the bill. Supporters, however, knew when compromise was necessary and when it was not. This time they had the votes to override a veto. The conference committee rejected HEW's offer. With a reduction in funding from $312 to $240 million and a waiver of matching requirements for some of the day care money, the revised legislation passed the House 281 to 71 and the Senate 72 to 15.

Congress did not enroll the measure until Ford's nomination as the Republican presidential candidate. With Ronald Reagan's right-wing pressure removed, they assumed a veto to be less likely. Their caution, though, was probably unnecessary; the override votes were there. HEW recommended approval. The bill, they observed, suspended staff ratios and was backed by a veto-proof majority. OMB, too, acquiesced in the undeniable probability of a veto override and recommended approval. Both agencies agreed a veto would be highly impolitic in an election year. Only the Council of Economic Advisers suggested Ford disapprove the measure. Apparently Chairman Alan Greenspan either had little cognizance of the situation's political realities or had made other career plans for 1977. The President signed the bill into law on September 7, 1976.[37] Postponed until October 1977, the FIDCR would become Jimmy Carter's problem.

TO THE APPROPRIATENESS STUDY

Placing the FIDCR debate subsequent to 1976 in its political and economic context is a useful starting point for analysis. In large part the debate over the FIDCR was a contest among different perceptions of the reality of day care. Data that were statistically indisputable were ambiguous policy-wise, while data that clearly mandated a policy course were disputed. Among the relevant data available in 1976 are the following: one half of women with children under 18 work; 40 percent of

women with preschool children work; and over 5 million
chidren under 13 (12 percent of the age cohort) spend 30
or more hours per week in the care of someone other than
their parents or their teachers. Of these 5.2 million
children, 1.3 million are cared for by relatives in the
relative's home, 960,000 by relatives in the child's
home, 620,000 by nonrelatives in the child's home, 1.2
million by nonrelatives in "family" day care facilities,
and a little over 1.1 million in centers including day
care centers, nurseries, cooperatives, and Head Start.[38]

Approximately $10 billion is spent on child care
annually. Individual payments account for roughly 60
percent, direct federal payments 18 percent, federal tax
credit 8 percent, and state and local payments the
remaining 14 percent. The FIDCR applies to 56 percent of
direct federal payments, mostly through Title XX's
$800-million outlay for child care. If federally funded
in-home care and family day care are discounted from the
FIDCR's purview, the dollar amounts decline by 40 percent
and leave approximately $600 million in center-based care
covering fewer than 500,000 children. The FIDCR, then,
governs less than 10 percent of the nonparental,
out-of-school, full-time child care. Significantly,
however, this total constitutes nearly half of all center-
based day care. Insofar as it might affect state regulations, the FIDCR could have an impact on all day care
centers.[39]

Forty-one percent of all centers are proprietary, that
is operated for profit; the remainder are nonprofit. Of
the approximately 8,100 federal financial participation
(FFP) centers, 23 percent are proprietary. Compared to
the nonprofit centers, the proprietary centers generally
spend fewer dollars per child and have higher child-staff
ratios. Among FFP centers, 79 percent of the nonprofit
centers meet the FIDCR's staffing requirements, while
only 45 percent of the proprietary ones do. Among the
non-FFP centers (those not governed by the FIDCR), 38
percent meet the staffing requirements. The upshot is
that just under half of all day care centers do not meet
the FIDCR's staffing requirements. More important, one
quarter of the centers subject to FFP sanctions fail to
meet the requirements; whence came the protest over the
FIDCR's enforcement.[40]

Day care is a labor-intensive industry: 75 percent of
all expenses involve staff salaries and benefits. The
National Association for Child Development and Education,
the trade association of the proprietary centers,

estimates that lowering child-staff ratios to the FIDCR's level from existing state regulations would double the average staffing cost per child. For the proprietary centers a lower staff ratio would increase costs and compel them either to lower profits, raise fees, or drop children receiving federal subsidies. A boost in fees, insofar as it is not offset by larger state and federal subsidies, would reduce demand for their services, lower center utilization rates, and, ultimately, cut their profits. If subsidies for FFP proprietary centers were increased to ease compliance to the FIDCR, fees still might rise. Centers with less than 100 percent of their children receiving federal subsidies would have to conform to the lower staff ratios or drop their subsidized children. Moreover, states might not raise their subsidy share or, worse, they might revise licensing codes to require staff ratios consistent with those of the FIDCR. The latter move was a more disconcerting possibility to non-FFP proprietary centers for it would increase costs without providing any offset through subsidies.[41]

The staff ratios, however, do not have the same import for nonprofit centers. These centers serve a higher percentage of children completely covered by government funding. Thus, they are much more directly dependent on federal and state subsidies. Since the size of government subsidies per child are roughly based on the staff ratios mandated in the FIDCR, the nonprofit centers generally adjust their staff size to conform with the requirements. Their interest lies in having large staffs, not in maximizing profits. Any increase in the allowable child-to-staff ratios could entail a decrease in government subsidies per child and consequently, reduce staff size. Unlike their proprietary cousins, the nonprofit FFP centers generally support low staff ratios. Although the staffing requirements of the FIDCR are very important to both proprietary and nonprofit centers, the reasons for their importance are antithetical.[42]

Among center-based providers, the proprietary centers comprise 20-41 percent of the total market. A multi-million dollar industry, they are expanding rapidly, particularly in the form of chain centers. As in most service industries, wages are low, $6,000 to $7,500 for care givers. Though they point to a "nickel on a dollar" profit, their rate of return on equity ranges between 13 and 20 percent--not quite that of IBM, but not quite that of a saving bond, either. They have a lobby in Washington and stress their "taxpaying not tax consuming" character.

The proprietary centers are strongly opposed to any
federal enforcement of child-staff ratios lower than
current state requirements. Their central argument is
that in an age of fiscal austerity, government aid cannot
be counted on to pay for "absurd" staff ratios. The
continued availability of day care depends on keeping
costs down. The employment-oriented advocates, as well
as feminist organizations seeking to ease the entry of
women into the labor force, join them in this position.

On the other side of the staffing issue stand the many
nonprofit centers, the comprehensive developmentalist
advocates, such as the Child Welfare League and the
Children's Defense Fund, and the American Federation of
Teachers of the AFL-CIO. For reasons already mentioned,
many nonprofit centers prefer lower child-staff ratios.
Among the developmentalists, the 1968 FIDCR as amended
are an article of faith. The Child Welfare League
perceives any attempt to increase staff ratios to be an
abrogation of the child's interest. Fiscal austerity and
profit-making centers are their bêtes noires--precursors
of "Kentucky Fried Children" and "Wee Willie Warehouses."
The American Federation of Teachers has joined the
advocates of comprehensive day care and presses for more
requirements: stringent licensing requirements as well
as low child-staff ratios. Its President Albert Shanker
has called for "a system of universal day care [and]
early childhood education" under public school sponsorship. It is no secret that the American Federation of
Teachers has been struggling for several years to find a
new market for unemployed teachers to offset declining
school enrollments.[43]

On the issue of teacher certification, groups within
the pro-1968 FIDCR coalition diverge. The teacher's
union argues that the education of preschool children
requires professional educators, i.e., their members.
Many nonprofit centers with their roots in the community
action programs of the 1960s feel threatened by any
legally mandated infusion of teachers. Like a feudal
baron fearing for his fiefdom if he relied too much on
the king's troops to defend his castle, the community-
based providers are wary of Shanker's legions protecting
their government subsidies and low staff ratios. "Perhaps
they were afraid," Barry Bruce-Briggs observes, "that
they could not stand up to a tough-minded operation like
the AFT. . . ."[44] The defenders of the 1968 FIDCR greet
the support of the American Federation of Teachers with
one hand extended; the other they keep on their purses.

The array of the FIDCR's interest groups is matched in
many respects by the differing concerns of agencies
within HEW. The Office of Human Development Services
(HDS) administers most day care funds within HEW. Within
HDS the Administration for Children, Youth, and Families
(ACYF) is the primary standard-setting body for children,
a legacy from the Children's Bureau. Like its predecessor, OCD, ACYF does not administer day care funds
other than those for Head Start. Direct administrative
responsibility for Title XX belongs to the successor to
the Social and Rehabilitation Service within HDS, the
Administration for Public Services (APS). The schism
between OCD's charge of enforcing the FIDCR and the Social
and Rehabilitation Service's charge of funding day care
programs persists in their descendants, ACYF and APS.

APS's chief concern is to avoid day care requirements
that exact a level of care undesired by the states. The
states are their clients and they do not want to impose
punitive sanctions on them. ACYF, on the other hand,
stands in the tradition of Head Start and the Children's
Bureau and its strong concern for the child's development
over other considerations. They support rigorous requirements, effectively enforced. No better example of the
different perspectives of these two offices can be found
than ACYF's (at that time still OCD) response to an APS
prepared "decision memorandum" for the undersecretary.
APS had written: "the decision to modify or refine the
HEW role as defined by the Title XX FIDCR is a political
decision." ACYF replied that "we disagree with the
statement. . . . We strongly believe it is a human value
decision."[45] These are positions not easily reconciled.

Overall, this is the array of actors within and outside
HEW in the years after the 1976 suspension of the FIDCR's
staffing ratios. In this context HEW began to prepare
the congressionally mandated appropriateness report and
determine the fate of FIDCR. The preparation commenced
in March 1975 with formation of the FIDCR Appropriateness
Committee under the assistant secretary for planning and
evaluation (ASPE). Chaired by career civil servant
William R. Prosser of ASPE, the committee included
representatives from HDS, ACYF, and APS. In addition,
OCD and APS had commissioned several major studies of day
care: three by Abt Associates (the National Day Care
Study, the Infant Day Care Study, and the Family Day Care
Study); the Comparative State Licensing Study; and APS's
own effort to assess compliance with the Title XX FIDCR.
By far the largest, most expensive, and most significant

study was Abt's National Day Care Study. It dealt with
the primary issue of center-based, child-staff ratios.

At the outset, Prosser's committee faced several
problems. Congress had provided little or nothing in the
way of direction for the study beyond its basic mandate.
The committee members had as yet no hard data from these
studies on the effects of day care regulation on children
nor did they have any criteria for evaluating appropriateness. Merely arriving at a set of such criteria absorbed
a year of their time. To aid them in identifying the
issues and bringing extant knowledge to bear on the
problem the committee commissioned 21 state-of-the-art
papers from specialists in different facets of day care.
Still, little progress had been made by the time the
presidential election and change of administrations threw
HEW's hierarchy into flux.

Carter chose Joseph A. Califano to be secretary of HEW.
Califano chose Peter Schuck as deputy assistant secretary
in ASPE and gave him oversight responsibility for the
appropriateness report. Over the first year of the new
administration an approach to the FIDCR's revisions and
appropriateness report was agreed on. In a meeting with
Califano the principals (Schuck, Prosser, and other relevant staff) briefed him on the report's format and the
key issues, such as staff ratios and cost-effectiveness.
Califano stressed the need for continued public involvement and a published set of regulations by January 1979.
Within the executive secretariat of the secretary's
staff, there was some sentiment for detailed regulations.
Although they were receptive to changes in staff ratios,
the executive staff worried about "mere custodial warehousing of children" and "franchise operations . . .
mak[ing] profits from cheap, low quality centers."
Despite the administration's policy opposing complex,
lengthy regulations, Califano was prepared to make an
exception for the FIDCR. Finally, he instructed Schuck,
through ASPE's assistant secretary, Henry Aaron, to keep
all options open in the appropriateness report.[46]

HEW contacted the appropriate congressional committees
to obtain a postponement of the June 30 deadline for the
report and the revisions. Not wanting to reenact the
enforcement crisis of 1976, Congress suspended the FIDCR
staffing requirement again, continued the basic Title XX
provisions, and postponed to April 1978 the submission
date for the report. Their only caveat, given informally,
was that the various interest groups and advocates be
consulted throughout the revision process.[47]

To aid in drafting the report, Schuck recruited an advisory panel of specialists in various fields relating to child care. This move raised a larger question concerning Califano's overall include-the-public approach to the report and the regulation-writing process. The secretary's approach can be interpreted as an effort to restrain potential critics through their inclusion at various stages in the process. A social scientist or advocate who was asked for advice or commissioned to write a paper might be less inclined to attack the final product. With such a strategy, the product might reflect the adviser's point of view; by the same token, a sense of loyalty, participation, or obligation could act to inhibit criticism. An ancillary effect is that criticism made of a draft is often criticism not made of a final document. Merely by acknowledging the early criticism in the final report authors could avoid its repetition. By then, the critic is either frustrated at having had no impact or satisfied at having had the opportunity to voice misgivings. Public involvement may be democratic, but in the case of FIDCR, Califano conceived of it as a good tactic to dissipate future criticisms of the regulations. Whatever larger political and economic considerations might mold the FIDCR, the advocates would have had their moment of protest.

The appropriateness report began with an introductory overview of American day care and the FIDCR. It then discussed the various provisions of the requirements, their costs, and their administration. The report ended with a set of inconclusive findings and innocuous recommendations. In February 1978, HEW held three large public conferences on the draft report. Conference participants severely criticized it for its failure to make policy recommendations, to take a stand on significant issues, and to present a clear, accurate exposition of the data. Some of the criticisms were comprehended in the final document, but the report still avoided any clear policy statement. This avoidance was consonant with Califano's wishes. As his staff explained, the criticisms were "probably an inescapable cost to be incurred for the benefit of keeping all major policy choices open to debate in the course of developing the new regulations."[48]

Ill feelings toward the appropriateness report were not limited to the child care community. In Congress, Senator Daniel P. Moynihan excoriated HEW Undersecretary Hale Champion for the report's writing style. After reading aloud one particularly obtuse passage, Moynihan

bellowed, "What illiteracy. Would you dare consign a
child to the care of someone who would write something
like this? . . . It is appalling. And you have a man
from Brookings [Aaron] who put this out, right? . . .
this junk, this disgrace. . . ."[49] Moynihan's histri-
onics notwithstanding, the report was not without its
problems. Califano's staff admitted that "given its bulky
format, and technical, wordy style the FIDCR report is
unlikely to have much immediate impact on its prescribed
audience--Congress and congressional staff."[50]

Audience expectations, too, contributed to the report's
reception. The interest groups and advocates anticipated
a document that would make definitive policy statements.
Califano, however, had decided against this approach;
Prosser and his fellow authors were left to face the
gales of criticism that ensued. Congress, on the other
hand, looked at the report as an instrument for postponing
the enforcement of the staff ratios. The report's preparation justified subsequent suspensions. Regardless of
intrinsic quality, any report would have encountered harsh
criticisms within this political milieu.

Many of the criticisms were well founded. Due in part
to the political constraints placed on the report writers,
their final product had flaws. Its attempt to include
all points of view resulted in its having none. Its
recommendations expressed the need for the requirements
to "reflect current research and expert judgment" on
child care, to "clarify roles and responsibilities of
providers and state and local administrations," to
"educate as well as regulate," to "accommodate the rich
diversity in child-care needs and arrangements," and to
"include participation of all interested individuals" in
writing them. In other words, the report recommended
that the revised FIDCR be appropriate to child care in
America.[51] Whether it successfully fulfilled its stated
purpose of informing the public debate remains to a great
extent in the eye of the beholder.

TOWARD THE FINAL REGULATIONS

Once ASPE had issued the appropriateness report the task
of drafting new regulations on day care fell to the
Office of Human Development Services, the administering
agency. Califano, however, had misgivings about leaving
the FIDCR in the hands of HDS, which was permeated with
client interests. The Administration for Public Services

was very much attuned to the states' concerns on regulations issues. The ACYF was composed of many child advocates opposed to custodial care for children; strict federal regulation was their chief method of ensuring a high quality of care. They were closely aligned with advocacy groups such as the Children's Defense Fund and the Child Welfare League. Regardless of which administrative unit had its way on the requirements, the whole decision-making process would be skewed. The secretary did not rely on the senior administrators in HDS to check the predispositions of its constituent units. Neither Assistant Secretary Arabella Martinez nor her deputy, T. M. Jim Parham, were among those Califano entrusted with decision-making authority over these delicate issues.

Since Califano felt that HDS could not be trusted with the policy decisions on the FIDCR, he restructured the responsibility for revision writing within HEW. In October 1978 he took overall responsibility from HDS and vested it in the Office of the General Counsel under F. Peter Libassi. Libassi was the point man for HEW's most controversial regulatory decisions and worked closely with Califano and members of the executive secretariat. He brought a broader political perspective to the FIDCR and, more important, he had Califano's confidence.[52]

In the large context the conflict between Califano and HEW's bureaucracy reflected a basic division between career civil servants and political appointees. The career people were, among other things, individuals with many years of government service. In HDS, many senior civil servants were child advocates with established ties to advocacy groups, the states, and congressional committees. Often jealous of their prerogatives, they resented what they perceived as the intervention of outsiders, usually political appointees of brief tenure, in the administration and regulation of their programs. While they might disagree among themselves, they could agree that intervention such as Califano's was unwarranted and insulting.

In the midst of the revision process, Abt Associates completed its National Day Care Study. Abt's four-year study involved 1,800 preschool children, 1,100 parents, and 120 classroom groups from 57 day care centers in Atlanta, Detroit, and Seattle. The study dealt with three basic questions: (1) How is a preschool child's development affected by variations in regulatable center characteristics; (2) How is cost per child affected by variations in regulatable center characteristics; and (3)

How does the cost-effectiveness of center day care change with regulatory variations? In essence they studied the impact of child-staff ratios, group size, and care-giver qualifications on the preschool child and the cost of care. Abt used a combination of test scores and observations to assess the effects of different staff ratios, group sizes, and care giver qualifications on the child. These measurements included reflection/innovation, cooperation, noninvolvement, aimless wandering, and performance on the Preschool Inventory Peabody Vocabulary tests.[53]

The potential relevance of the Abt study to the FIDCR policy debate was as much a matter of coincidence as deliberation. The basic idea of examining these aspects of day care originated in the research and planning unit in OEO years before. When the Nixon administration dismantled OEO, its research staff was dispersed into OCD, ASPE, and elsewhere. One of these people, Allen N. Smith, resurfaced in OCD and in 1974 contracted with a research organization, Abt Associates, to conduct a study of day care. The study was commissioned prior to the Title XX-FIDCR controversy and the appropriateness report. Its relevance to these matters, however, soon became evident.

By 1977, Abt had spent its entire $7-million budget on gathering data for the study. They went to their project director at OCD, Allen Smith, and asked for an additional $1 million to analyze the data and prepare their report. Having little choice, Smith agreed and began building support within OCD (now ACYF) and HEW for the additional money. There was, of course, opposition within HEW and among the research community to serving Abt so large a share of the funding pie for what seemed like a study with an unsatiable appetite. Smith needed allies, and in ASPE he found one.

Prosser and his FIDCR appropriateness committee were still mired in their report when Smith came to him with an offer of help. If Prosser would support the $1-million extension of the Abt study, Smith would share Abt's early findings with him to assist in completing the report. After some hesitation, assuaged by a quick trip to Abt's headquarters in Cambridge, Prosser agreed. With his support Abt received the additional funds. Both sides were pleased. Prosser anticipated decisive help in what was becoming his own Vietnam, and Abt rejoiced in the hope that their study would be completed and sail in the appropriateness report to the sea of policy relevance.

Smith was among the first to realize that the appropriateness report was headed toward serious difficulties.
Any strong link between the Abt study and the report meant
only problems for his project. Critics at the early
stages of reviewing the draft had already begun to con-
fuse Abt's study with the report. Wary of Prosser's
attempts to infuse portions of Abt's preliminary findings
into the text of the report, Smith prevailed on him to
publish the findings, delivered as part of the research
funding deal, as a separate appendix to the report. All
Prosser reaped from his early support of Abt's funding
was a further delay in his report's completion and
another appendix.

Abt's study did survive the appropriateness report,
and during 1978 and 1979 Abt publicly disseminated its
findings. Group size, Abt concluded in its briefing for
HEW, was the "most powerful and pervasive factor related
to NDCS [National Day Care Study] measures of quality."
Children in groups of 12 with two care givers performed
in a consistently superior manner to children in groups
of 24 with 4 care givers. More desirable care giver
behavior was also "associated with smaller groups." Then
Abt turned to the crux of the FIDCR controversy, "For
children, staff/child ratio is ambiguously related to
child behavior [and] not related to test score gains."
Only infants benefited from the low child-staff ratios.
In one social scientific stab, Abt had killed the intuitive, experiential assumption of decades of preschool
education.

Low child-staff ratios in themselves did not matter
for the child's cognitive or social development. Staff
ratios, however, were not unimportant. The Abt study
concluded that they were "the most important determinant
of difference in costs." In cost-benefit terms the
ultimate conclusion became obvious. As long as group
size was controlled, the center could reduce costs and
increase the benefits of care to the child. As Keynes
had once told governments, not only should they spend
money they did not have, but also by spending it they
would receive more; now Abt was telling HEW that not only
could it spend less money per child on day care, but also
that while spending less the children would benefit
more.[54]

Their identification of group size as the most significant factor related to outcome was somewhat surprising.
Group size had consistently been included in standards
for day care, but in a manner clearly subordinate to

staff ratios. Abt's researchers admit it was a "sleeper."
Indeed, group size emerged in the wake of the study's
early findings that staff ratios had no significant
effect on outcome. Within ACYF project director Smith
strongly suggested that Abt's results needed to establish
more than the insignificance of regulatable center characteristics. Subsequent analysis of the data revealed
group size as a significant regulatable characteristic;
soon it was made a major finding of the study.

In their recommendations Abt also suggested that
regulators set less stringent staff ratios than the 1968
FIDCR had required. "The staff/child ratio requirement
for three, four and five year old children should be no
more stringent than 1:7." That ratio was for actual
attendance; the enrollment ratio (the one generally used
in calculating staff ratios) should be no lower than
8:1. Abt offered three policy options ranging from 8:1
to 10:1 for enrollment, and 7:1 to 9:1 for attendance.[55]
These policy options traded cost reduction for program
quality. The minimum-quality policy promised that all
centers would attain current average program quality at a
cost savings of 10-12 percent from current average
expenditures. The middle policy option offered a 5-10
percent increase in program quality and a 6-8 percent
savings from current costs. The high-quality option
offered a 10-20 percent improvement in program quality at
a 1-2 percent savings from current expenditures. These
three options involved enrolled child-staff ratios of
10:1, 9:1, and 8:1, respectively. "All three of the
policy options," Abt observed, "have the potential of
reducing costs." More important, "none of the three
policy options would severely disrupt current subsidized
center practices, Policy C [the minimum-quality option]
would require the smallest changes."[56]

Politically, Abt's policy recommendations were significant. In shifting the emphasis to group size, Abt change
the de facto compliance of FFP centers. If HEW chose the
high-quality option, 72 percent of FFP centers would be
in compliance with the recommended staff ratios and 77
percent with the recommended group size. If HEW chose
the minimum-quality option (i.e., all centers reaching
the average quality of current care) 83 percent would be
in compliance with the recommended staff ratios and 89
percent with the recommended group size. The minimum-
quality option would increase the number of centers
complying with the FIDCR's staff ratios from 60 to 83
percent. Moreover, since 79 percent of the nonprofit

centers were already in compliance with the current FIDCR, this increase in compliance would be almost entirely among the 55 percent of proprietary centers that were not in compliance.[57]

The study's results offered something for everyone involved in the revision of the FIDCR. It confirmed ACYF's long-standing belief that federal regulation of day care could indeed affect a child's development in measurable ways. It also sat well with APS. Since the study recommended staff ratios higher than those in the 1968 and 1972 requirements, APS's clients--the states and their day care centers--would be relatively unaffected by requirements based on these recommendations. For the cost-benefit people in ASPE the study provided quantitative data on which the decisions could be based. Finally, at the secretary's level, the results placed a social scientific seal of approval on a relaxation in staffing requirements. Such approval would buttress Califano against attacks by those advocating either higher or lower staff ratios. The results would depoliticize an essentially political decision. Abt's study pleased most decision makers in HEW, and its impact soon became apparent through the Office of the General Counsel.

There were some critics of the study's data gathering and the strength of the evidence supporting its conclusions. Nonetheless, Abt's careful presentations and efforts to incorporate the criticisms in their findings or the critics on their consulting staff mitigated much of the outcry that might have otherwise engulfed it. Moreover, Abt's finding of a positive correlation between center characteristics and child performance helped to preclude vehement opposition. Whatever else the study concluded about costs and staff ratios, that one finding pleased actors throughout the child advocacy establishment. Perhaps the most striking aspect of this finding, however, was that though the correlations between center characteristics and performance were real and statistically significant, they were weak. Indeed, in assessing the study one social scientist observed that had federal regulation of day care never been attempted and had this study been the sole basis for determining whether or not to regulate, the results would not have justified the costs and the complexities of regulation. In the face of political reality that particular policy recommendation was simply untenable.

Abt Associates' official briefing of HEW on their findings came in January 1979. Although their final report was not released until spring, HEW's hierarchy had known of its general results for over a year. In the first public statement on the post-study "present thinking" of HEW, General Counsel Peter Libassi spoke to a group of advocates, center operators, and state and local administrators at a seminar in Washington on March 2, 1979. Although carefully qualifying his pronouncements with "we are leaning," "we are inclined" and "we want to hear from all of you on this issue," Libassi indicated in unambiguous terms that HEW was taking Abt's findings and recommendations very seriously.

"The [FIDCR] task force," Libassi began, "leans toward accepting the conclusion that group composition should be used in the new regulations. . . . We believe that group composition strongly affects the benefits which children receive from day care." In the ensuing sentence he recounted Abt's recommended child-staff ratios. Though he made no explicit affirmation of these ratios, he clearly implied in the context of his remarks that these ratios were in the forefront of HEW's policy mind. Indeed, the leitmotif of Libassi's statement was that "sensible requirements are enforceable requirements." It would not be sensible to create a set of requirements beyond the reach of a large number of centers. Sensible, enforceable requirements were those easily attained by the centers. Regulation, like law, had to be in large part a recognition of fact--something Libassi understood.

Many of the doubts he might have had concerning the Abt ratios were assuaged by the responses of participants. William Pierce of the Child Welfare League rose to condemn HEW's "inclination." Significantly, however, he was alone in this proscription. The local center operators and administrators greeted Libassi's statement with approbation. They opposed the Title XX FIDCR and "excessive" regulation of their centers. Besides Pierce, no one assailed the higher child-staff ratios or any further relaxation in the requirements. Indeed, at the conclusion of his appearance a sanguine Libassi noted the absence of any widespread acrimony over the staffing issue. After the conference, the Abt ratios were, if anything, more firmly rooted in the FIDCR's policy soil at HEW.

The preliminary publication of the new revised FIDCR took place in June 1979. Generally, the new FIDCR proposed the staff ratios recommended by the Abt study, though a range of options was offered. Neither the states nor the FFP centers desired requirements that might result in punitive sanctions against them. HEW's

hierarchy and, presumably, OMB also wanted to avoid
raising the costs of child care or penalizing the states'
Title XX funds. More than once the states and day care
centers had demonstrated their political muscle in
inducing congressional suspensions of child-staff ratios
that they could not attain. Although the 1976 offer of
additional Title XX funds for compliance did dampen state
opposition, a fiscally austere Congress was unlikely to
sweeten compliance with more money. Since the alternative
to funding additional staff was more "sensible" requirements, most members of Congress were not inclined to
oppose HEW's relaxation of staff ratios. Moreover, the
Abt study provided all parties interested in less strict
child-staff ratios with a scientific justification.

After preliminary publication, HEW sponsored a series
of meetings across the country on the requirements.
Participants generally approved the requirements, though
there was some dissent over the exact child-staff ratios.
While these meetings progressed, decision makers within
HEW were replaced by new people. While Patricia Harris,
who replaced Califano, and Jody Bernstein, who replaced
Libassi, learned anew about the issues, the FIDCR
revision process came virtually to a halt in fall 1979.

In the face of this hiatus the advocacy groups split
into three camps. In one camp were the proprietary day
care centers. They believed that the changes in HEW
accorded them an excellent opportunity to delay the
FIDCR's promulgation and relax the staffing ratios. To
this end they distributed anti-FIDCR postcards to parents
who used their child care facilities, newspapers, members
of Congress, and HEW. The message was simple: the new
FIDCR will close the day care centers or raise costs or
both and we oppose them.

At the other extreme was William Pierce and the Child
Welfare League. Pierce refused to accept the staff ratios
that the Abt study had recommended. He, too, wanted the
new FIDCR blocked and replaced by the 1968 requirements.
Pierce, however, was respectfully ignored.

Somewhere in the middle was a coalition of advocacy
groups led by the Children's Defense Fund. They had
accepted Abt's recommendations and strove to have the new
FIDCR promulgated with the strictest staff ratios within
those recommendations. To this end they organized their
own campaign to compel HEW Secretary Harris to promulgate
the new FIDCR.

In response to this coalition and the personal lobbying
effort of the Children's Defense Fund's leader Marion

Wright Edelman, Harris agreed to a March 1980 deadline
for the new FIDCR. Although the deadline was a small
victory for the Children's Defense Fund, the exact staff
ratios remained unresolved. Here the proprietary centers
made some headway. Joan Bernstein, HEW's general counsel,
had a reputation for being somewhat antiregulatory from a
previous stint at the U.S. Environmental Protection
Agency. Bernstein and her staff produced a memorandum on
the new FIDCR for Harris that essentially argued for less
stringent staffing ratios. In conjunction with the
proprietary centers' campaign, Bernstein's memo began to
sway Harris toward less strict requirements--particularly
staffing ratios.

Bernstein's memo, however, was leaked to the Children's
Defense Fund and to their allies within HEW--specifically
ACYF. Proponents of the stricter FIDCR realized that
only a strong response could salvage their course. In
desperation they turned to White House domestic adviser
Stuart Eizenstat. Access to Eizenstat depended on the
personal relationship of one of the proponents with
Eizenstat's wife. They presented their case for the
stricter FIDCR to Eizenstat at his home one night and
convinced him to send a memo--drafted by the Children's
Defense Fund--to Harris expressing strong White House
support for the stricter FIDCR. Armed now with White
House support, proponents of the stricter FIDCR managed
to overcome their opponents' objections based on costs
and promote staff ratios as strict as (or stricter than)
those recommended in Abt's Policy A option.

The final regulations were issued in March 1980.
Although the staff ratios for the key preschool age
cohort--3-5-year olds--were in the range of Abt's Policy
A option, they were still less stringent than those in
the other revisions of the FIDCR. The new requirements
are "enforced" because 80 percent of the day care centers
are already in compliance with all or most of the new
requirements. Moreover, the requirements allow, upon
application to HEW, a two-year phase-in period. Thus
enforcement means affirmation of continuity in existing
conditions, not disruption and proscription. Indeed, one
of the general survey findings of the Abt study was that
centers, regardless of regulations, tend to gravitate to
certain staff and group patterns that quite simply work
better than others. In the final analysis, effective
regulation may be no more (and no less) than an authorita-
tive imprimatur on situations ordered by forces more
profound than any policy maker's decision.

197

NOTES

[1] Sara Pope Cooper, A History of the Federal Interagency Day Care Requirements" (HEW, 1976); Sheila Rothman, "Other People's Children: The Day Care Experience in America," Public Interest, #30 (Winter 1973), 15-19; and Michael B. Katz, The Irony of Early School Reform (Harvard University Press, 1960), passim.

[2] Rothman, "Other People's Children," 18-19; Planning Services for Children of Employed Mothers (U.S. Department of Labor Publication, 1953), 7-11, 14-15.

[3] Gilbert Y. Steiner, The Children's Cause (Washington, D.C.: 1976), 16-18; Planning Services, 7-10, 14-15; Rothman, "Other People's Children," 20-21.

[4] Planning Services, 10; Bureau of the Budget, Legislative Reference File: G-1-2154.1, [hereafter cited as BOB-LRF:] (1954), Record Group 51, National Archives [hereafter cited as NA].

[5] Standards for the Day Care of Children of Working Mothers (Children's Bureau Publication No. 284, 1942), passim.

[6] Planning Services, passim.

[7] Child Welfare League, Standards for Day Care Service (New York, 1960), passim.

[8] BOB:LRF:R1-4/67.4 (1967), RG 51, NA; Congressional Quarterly Almanac: 1967 (Washington, D.C.: 1968), 1058-1086 [cited henceforth as CQA:].

[9] Federal Interagency Day Care Requirements (HEW Publication #(OHDS)78-31081, 1978 [1968]), passim.

[10] Cooper, "History of FIDCR," 19.

[11] Gwen Morgan, "Legal Aspects of Federal Day Care Standards" (HEW, 1976), 39.

[12] Rothman, "Other People's Children," 22.

[13] Edward Zigler and David Cohen, "Federal Day Care Standards: Rationale and Recommendations" (HEW, 1976), 6-8.

[14] Zigler to R. P. Nathan, April 18, 1972, File CY-1-3, HEW: Office of the Secretary [cited henceforth as OS].

[15] OMB:LRF R1-4/71.2 (1971), RG 51, Federal Records Center [cited hereafter as FRC]. In The Children's Cause Steiner apparently overstates the conservative appeasement motivation for the veto.

[16] Richardson to Quie, August 31, 1972, File CY-1-3, HEW:OS.

[17] OMB:LRF R1-4/7112 (1971), RG 51, FRC.

[18] Note for Mr. O'Neill, June 21, 1972, OMB File A7, RG 51. New Executive Office Building [cited hereafter as NEOB].

[19] Ibid.

[20] Veneman to Richardson, July 10, 1972, File CY-1-3, HEW:OS.

[21] Zigler, "Federal Day Care Standards," 8-11; Morgan, "Legal Aspects," 39.

[22] OMB:LRF R1-4/74.6 (1974), RG 51, FRC.

[23] Ibid.

[24] House Report 93-1490.

[25] Senate Report 93-1356; House Report 93-1543; CQA: 1974, 505-508.

[26] OMB:LRF R1-4/74.6 (1974), RG 51, FRC.

[27] Memorandum to the Secretary, September 16, 1975, File FIDCR-Title XX, HEW:ACYF.

[28] Memoranda to the Secretary, August 27 and September 16, 1975, File CY-1-3, HEW:OS; Weinberger to Mondale, June 12, 1975, CY-1-3, HEW:OS.

[29] See the letters in File CY-1-3 (1975), HEW:OS.

[30] These responses are attached to the Social and Rehabilitation Service's draft memorandum, September, 1975, ibid.

[31] Matthews to Carl Albert, October 1, 1975, ibid.

[32] See CQA: 1975, 691-692, and CQA: 1976, 620-625, for the details of these legislative actions.

[33] CQA: 1976, 621-625.

[34] Matthews to Lynn, October 16, 1975, OMB:LRF 73-1(G)/75.2 (1976), RG 51, NEOB.

[35] CQA, 1976, 625-628.

[36] Morrill to Secretary, May 6, 1976, File CY-1-3, HEW:OS.

[37] OMB:LRF R3-1/76.4 (1976), RG 51, NEOB.

[38] These statistics are drawn from UNCO's, National Child Care Consumer Study: 1975 (HEW-OCD, 1975) and ASPE documents.

[39] Abt Associates, Inc., National Day Care Study: Preliminary Findings. . . (HEW:OCDS, 1978), passim.

[40] Ibid., 23-25; Abt Associates, Inc., Day Care Centers in the U.S.: A National Profile, 1976-1977 (Cambridge, 1978), 63; Abt Associates, Inc., Children at the Center: Summary Findings and Their Implications (Cambridge, Mass.: 1979), 194-195.

[41] This information is derived from statements and handouts by participants in the Day Care and Child Development Reports' Conference, Washington, D.C., March 2, 1979.

[42] Ibid.

[43] Quoted in Barry Bruce-Briggs, "Child Care: The Fiscal Time Bomb," Public Interest (Fall 1977), 100.

[44] Ibid.

[45] S. R. Rosoff, OCD, to Margaret Watson, HDS, March 22, 1977, File FIDCR, HEW:ACYF.

[46] Aaron Memorandum on his meeting with Califano, April 13, 1977, File FIDCR, HEW:ACYF; CQA: 1977; P.L. 95-59 and P.L. 95-171.

[47] Memorandum for the Record, September 28, 1977, File FIDCR, HEW:ACYF; Cotton to the Secretary, September 15, 1977, File CY-1-3, HEW:OS.

[48] Note for the Secretary (Bohen), June 21, 1978, File CY-1-3, HEW:OS; Note to the Secretary (Schuck), March 13, 1978, ibid. The latter note contains handwritten comments on the report and ASPE by a staff member of the executive secretariat.

[49] From an unedited transcript of Moynihan's comment before the Senate Subcommittee on Welfare Reform in July, 1978.

[50] Note for the Secretary (Bohen), June 21, 1978, File CY-1-3, HEW:OS.

[51] The Appropriateness of The Federal Interagency Day Care Requirements (FIDCR): Report of Findings and Recommendations (HEW:ASPE, 1978), XXXV.

[52] Califano to Libassi, October 2, 1978, File CY-1-3, HEW:OS.

[53] Abt Associates, Inc., National Day Care Study: HEW Briefing (Cambridge, Mass.: January 19, 1979), 1-4.

[54] Ibid., 4-15, 21.

[55] Ibid., 22-25.

[56] Ibid., 25-30.

[57] Abt Associates, Inc., Final Report of the National Day Care Study: Children at the Center (5 vols., Cambridge, Mass.: 1979), I, 159.

[58] Statement by F. Peter Libassi, General Counsel, HEW (March 2, 1979).

Appendix A

Proposed Child-Staff Ratios, 1942-1978

Source	Year	0-6 Weeks	7 weeks- 18 mo.	19 mo. 24 mo.	25 mo. 36 mo.	3 yr. old	4	5
Children's Bureau	1942	NR	NR	10	10	10	10	
Child Welfare League	1960	NR	NR	NR	6-7.5	7.5-10	7.5-10	10-12.5
Head Start	1965	--	--	--	4	5	5	--
FIDCR	1968	NR	NR	NR	NR	5	7	7
Child Welfare League	1969	NR	NR	NR	NR	6-7.5	7.5-10	7.5-10
American Academy of Pediatrics	1971	4	4	4	4	--	--	--
FIDCR (Zigler's Revision)	1972	3	3	4	4	4	10*	10
HEW guides for state licenses	1973	4	4	4	5	10	10	12
Title XX legislation	1975	X	X	X	X	5	7	7
Title XX FIDCR	1975	1	4	4	4	5	7	7
State licensing average	1977	--	6	8	10*	11.4	13.7	16.5
Abt study recommendations	1978	1	5	5	5	8-10	8-10	8-10

NOTE: Figures given in table are numbers of children per staff member.

NR: Center-based care not recommended for this age group.

(-): No ratios specified/not applicable

X-: To be set by the Secretary of HEW.

S: "standards"

G: "goals"

R: "requirements"

*over 54 months

**over 30 months

6	7-8	9	10	11	12	13-14	Objective
--	--	--	--	--	--	--	S
10-12.15	10-12.5	10-12.5	10-12.5	10-12.5	10-12.5	--	G
--	--	--	--	--	--	--	R
10	10	10	10	10	10	10	R
10-12.15	10-12.5	10-12.5	10-12.5	10-12.5	10-12.5	--	G
--	--	--	--	--	--	--	S
12	13	13	16	16	20	20	R
12	16	16	16	16	20	20	S
15	15	15	15	20	20	20	R
15	15	15	15	20	20	20	R
18.8	18.8	18.8	18.8	19.6	19.6	--	--
8-10	17	17	17	23	23	23	R

Appendix B

Federal Expenditures for Child Care, 1977 ($ millions)

	Fiscal 1977 Obligations
U.S. Department of Health, Education, and Welfare	
Title XX Social Services--FIDCR Applies	$ 809
Title IV-A Work Experience (Income Disregard)	84
WIN--FIDCR Applies	57
Head Start	448
Title IV-B--FIDCR Applies	5
ESEA (optional, as determined by state)	172
HEW TOTAL	$1,575
U.S. Department of Housing and Urban Development	
Community Development Block Grant Entitlement Programs	43
U.S. Department of Agriculture	
Child Care Food Service--FIDCR Applies	120
Food Stamp Deduction	30
TOTAL BUDGET EXPENDITURES	$1,768
TAX EXPENDITURES--TREASURY	517
TOTAL	$2,285

Appendix C

Distribution of Children Receiving Full-Time Nonparental Care, 1977 (thousands)

	Total Child Care[1]				Child Care Under Title XX[2]		
	More Than 30 Hours Per Week	Subtotals	% of Total Full-Time Arrangement	Subtotals	% of Total More Than 32 Hours Per Week (Full-Time)	Full-Time Arrangements Under Title XX	% of Total Child Care
In-Home Care							
Relative	957		18.5				
Nonrelative	620		12.0				
Subtotal		1,577		30.5%	65	16	4
Family Day Care							
Relative	1,258		24.3				
Nonrelative	1,184		22.9				
Subtotal		2,442		47.2%	97	24	4
Center Care							
Day Care Center	536		10.4				
Nursery/Preschool	533		10.3				
Cooperative	29		0.6				
Head Start	42		0.8				
Subtotal		1,140		22.0%	242	60	21
Other		16		0.3%			
TOTAL		5,175		100%	404	100	8

*Includes group home day care.

Sources: (1) The National Child Care Consumer Study: 1975 Basic Tabulations. Volume 1. The National Child Care Consumer Study is based on a stratified national probability sample of telephone households with children under 14 years of age. A total of 4,609 interviews were conducted concerning child care arrangements. (2) Final Draft, Social Services, U.S.A. A compilation of state reports from the 50 states and the District of Columbia on the delivery of Title XX social services.

Care Modes: A Consumer Survey

Care Mode		Age and Numbers of Children			
		0-2		3-6	
		10-29 Hours per Week	30+ Hours per Week	10-29 Hours per Week	30+ Hours per Week
Center (group) Care	No. %	106,000 8	180,000 15	494,000 26	708,000 40
Family Day Care (Relative)	No. %	402,500 32	287,300 24	471,300 25	346,700 20
Family Day Care (Nonrelative)	No. %	286,000 22	364,600 30	302,800 15	394,100 22
In-Home Care (Relative and Nonrelative)	No. %	485,000 38	371,000 31	642,000 34	328,000 18
TOTAL IN CARE	No. %	1,279,500 100	1,202,900 100	1,910,100 100	1,776,800 100

Type of Care	Number and Percentages of Children in Care			
	0-2		3-6	
	%	No.	%	No.
In Own Home by Relative				
10-29 hours per week	3	245,900	3	302,100
30+ hours per week	3	239,900	2	178,200
In Own Home by Nonrelative				
20-29 hours per week	3	238,500	3	340,400
30+ hours per week	1	130,500	1	138,600
Relative's Home				
10-29 hours per week	4	402,500	4	471,300
30+ hours per week	3	287,300	3	346,700
Nonrelative's Home (Family Day Care)				
10-29 hours per week	3	286,000	3	302,800
30+ hours per week	4	364,600	4	394,100
Nursery and Day Care Center				
10-29 hours per week	<2	106,300	5	493,800
30+ hours per week	2	179,700	6	708,700

Appendix E

Households Using Various Types of Care, Classified by Youngest Child's Age

Service Used	Main Method Youngest Child 0-2	Main Method Youngest Child 3-5	Over 30 Hours Youngest Child 0-2	Over 30 Hours Youngest Child 3-5
Relative (In Child's Own Home)	20.3	11.1	5.0	2.7
Nonrelative (In Child's Own Home)	16.8	17.0	3.1	3.2
In Relative's Home	22.1	17.0	5.3	6.5
Nonrelative Home (Family Day Care)	10.7	10.8	6.2	5.6
Nursery School	4.4	8.2	2.1	4.3
Day Care Center	1.5	5.0	1.2	4.2
Cooperative Center	1.2	0.7	0.3	0.2
Before and After School Program	0.4	0.6	--	0.3
Head Start	0.2	0.7	0.1	0.4
No Extramural Care	22.4	28.7	22.4	28.7

Source: Sheila B. Kamerman and Alfred J. Kahn, Child Care, Family Benefits and Working Parents (1980).

The Child Care
Tax Deduction/Credit
John R. Nelson, Jr., and Wendy E. Warring

INTRODUCTION

The child care tax deduction/credit originated in 1954 as
an itemized deduction for work-related day care expenses.
It was limited to $600 and to households in which both
the husbànd and wife worked and that had an adjusted
gross income of $4,500 or less. Designed as both a labor
supply and a relief measure, the deduction reached an
average of 290,000 households in the first decade after
its enactment. (For these data and their sources see
Appendixes A and B.) To reflect the rise in family
incomes, Congress updated it in 1964 by increasing the
income ceiling to $6,000 and the maximum deductible
amount to $900 for two or more children. These changes
allowed an additional 125,000 households to claim the
deductions, but the tax savings per household still
remained the same--approximately $70 per year. By 1971,
constant agitation for revision of the deduction culminated in several significant changes. It was renamed
the "job development deduction," and Congress, specifically the Senate, tripled the income ceiling to $18,000,
increased the deductible amount eightfold to $4,800 per
year, and allowed the deduction of housekeeping services
to stimulate the employment of low-income persons as
domestic housekeepers. These changes doubled the annual
average tax saving per household to $135. Less biased
against working mothers, Congress sought to provide tax
relief to dual-career families in middle- and upper-income
brackets. This revision altered one major purpose of the
original deduction: relief for low-income families. It
became instead a tax incentive for their employment in
higher-income households.

In 1975, Congress updated it again by raising the income ceiling to $35,000, but this change was principally a compromise measure to postpone for further deliberation a major overhaul of the deduction. That overhaul finally came to fruition in 1976 when Congress dropped the job development title, removed the income ceiling, and transformed it into a 20-percent tax credit on care-related expenses up to $2,000 for one dependent and $4,000 for two or more dependents. As a credit, all eligible households could claim the tax benefit whether or not they itemized deductions on their tax returns. In 1977, 2.85 million households claimed the child care credit and saved $517 million in income taxes--an average savings of $177 per household. This case study examines each of these four major revisions in the child care deduction/credit.

In many respects the subject of this study represents a different genre from the other two cases. It is not a federal program or regulatory policy. Its enactment entails no new bureaucratic structures and very little administrative history. Yet income is transferred, regulations are promulgated, and the society is affected. Indeed, taxation is the one federal policy that touches virtually every citizen in a regular, direct, and visible manner. Three elements affect this policy formation process: the revenue and distributional effects of proposed changes, the equity of such changes, and the maintenance of incremental increases and decreases in progressive tax rates. The first consideration is an obvious outgrowth of the purposes of taxation: to raise revenue. The second seeks to ensure equal treatment for taxpayers in similar situations. The third is to avoid abrupt shifts in tax rates across small changes in income.

The policy-making processes are confined chiefly to the House Ways and Means Committee, the Senate Finance Committee, the Office of the Assistant Secretary of the Treasury for Tax Policy, and the Joint Committee on Taxation. Each has an institutional role. The Joint Committee staff serve as technical adviser to the Congress. The bills originate in Ways and Means, which tends to be conservative in its measures. It is distinctive among congressional committees in its careful deliberations, its close alliance with professional staff, and, until recently, its lack of subcommittees. Moreover, its legislation generally comes to the floor under a closed rule, though amendments are sometimes permitted. Since Wilbur Mills's departure as chairman,

however, these committee attributes have changed somewhat.
The Senate Finance Committee has similar attributes, with
one major difference. Finance Committee bills are open
to amendment on the Senate floor. Consequently, its
measures are often amended to provide more generous tax
benefits than House measures. The committee has less
than final determination over its legislation, yet the
Senate debates over tax provisions, Joseph A. Pechman
observes, "rank among the most informed discussions held
on the Senate floor."[1]

The role of the U.S. Department of the Treasury and
its Internal Revenue Service (IRS) is to maintain the
structural integrity of the tax system, to curb revenue
losses from the special benefits so popular with Congress,
and to represent the President's tax proposals before
Congress. Treasury works to accomplish this through
direct negotiations with congressional committees at each
stage in the tax-writing process. Once passed by Congress, the tax bills become operative in substantially
the same form in which they are written. Since 1948 only
once has a president vetoed a tax bill: that veto by
Gerald Ford in 1975 was the result of a conflict with
Congress over a concomitant spending ceiling, not the tax
provisions themselves. Although numerous judgments are
made by the IRS and federal tax courts on specific
applicability in individual cases, the basic principles
and structure of the policy remain unimpeded between
legislative enactments.

The mechanics of the income tax are straightforward,
though the nuances are often obscure to the point of
unintelligibility. In principle, a taxpayer totals all
income from wages, interest, dividends, alimony, etc., to
arrive at a gross income. He or she then subtracts the
allowable expenses incurred in earning that income (e.g.,
business and moving costs) to reach an adjusted gross
income. These adjustments are "above-line" and open to
all eligible taxpayers regardless of whether they elect
the standard deduction or itemize. After calculating the
adjusted gross income a taxpayer can either take a fixed
standard deduction (now referred to as the "zero-bracket
amount") or itemize deductions to arrive at his or her
taxable income. In either instance the taxpayer is
allowed a fixed exemption of a particular dollar amount
from the taxable income for himself or herself and each
dependent. The actual tax is based on the taxable income.
From the tax itself a credit is allowed for certain items
(or portions of items). A credit represents a specific

dollar amount subtracted directly from the tax liability. An adjustment to gross income or a tax credit benefits all eligible taxpayers regardless of their decision to itemize deductions. A deduction benefits only those who elect to itemize. Generally speaking, a deduction and an adjustment benefit higher-income groups more than lower-income groups, while a tax credit has the opposite effect.

THE ORIGINS OF THE CHILD CARE DEDUCTION

In 1861 the federal government levied the first tax on individual incomes to raise urgently needed revenue for the Civil War.[2] Until that time customs duties, excise taxes, and land sales provided all federal tax revenues. The income tax was a straightforward 3 percent levy on incomes up to $10,000 and 5 percent on incomes above that amount. The law allowed each taxpayer an exemption of $600. Congress raised tax rates in the next years to 10 percent on a net income between $600 and $5,000, 12.5 percent on income between $5,000 and $10,000, and 15 percent on income above $15,000. When the income tax law expired in 1871, the rate was 2.5 percent and the exemption $2,000. After its expiration, excise taxes and customs duties resumed their function of supplying revenue for the government until 1909. Congress attempted to revive the income tax in 1894. The tax was 2 percent on individual and corporate net income, with a $400 exemption for individuals. Personal property received by gift or inheritance was included in net income. The Supreme Court, however, declared the act unconstitutional in 1895. It ruled that the portion of the personal income tax levied on income from land was a "direct" tax and in violation of the constitutional requirement that direct taxes had to be apportioned among the states according to population.

Despite the decision, agitation for an income tax continued. As the American economy matured and industry gained the strength to withstand foreign competition, Congress reduced tariff rates. Many groups saw the income tax as a way to compensate for the resulting revenue losses and inject a progressive element into the revenue system. In 1913 the necessary states ratified the 16th amendment to the Constitution and gave Congress "the power to lay and collect taxes on incomes, from whatever source derived, without regard to any census or enumeration." Shortly thereafter, Congress passed the income tax law. The tax applied to wages, salaries, interest dividends, rents, entrepreneurial incomes, and capital gains. There were two categories of tax levies: normal, a flat 1 percent rate on all income above $3,000 ($4,000 for married couples), and surtax, a progressive rate from 1 percent to 6 percent on larger incomes. It allowed deductions for interest on debts, nonincome tax payments, and business expenses. State and local government employees were exempted from paying the tax; the interest on federal, state, and local government bonds was also exempt. The surtax, however, applied to income exempted from the normal tax.

In 1917, Congress introduced a credit for dependents and a deduction for charitable contributions. Successive changes continuously complicated the 1913 law. Not until 1939 did Congress codify the revenue acts that had accumulated over the years. By today's standards exemptions were high and few incomes were large enough to be subject to even the lowest tax rate. Prior to World War II the income tax applied mainly to a small number of people with high incomes and created tax liabilities of approximately $1 billion.

The 1939 code did not remain unmolested for very long. World War II brought a new dimension of complexity to the tax laws. In the national effort to raise revenue, exemptions were greatly reduced, rates were increased, and substantial growth coupled with an upward shift in income occurred in the tax base. Congress also made a series of structural changes in the tax code. Beginning with taxable year 1941, taxpayers whose gross incomes did not exceed $3,000 from specified sources were able to submit a simplified return. The return allowed them to deduct a standard percentage of earned income from their adjusted gross income. Those who did not use the short form were required to itemize their deductions. In 1944 legislation further simplified tax returns by making the standard deduction part of the Internal Revenue Code. Taxpayers had the option of deducting 10 percent of their adjusted gross income up to $500 from 1944 to 1947 and $1,000 from 1948 to 1970. When it was first introduced, over 80 percent of taxpayers used the standard deduction.

The growing complexity and the residue of anachronistic provisions had rendered the tax code difficult to understand and administer. At the outset of the 1950s the Treasury Department and the Joint Committee on Taxation made preparations to simplify and reorganize the 1939 Code. These resulted in the Internal Revenue Code

of 1954, the last codification of the tax law to the
present. The groundwork for a major tax revision began
as early as 1951, but most of the legislative tax writing
took place in the House Ways and Means Committee during
the first session of the 83rd Congress. In that session
the committee began drafting H.R. 8300, the nucleus of
the 1954 code. The bill contained approximately 27 major
new tax provisions affecting both corporate and individual
taxpayers. Among these was an itemized deduction for
child care expenses. As one might anticipate, the child
care deduction ignited some controversy in Congress.

The issue of a child care deduction was not new.
Litigation on the subject began as early as 1939. In
that year a married couple contested the IRS's exclusion
of child care as a business deduction. The plaintiffs
argued that expenditures for nursemaids should be considered an ordinary and necessary business expense of the
wife. They contended that expenses incurred to care for
their young children were necessary to earning an income
because without some provision for care the wife would
not be free to leave her children to pursue employment.
The court characterized their argument as the "but for"
test and rejected it as too broad:

> The fee to the doctor, but for whose healing
> services the earner of the family income could not
> leave his sickbed; the cost of the laborer's
> raiment, for how can the world proceed about its
> business unclothed . . . might all by an extension
> of the same provision be construed as necessary to
> the operation of business and to the creation of
> income. Yet these are the very essence of those
> personal expenses the deductibility of which is
> expressly denied.[3]

The court explained that child care, like other
aspects of family and household life, was nothing other
than a personal concern because "the wife's services as
custodian of the home and protector of its children are
ordinarily rendered without monetary compensation." The
same work performed by others is still of a personal
nature. Although the court conceded that certain business
expenses were often personal, such as entertainment,
traveling expenses, or the wardrobe of an actor, it drew
a fine line between activities that are ordinary to the
direct accompaniment of business pursuits and those that
relate "in some indirect and tenuous degree" to employ-

ment but are "of a character applicable to human beings generally."[4] Expenditures for child care, the court concluded, existed on a personal level regardless of an individual's occupation.

Taxpayers did not give up after the 1939 decision. Several subsequent cases claimed a child care deduction as an allowable expense for the production of income under Section 213. In each case, the court affirmed that child care expenses were not deductible under existing tax laws. The thrust of the court's decisions was that all personal deductions were granted by legislative discretion and could not serve as precedents for new deductions, however similar they might be in principle. Indeed, the same argument was applicable to business deductions. What constituted an expense "ordinary and necessary" to business was by no means unambiguous. The courts generally followed the legislature and IRS in their determinations of proper business expenses. Like personal deductions, business expenses were as much a matter of fiat as principle.

No single consideration readily explains why members of Congress and the administration proposed a child care deduction in the 1954 code. Apparently, several circumstances turned the cases brought by a few determined taxpayers into law. In 1953 there were 19 million women in the labor force, who constituted 33 percent of the entire working population: 27 percent of all married women worked, and there were approximately 9 million working mothers. About 25 percent of working mothers (2.25 million) had children under the age of 18, and 16 percent (1.44 million) had children under 6 years old. In other words, 64 percent of the working mothers with minor children had preschool children.[5] Social mores notwithstanding, working mothers were fast becoming a fact of American life.

There was some precedent for federal involvement in helping working mothers care for their children. In 1942 the Federal Works Agency obtained an interpretation of the Lanham Act for defense housing and public works that allowed funding of day care facilities. This program spent $52 million over three years to care for 109,000 children across the country. When World War II ended so did federal aid, but during the Korean War, Congress passed an authorization for day care grants: the Defense Housing and Community Services act. Although with this act Congress had formally acknowledged the need for day care services due to the steady influx of women into the

labor force, the provision was never funded and the
authorization lapsed with the armistice. In 1953 the
Children's Bureau and the Women's Bureau of the Department of Labor sponsored a conference on services for the
children of working mothers. They stressed the growing
number of mothers entering the labor force to fill vacant
jobs and to supplement family income. The conference
concluded that these women, many the sole support of their
children, required government aid for their children's
care. The issue, therefore, was far from dormant.[6]

There was much support for some sort of child care
deduction. The CIO, the American Nurses Association, the
American Hospital Association, the American Federation of
Government Employees, the Office Employees International,
the American Bar Association, and the American Institute
of Accountants all supported a deduction. A report of
the Joint Committee on Taxation observed that a "large
number of letters" had recommended special tax treatment
for child care expenses;[7] 29 members of Congress
proposed or spoke in favor of such provision. The
deduction was not a partisan issue. It turned upon
considerations less cosmic than the then heated battle
between Democrats and Republicans over redistribution and
balanced budgets. Proponents offered three rationales
for the deduction. First, child care expenses were
necessary to the conduct of business and hence deductible.
Second, working mothers were compelled to seek employment
by economic necessity, thus defraying their child care
expenses was a justifiable relief measure. Finally, tax
subsidies for child care would enable welfare mothers to
avoid the dole and support their children through employment. The costs of the Aid to Dependent Children (ADC)
program would thus decline.

Within these basic overlapping rationales, there were
many nuances among the bills. Generally, however, they
raised two major questions: Should child care be treated
as a business or personal expense, and what should define
a taxpayer's eligibility for the deduction? The first
question involved where the deduction should be allowed.
Business expenses, as adjustments to gross income, were
deducted before personal items, thereby reducing the
taxpayer's liability regardless of whether he or she took
the standard deduction. If the child care deduction were
incorporated as a business expense, then the qualified
population would include all otherwise eligible taxpayers
with a dependent, whether or not they itemized their
returns. The 75 percent of the taxpayers who took the

standard deduction in 1954 would then be able to deduct
child care expenses. The second question involved which
taxpayers were eligible for the deduction. The taxpayer,
naturally, had to have a dependent child and be gainfully
employed. Some bills extended the deduction only to
widows, widowers, and divorced or separated mothers.
Others allowed all families with both parents working to
claim it. Some placed income limits on families and
varied the age limits for eligible dependents.

Supporters of the deduction, who equated child care
with a business expense, included the American Bar
Association, American Institute of Accountants, and
American Nurses Association. An institute representative
summarized this rationale in testimony before the Ways
and Means Committee: "Taxable income," he stated, was
only that portion of the gross amount earned that remained
after expenditures "necessary and ordinary to the production of income" were subtracted. Since child care was an
ordinary expense to the production of income, deducting
it was therefore legitimate under the current code. An
amendment to Section 23 of the 1939 code covering business
deductions would only affirm what was true though miscon-
strued by the courts. The American Nurses Association
advanced a similar case. Congress, they argued, had
recognized that it is equitable to tax only net income--
income actually available for the taxpayer's discretionary
use. The association added that expenses such as alimony
and entertainment, currently deductible under this principle, were more in the nature of personal expenses than
are the payment of wages for services to a custodian of
one's child.[8]

Representatives in Congress echoed the belief that a
child care deduction was consistent with the principles
of a business deduction. Many of their arguments, moreover, stressed not only the equitable nature of the deduction, but also that a failure to enact the provision
would prove discriminatory and inhumane. Representative
Kenneth Roberts of Alabama, for example, argued that
women and working mothers bore an unjust burden because
of an outdated court decision. "It is a little hard,"
Roberts concluded, "to reconcile the present insensitive
attitude on the part of the government which allows a
lawyer to deduct entertainment fees lavished upon a
prospective client . . . which will not grant this
privilege to the working mother who toils all day in the
factory and works for her family in the evening in the
hope that her children may have a better life."[9] In

sum, several members of Congress and advocates from various interest groups in favor of a child care deduction saw the principle of a business expense deduction as a precedent for allowing a deduction for child care.

The second basic rationale advanced the child care deduction as a relief measure for working women. Supported by the CIO and other unions with female members, this argument involved debate on a wider range of issues. The legislators favoring this position needed at the very least to prove that women were compelled to work. They had to disabuse their fellow legislators of the current notion that women worked only for personal pin money.[10] They had to demonstrate, in the words of one representative from New York, that the "great majority of these (working) mothers would sooner prefer to remain at home and devote themselves to raising their children were it not for economic circumstances which force them to become the breadwinners of their family."[11]

The most obvious and persuasive example of economic compulsion was that of widows and widowers who were the sole means of support for their children. The case became more difficult to prove when mothers worked despite the presence of a working husband. Opponents of a broad deduction asked why these wives could not stay home where they belonged. Why, in other words, should the deduction not be restricted to single parents? Supporters answered that most women worked because their families desperately needed the money. The low income of households with working women demonstrated that necessity, not choice, dictated these mothers' entry into the labor force. The deduction was a relief measure for them and not an inducement for those mothers still at home to seek employment. The evidence, they concluded, demonstrated that very few mothers work if they have a choice.

The third rationale involved the potential of lowering welfare costs by providing a tax incentive for ADC families. Representative James Davis of Georgia observed that "this nation spends hundreds of millions of dollars each year for child welfare, aid to dependent children, etc., but when a mother has the courage to support her children by working rather than accepting government aid, she is penalized by the law." Others praised the working mother for her "courage" and "independence" in working when the cost of day care rendered it more lucrative to stay home "in idleness and rely on the country welfare board to take care of her." The child care deduction, Davis emphasized, would guarantee working parents the

money to find "proper care" for their children. He
promised that the deduction would aid in "keeping
families together, preventing juvenile delinquency, and
having children reared under influences conducive to good
citizenship."[12]

The implicit counterpart of women's needing to work
was the economy's need for women workers. "An important
point to make," one member of Congress explained, "is
that not only do women work because they have to, but
under our present economic system we need these women
workers."[13] The memory of World War II was fresh, and
the United States was involved in the Korean War.
Testifying before the Ways and Means Committee, one
witness adduced that if the country's defense production
and military requirements continued to expand, more women
would be called to work. Women, she added, are the
nation's greatest source of reserve labor needed not only
in times of emergency, but also in peacetime professions
such as teaching and nursing.[14] In the early 1950s
there was a serious labor shortage in these professions
traditionally filled by women. Many contended that the
low wages prevented women from continuing to work in
these fields after having children. They simply could
not afford to work and pay for the care of their children.

Representative Roberts explained that "the present
inequitable tax law has an adverse effect on the welfare
of the country by making it difficult to keep women in
the fields of teaching and nursing where a critical labor
shortage exists." These jobs were underpaid to begin
with, and "nondeductible child care expenses" made it
"hardly worthwhile for these women to continue to work
once they have families."[15] The American Hospital
Association and the American Nurses Association agreed.
The nurses association contended that although more
nurses were working in 1954 than at any other time, a
critical shortage of nursing services in cities and rural
areas still existed. The shortage could be remedied in
part by allowing working women to deduct expenses for the
care of their children. They pointed out that although
60 percent of all registered nurses were active in
nursing, only about a third of those with dependent
children were practicing their professions. Inactive
nurses, who were otherwise willing to work, simply could
not afford to do so. Tax relief, they contended, would
create incentives for women to return to work.[16]

There was a certain paradox between the labor supply
and rationales of economic necessity. Those who argued

for passage of the deduction to relieve mothers compelled
by circumstances to work contended that it would not act
as a work incentive. Those who argued on the grounds of
labor shortages were implicitly contending that the
deduction would be a work incentive. This paradox,
however, appears to have mattered little to congressional
supporters of the deduction.

Most members did not object to facilitating the return
of nurses and teachers to the work force or encouraging
mothers to seek employment in the country's labor-short
defense plants. Neither did most legislators object to
encouraging poor or husbandless mothers to work to support
themselves and their families. Nevertheless, some legislators thought that by granting the benefits of the deduction to all working mothers the wrong group of mothers
would find an incentive to seek employment. Representative Noah Mason of Illinois did not want to give the
deduction to the kind of mother who might neglect her
responsibilities to her family in order to earn some
extra spending money. As he saw it, the problem in
drafting the child care deduction was to draw a line
"between those women who have to work, are compelled to
work because their husbands do not care enough, or because
they are unable to earn money or incapable of earning it,
and those women who want to work to earn extra money to
buy things they want that their husbands cannot afford to
buy them."[17]

In congressional considerations of the child care
deduction a tension surfaced between those who viewed
women as working individuals and taxpayers and those who
viewed women as mothers--sentinels of home and family.
Delimiting eligibility for the deduction was essentially
a matter of assuming a position on these views. The
question of eligibility brought the legislative debate
into the realm of values and assumptions about family
life. The following exchange between Mason and Nancy
Henderson, a working mother, illustrates this debate
particularly well:

> Mr. Mason: But you think that when a young
> career woman gets married she should not give
> up her career. She should then adopt the dual
> obligation and responsibility of raising a
> family, keeping a home and holding on to her
> career; is that it?
> Mrs. Henderson: That, of course, is up to the
> individual's personal decision whether or not

she wishes to continue to do that. I don't
think the law should discriminate against her
if that is what she wants to do.
Mr. Mason: Just at present our employment is
almost full capacity, but suppose we have a
slight depression and we have several million
unemployed men. Then would you say that she
should have the right to her career as well as
her married privileges?
Mrs. Henderson: I would say yes, certainly,
if she is more capable. I do not think you
would prefer to fire a woman who was producing
more than a man who was producing less. She
is going to be kept if she is an economic unit.
Mr. Mason: I am thinking of the thousands, if
not millions, of women who are married who
have families who have responsibilities but
who prefer to neglect these obligations and
responsibilities in order to go to work and
earn money which they can spend upon themselves in spite of the fact that their
husbands are earning enough for a pretty fair
living.[18]

At stake in determining who was eligible for the
deduction was the fate of the deduction as an instrument
of economic policy as well as social policy. The eligibility criteria would control the amount of relief given
to taxpayers. Moreover, they might influence which
mothers went to work and therefore which children would
receive nonparental care. With respect to the deduction's
economic impact, the eligibility criteria might curb the
extent to which the deduction acted as an influence on
the entry of women into the labor force--whether to meet
a general demand or to fulfill specific needs in certain
professions. Eligibility restrictions might also limit
the deduction's affinity to a business deduction and
consequently limit the degree to which a working woman
received "equitable" tax treatment.

In a detailed report on the various proposals,
analysts within the Treasury Department and Internal
Revenue Service (then the Bureau of Internal Revenue)
raised several major questions concerning the child care
deduction. The report expressed concern over the number
of taxpayers eligible for the deduction and consequent
revenue loss. It warned of establishing a precedent for

other "special expenses associated with employment" if
child care were treated as a business expense. Finally,
the report noted the "significant administrative difficulties" that a deduction presented. It concluded that
"these questions may raise serious doubts as to the
desirability of providing the proposed tax benefits to
[all] working parents." The report in effect opposed any
deduction that extended the administration's original
proposal. In his tax message President Eisenhower had
suggested "some tax allowance" for the actual costs of
providing care for small children of widows and widowers
compelled to work outside their homes. In addition to
widows and widowers, a mother forced to support her family
because of her husband's incapacity was also eligible.
In their consultations with the Ways and Means Committee,
Treasury personnel advocated this proposal.[19]
     Underlying this debate was a more fundamental issue
of the infrastructure of the tax code. If one desired
equity in the code, then the putative value of homemaker
services should be included in a household's income and
taxed accordingly. Since assessing the value of these
services and levying a tax on them were so alien to common
perception of income, Congress had not incorporated such
a provision in the tax laws. The effect of this was to
create a disincentive for homemakers to seek outside
employment. Not only would they have to compensate for
the loss of homemaking services, but their outside income
would be subject to taxation. The tax structure created
a distortion in the labor market. Since Congress did not
consider taxing homemaker sevices, the question then
arose, to what extent, if any, did Congress and Treasury
want to create another tax distortion to compensate for
it. At this point in the decision-making process constituent demands, lobbyist pressures, and the ideological
preferences of individual members of Congress entered.
Once one acknowledged that the tax system was distorted,
the issue then became, in the words of one former congressional and Treasury staffer, "are we distorting it in a
good or bad way?" The ultimate decision rested less on
the structural integrity of the tax system than on the
legislators' ideologies and the constituencies to which
they responded.
     When passed by the House as part of the general tax
revision measure, the child care deduction (Section 214)
conformed substantially to the administration's proposal.
The bill specified that the deduction could not exceed
$600--a figure based on the estimated median monthly cost

of child care, $50. Deductible expenses could include
only those incurred in pursuit of gainful employment.
The committee considered child care as care for children
under the age of 10 (16 if the child were physically or
mentally unable to attend a regular school), since the
available data indicated that such costs declined for
school-age children, becoming negligible for children
over 12. Payments made to dependents of the taxpayer for
the care of her children were not considered eligible
under the section. Only widowed or divorced mothers,
widowers with children, and mothers with incapacitated
spouses were eligible to deduct, if they itemized, the
child care expenses they incurred while working. The
House report on the tax bill explained that this provision
was consistent with the principle of a business deduction.
Women under these circumstances had to pay child care
expenses in order to earn a livelihood. The expenses
could thus be compared to an employee's business expense.
This justification was only a partial explanation. Widows
and widowers evoked an image of needy parents struggling
to provide for their children. Tax breaks granted to
these individuals apparently accorded with a portrayal
acceptable to most House members of which women should be
working and which should not.[20]

Upon receiving the House version of H.R. 8300 in early
April 1954, the Senate Finance Committee held extensive
hearings on the general topic of tax revision. Little,
however, was heard from those concerned with the child
care deduction in particular. Although retaining the
basic structure of the House version, the Finance Committee made several significant changes in Section 214.
The committee allowed the deduction for all working
mothers provided that they filed a joint return with
their husbands. However, they placed an income ceiling
of $4,500 on any dual-career household claiming the deduc-
tion. The amount of allowable deduction decreased by the
amount by which the combined adjusted gross income of a
husband and wife exceeded $4,500. The Senate report
pointed out "that in many low-income families, the earnings of the mother are essential for the maintenance of
minimum living standards, even when the father is also
employed. . . . in such situations . . . child care may
be just as pressing as in the case of a widowed or
divorced mother."[21]

The Finance Committee also included expenses paid for
the care of any dependents who were mentally or physically
incapable of caring for themselves, on the assumption

that such expenses were effectively the same as child care
costs. Finally, it raised the age limit for children from
10 to 12. The committee retained an important provision
of the House bill: the maximum amount deductible for
child care in any single tax year could not exceed $600.
The reasons for retaining this provision apparently
involved Senate concerns over containing the revenue loss
of the deduction.[22]

In conference the House acceded to the Senate's amendments. The House version of child care deduction would
have meant $40 million in revenue losses in fiscal 1955
and would have benefited approximately 300,000 taxpayers;
the final version was estimated to cost $140 million and
to benefit potentially 2.1 million taxpayers. When
enacted, Section 214 contained measures associated with
business deductions on one hand and measures that stressed
the personal nature of child and dependent care expenses
on the other. The personal nature of child care deduction
was affirmed by the fact that the deduction was not added
to the business deduction section of the tax code.
Excluded from this section, child care expenses could
only be deducted by taxpayers who itemized deductions on
their returns. The provision also restricted the deduction to $600 for a taxable year and set an income ceiling
on the adjusted gross income of a married couple who could
use the deduction. No income limitation was imposed on
those claiming business deductions.[23]

The business nature of child and dependent care
expenses was reflected in one of Section 214's fundamental
rules. The section stated that a deduction for dependent
care could be taken only "if such care is for the purpose
of enabling the taxpayer to be gainfully employed." The
deduction was clearly linked to the production of income.
Deductions for the expenses of child care were legitimate
only for periods in which the taxpayer was gainfully
employed or in active search of gainful employment.
Thus, a woman who worked part time and employed a babysitter for the full day could deduct only the portion of
the expenses attributable to her working hours. Furthermore, if a taxpayer employed a housekeeper who cooked and
cleaned in addition to providing care for the taxpayer's
children, only the portion of the housekeeper's salary
allocable to child care could be deducted.[24]

Many compromises had been made in passing the child
care deduction. Retention of the deduction in a separate
section of the code helped to ensure that its passage
would not serve as precedent for wholesale expansion of

eligible business adjustments to gross income. As an
itemized deduction, child care expenses still possessed
the character of personal expenses. They were, however,
deductible expenses not only for single women or widowers
with children, but for all families within the income
limits, provided that both parents worked. Although the
final bill expanded both the site and scope of its proposal, the administration would not consider vetoing a
very large, complex tax revision for the sake of changing
one very minor deduction. The President signed the new
tax code, child care deduction and all, into law in 1954.

IMPACT AND REVISION: 1954-1964

The child care deduction brought much less tax relief
than Congress had estimated. In contrast to their
estimate of $140 million in tax savings to 2.1 million
households, the deduction provided only $18 million in
savings to 273,000 households in 1954 and $24 million in
savings to 329,000 households in 1956. Either most of
those paying for child care were unable to claim it due
to the restrictions, or most working mothers were not
using formal child care arrangements. Members of Congress
appeared to have assumed that the former was true and, in
1957, began introducing legislation to liberalize the
deduction. Two bills would have permitted a married male
taxpayer to deduct the expenses for the care of his dependents, if his wife were mentally or physically disabled.
Another would have increased the amount that a taxpayer
could deduct for the care of dependents. The following
year a member of Congress offered a bill to remove the
income limits on taxpayers deducting child care expenses.
This bill also sought to increase the dollar amount of
the deduction. In 1959, two more congressmen proposed
bills to amend the deduction by increasing the amount
that a taxpayer could deduct. One also recommended
allowing a taxpayer to deduct expenses for the care of
certain dependents, if one spouse were incapacitated.
Unsuccessful attempts to liberalize the deduction continued into the early 1960s. In October 1962 a bill to
make the child care deduction available to "a wife who
has been deserted by and cannot locate her husband on the
same basis as a single woman" passed the House unanimously
but, in the preelection chaos, never reached the Senate
floor.[25]

Several circumstances coalesced to change the fortunes
of the child care deduction in 1963. The election of
John F. Kennedy in 1960 brought the Democrats to power
for the first time in 8 years. Although cautious during
his first year in office, Kennedy subsequently broached a
series of economic and social intiatives that focused
attention on the nation's poor and, more important,
incorporated a Keynesian approach to fiscal policy. The
centerpiece of his fiscal policy was a broad tax cut.[26]
In his message to Congress on taxes, he outlined the
economic problems of the country that necessitated such a
cut. The chief problem, he declared, was the economy's
unrealized potential--slow growth, lack of investment,
unused capacity, and persistent unemployment. The tax
system as it currently stood stifled economic growth by
withdrawing from the private sector too large a share of
personal and business incomes. It also narrowed the tax
base with the special preferences and provisions it
contained. A narrower base required higher tax rates,
added complexities, and promoted inequities that undermined the morale of the taxpayer and inhibited capital
formation. Kennedy's proposals for the reform of the tax
code included reducing individual and corporate income
taxes, broadening the tax base, and removing certain
inequities and hardships. Under the rubric of removing
inequity and hardship, he recommended a liberalization of
the child and dependent care deduction.[27]

The President's proposal on the child care deduction
was in large measure shaped by the recommendations of his
Commission on the Status of Women.[28] Created by executive order in December 1961, the commission received a
broad mandate to explore virtually all social and economic
issues affecting women. Chaired by Eleanor Roosevelt and
Assistant Secretary of Labor Esther Peterson, the commission included cabinet heads, members of Congress, and
civic, labor, and business leaders. The commission dele-
gated several major topics for study to seven committees,
two of which--social insurance and taxes and home and
community--dealt specifically with the child care deduction. Both committees issued reports critical of the
existing deduction.

The committee on social insurance and taxes concluded
that the $600 limit on the deduction was inadequate when
more than one dependent required care. As evidence they
offered a 1961 study in Texas revealing that expenditures
for nursery and baby-sitting services averaged a minimum
of $58.22 per month ($700 a year) for mothers with

children under 17. They suggested increasing the maximum
deductible amount for each child and removing any restrictions on the number of children whose care expenses were
deductible. They criticized the income limitations of
the deduction as too restrictive due to the sharp rise in
family income since 1954. At that time the median income
of families with working husbands and wives was approximately $5,336; by 1961 it was $7,188. The committee
proposed an increase in the income limitation on dual-
career families from $4,500 to $7,500. The maximum
allowable deduction would be reduced by one dollar for
each dollar of income above that level. They believed
that the higher income ceiling would allow more taxpayers
to use the deduction. In proposing a new limit on the
joint income of families of working wives, however, the
committee supported some limitation as "justifiable in
the case of wives whose husbands are able to work."[29]

The committee on social insurance and taxes also
suggested raising the age level of eligible children.
Although they found it difficult to pinpoint the exact
age beyond which children no longer required supervision,
14 seemed attractive as a compromise. They recommended
allowing the deduction of child care expenses if the
mother were confined to an institution. The problem they
encountered was the technical difficulty of defining a
noninstitutionalized spouse's "incapacity" to care for
her children. The committee noted that the criterion,
"ability to earn," which determined if a husband was
incapable of self-support, could not be applied to a
housewife. Although they suggested that the Treasury
Department "give sympathetic study to the feasibility of
extending the deduction to all cases in which the wife is
not able to care for the children," the committee concluded that institutionalization was the only unambiguous
criterion for judging a mother's capability of caring for
her children. Their final recommendation was that any
government aid received by the child, either directly or
through parent-guardians, should not be taken into consideration in determining a child's eligibility for tax
purposes. They believed that low-income widows had
greater difficulty than higher-income widows in proving
that they provided 50 percent or more of their child's
support.[30]

The committee on home and community also discussed
the deduction and made recommendations similar to those
of the committee on social insurance and taxes. In
establishing the general importance of the child care

deduction their report cited a 1958 census survey. The
survey ascertained that 5 million children under 12 had
working parents. Of these, 12 percent (600,000) were
cared for at least for some time by nonrelatives, and 8
percent (400,000) had no alternative care arrangements
while their parents worked. There were 500,000 families
with children in which the mother provided the sole
support, 117,000 families in which the father alone was
present, and 3 million families with children under 6 in
which both parents worked. The committee concluded from
these data that 3.6 million families required child care
services; current facilities, however, cared for only
185,000 children. Their report regarded these facilities
as extremely inadequate. Although the committee lamented
that so many women had been "forced by economic necessity
or by the regulations of welfare agencies" to work despite
the presence of young children, they affirmed the right of
all women who elected to work to have child care services
available.[31]

Even on the part of the commission's committees, the
tenor of the discussion on reform of the child care deduction retained the traditional perception of the tax
measure as justified chiefly by economic necessity. While
expressing the belief that child care services should be
available and accessible to all women who choose to work,
the committee on home and community found it, nonetheless,
"regrettable" that women with very young children sought
employment. The commission left the purpose of the child
care deduction ambiguous. It was a welfare measure that
allowed families to retain their financial viability without the dole as well as a measure of equity that allowed
any married women with children to enter the labor force
without the unremitted burden of child care.

In its proposals to Congress the Kennedy administration adopted many of the commission's recommendations.
Articulating the administration's position, Secretary of
the Treasury Douglas Dillon explained that the deduction
was too restrictive in light of current income levels and
costs. Specifically, he proposed that the deductible
amount be raised to a maximum of $1,000 for three or more
children. The present limit of $600 placed an unfair
burden on those families with more than one child, particularly if the children were provided care outside the
home. The costs of such care rose in proportion to the
number of children. Second, Dillon asked that the deduction be allowed at higher income levels for married
women. Raising the income limitation on the deduction

from $4,500 to $7,000 would, he argued, provide more
effective aid to working mothers at current income levels.
The administration also wanted to raise the age limit of
eligible children from 12 to 13. Finally, Dillon recommended that the deduction for child care expenses be
extended to a married man with an institutionalized wife.
He argued that these circumstances were comparable to
those of a widower who was allowed the deduction under
current law.[32]

Offering a different, though not unprecedented
rationale, Secretary of Labor Willard Wirtz also testified
for the liberalization of the child care deduction. Wirtz
explained that despite current high unemployment levels,
there were actually labor shortages in some occupations.
"[Some] of those areas in which we presently experience
the worst shortages, as nursing being perhaps the most
obvious illustration, are occupations which involve
women." Women with these key occupational skills could
not assuage the shortages without some tax relief for the
care of their children. He concluded that the current
deduction was clearly insufficient to this end.[33]

Congress revised a small part of the child care
deduction in early 1963. On February 4, the Ways and
Means Committee unanimously reported the deserted wife
bill, which had died at the end of the last session in
the Senate. The Committee explained "that where women
clearly have been deserted by their husbands, they should
be eligible for any child care deduction in the same
manner as a widow." The House adopted the bill for a
second time on February 26. Three weeks later the Senate
passed the new measure, and in April Kennedy signed it.[34]

It is unclear why this provision was singled out for
quick passage among the several bills seeking to amend the
child care deduction. The Treasury Department supported
it, though preferred "to consider the instant amendment
in light of the overall proposals with respect to Section
214." One distinction between this amendment and the
others might have influenced its separation: It was more
closely associated with the basic principles of the 1954
tax measure. It maintained the tradition of the child
care deduction as a limited relief measure for those women
compelled to work. In presenting the provision to the
House Ways and Means Committee, Chairman Wilbur Mills
placed deserted women in the same category as single
mothers. "The woman," he observed, "who has been deserted
must normally work and provide child care." In this
rationale, the Treasury Department concurred: "Since the

child-care deduction was originally authorized to allevi-
ate the burdens on families where the mother had to work
in order to maintain minimum living standards and had to
pay for child care while outside the home, it seems
inequitable to deprive deserted wives of this form of
assistance when they are in similar circumstances."
Unlike the many other proposed amendments to the child
care deduction, this one was a clear extension of an
already acknowledged goal of the deduction--subsidizing
mothers who had no choice but to work.[35]

The House bills embodying the other administration
amendments for the deduction, however, had much tougher
going in Ways and Means. At the initial meeting between
Treasury personnel and committee members and their staff,
the latter agreed to the major administration proposals
on raising the income limit to $7,000, the deductible
amount to $1,000, and the age limit to 12. They also
agreed to extend the deduction to single fathers and
husbands with incapacitated wives. Participants considered changing the deduction to an above-line adjustment to gross income, which would allow its benefits to
families electing the standard deduction. They decided
against this change despite the fact that such a change
would make the deduction a more effective aid to low-
income families. "More importantly," they determined,
"there is the problem of integrating the deduction within
the general objectives of the reform program and giving
it its proper emphasis within the code." Child care
expenses "are essentially personal expenses, as distinguished from business expenses . . . [;] it would set an
undesirable precedent to grant [them] a more favored tax
treatment than is now generally allowed to other types of
personal expenses."[36]

The favorable decisions of this early meeting were
reversed in the full committee a few months later.
Chairman Mills, the Treasury staff reported, "did not
appear to favor the increase in the child care deduction
and there did not seem to be much sentiment in the committee for it." Members simply wished to avoid any tax
incentives for mothers to seek employment.[37] The
committee's final bill excluded most of the President's
major recommendations with respect to the child care
deduction. The committee did raise the limit of the
deduction from $600 to $900 if the taxpayer had two or
more eligible dependents, but refused to increase the
income ceiling of $4,500 on dual-career families. They
granted the deduction to a husband whose wife was incap-

able of caring for herself or institutionalized for a
period of at least 90 consecutive days. For the purposes
of the deduction, deserted wives were placed in the same
category as widows and divorcees, and the age of qualified
dependents was raised from 11 to 12. Significantly,
working mothers whose husbands were present were excluded
from all these changes. For the most part, the committee
explained their actions as an effort to "update" the 1954
provisions. In raising the maximum deduction to $900 for
single parents with two or more children, they reiterated
the rationale of the provision (aiding mothers forced to
work) as their "general explanation" for the change. The
House passed their tax bill without amendment.[38]

Since the House bill incorporated most of the major
tax reductions sought by the administration, Treasury was
unwilling to challenge the measure over the relatively
minor issue of the child care deduction. It was not
politic to risk alienating the Ways and Means Committee
in a Senate battle over the deduction's provisions; the
administration proffered only tacit support.[39] Several
senators, however, were determined to see the administration's and the commission's proposals realized. On the
floor, Senator Maurine Neuberger of Oregon offered a bill
to amend the House version of the deduction. Neuberger,
a member of the Commission on the Status of Women,
proposed an increase from $4,500 to $7,000 in the income
ceiling of the deduction. "The question," she explained,
"is not whether women and mothers would be encouraged to
work through the child care tax deduction. Twenty-four
million women [one third of the labor force] are presently
employed in our working force, and I think it desirable
to accept facts as they are. . . . By 1970, it is forecast
that the workforce will contain 30 million women."
Neuberger concluded that expansion of the child care
deduction would be consonant not only with achieving
equity in tax laws, but also with the spirit of the Equal
Pay Act of 1963 mandating equal pay for equal work.[40]

Her explanation was not far removed from previous
efforts to justify the extension of the child care deduction to all working mothers as a business expense.
Neuberger's amendment did not attempt to differentiate
among working mothers on the grounds of economic
necessity. Rather she based her proposal to alter the
child care deduction on a general perception of social
conditions, in this instance the number of women in the
work force, and on the applicability of the principle of
equity in taxation. In these respects she did not deviate

from the President's own rationale for changes in the
child care deduction. Neuberger was, however, more
direct in her assertion of the principle of equity and of
a mother's right to work. In effect she challenged the
implicit assumption of the 1954 child care tax provision
that a mother's only justification for working was
economic necessity.

The sentiments of Neuberger and others carried some
weight with the Senate Finance Committee. While agreeing
with the changes made by the House bill in the child care
provision, the Finance Committee found them "too narrow."
As a result, the committee followed more closely the
administration's recommendations. Their most important
amendment raised from $4,500 to $7,000 the income limit
applicable to working mothers whose husbands were present.
Affirming the original intent of Congress in providing
the deduction to working wives--that the maintenance of a
minimum standard of living sometimes required that a wife
work--the Finance Committee explained that the current
higher median income made the $4,500 limitation unreal-
istic. It was below the median income of two-parent
families in which the wife worked. They concluded that
"the $4,500 limitation falls far short of covering the
average case where the wife has found it necessary to
supplement the husband's income by working."[41]

The Finance Committee aided working wives in another
way. They made the deduction for each child comparable
to that allowed for single-parent families in the House
version. "These expenses," they explained, "are as likely
to increase on a per-child basis in the case of a married
couple as in those cases where there is only one parent."
Moreover, the Senate bill carried the House provision one
step further in providing a maximum deduction of $1,000
for three or more eligible dependents. Otherwise it
substantially conformed to the House version. Nevertheless, the changes made by the Finance Committee added $15
million to the estimated revenue loss of the House bill
and 200,000 taxpayers to the universe of those eligible.
The new totals were $20 million and 444,000 taxpayers.
While aligning itself with the administration's position,
the Senate bill still skirted the issue of equity. Like
the House, the Senate explained that its amendments were
necessary updates to the 1954 measure--principally a
function of the change in median family income over the
decade. Apparently, Congress was neither more comfortable
with the idea of mothers working nor more certain of the
connection between business and child care expenses.[42]

As a result of their differences the two versions went
into conference. The final bill was a compromise between
the Senate and the House versions. It raised the maximum
amount of the deduction from $600 to $900 for eligible
taxpayers with two or more children. Congress extended
this benefit to all working mothers regardless of the
presence or absence of their spouses. In addition, the
final bill raised the joint income level, which determined
a working wife's eligibility for the deduction, from
$4,500 to $6,000. Both these increases were below the
recommendations of the administration and the Senate.
The law provided a new rule to cover a taxpayer with an
incapacitated or institutionalized spouse. Finally, the
bill specified the age of a dependent qualified to receive
care at 13 rather than 11. In April 1963, with the
President's signature, the measure became law.[43]

FROM TAX RELIEF TO "JOB DEVELOPMENT": 1964-1971

Although the revised deduction increased by one third the
income limitation and by one half the deductible amount
for more than one dependent, the impact was very slight.
Comparing the figures before and after the revision in
the years for which the data are available (1960 and
1966), households claiming the deduction declined by 7
percent from 272,000 to 254,000. Despite an increase of
27 percent in the dollar amount deducted ($103 million to
$131 million), the 1964 reduction in tax rates left the
net revenue loss virtually unchanged at $21 million. More
households in the $5,000-$10,000 income range took the
deduction, fewer in the under-$5,000 group. Nevertheless,
the low income ceiling and limit on the amount deductible
made the child care deduction of little value in an era
of rapidly rising incomes.

To deal with this situation, members of Congress
introduced 15 bills to increase the amount of the allowable deduction, 9 to raise the income ceiling, 5 to raise
the age of children qualified to receive care, 5 to change
child care expenses from a personal to a business deduction, and 2 to remove all restrictions on marital status.
Often proposals to raise the amount deductible for child
and dependent care expenses also increased the limitation
on income. In all, members of Congress proposed approximately 43 bills between 1964 and 1971; many introduced
the same bill two or three times. Others simply offered
amendments of a general nature. In 1971, for example,

two bills "to amend the Internal Revenue Code of 1954 in relation to expenses for the care of certain dependents" had 36 sponsors and cosponsors.[44]

The impetus for and shape of the proposed revisions came to some extent from organized groups. While introducing a bill to revise the deduction in 1966, Representative Joseph Resnick (D-New York) acknowledged Howard Coughlin, president of the Office and Professional Employees International Union (AFL-CIO), as a "spokesman for thousands of working mothers." It was Coughlin, Resnick noted, who had called the attention of Congress to inadequacies in the child care deduction with respect to this group of women and inspired his bill.[45] In the course of shaping a new deduction, the American Bar Association also had a direct impact. At one point, for example, Acting Assistant Secretary of the Treasury John Nolan wrote the American Bar Association to observe that "we could convince the conference committee only to go part of the way as urged in your brief with respect to [the deduction]."[46] In addition, there is evidence that women themselves were organizing around the deduction issue. Judith Viorst organized a group called Working Mothers United for Fair Taxation to lobby for a bill that would "make all necessary and ordinary business-related child care expenses tax deductible regardless of income."[47]

Less-organized constituent pressure also had some impact. "[A]s it stands now," Senator Russell Long explained, "when one goes home and talks with his constituents, about half of the working mothers are not getting the benefit of the deduction under present law while half of them are, and a senator must spend half of his time explaining why one-half of the working mothers do not get the benefit of the deduction while the benefit is available for the others." Television programs publicized this issue. A mother on the "Today" show raised a classic example of the tax law's inequity: If David Rockefeller could deduct as a business expense the salary of a secretary, why shouldn't every working mother be able to deduct the cost of hiring someone to take care of her house and children while she was at work?[48]

Much of the rationale for enacting amendments to the child and dependent care deduction recapitulated past arguments. Some argued that the hardships of working mothers were not adequately redressed by the 1964 revision. Others pointed to changes in the labor force participation of women and in median incomes to urge revisions to achieve the promised relief to working mothers of both the 1954 and 1964 deductions. This reasoning essentially affirmed the purpose of the child care deduction as a relief measure for those taxpayers whom circumstances compelled to work.

On the other hand, a growing aspect of the rationale for amendments to the deduction attributed a very different meaning to the child and dependent care section. The growing women's liberation movement recast the principle of equity in taxation to include not only equal treatment for all working mothers but also equal treatment for men and women. Men, the traditional breadwinners, had benefited the most from the business deduction; for women, whose traditional responsibility was the care of their children, the child care deduction offered a social equivalent. Child care expenses were as "ordinary and necessary" to a working mother as lunches, sales trips, etc., were to a working man. Overall, despite one's particular position, a consensus was slowly developing to eliminate the tax stigma attached to mothers who elected to work voluntarily. Each proponent implicitly agreed that all working mothers, regardless of income or circumstances, should be eligible for the deduction.

This new consensus was not without tensions--some of which surfaced in the reports issued by the Citizen's Advisory Council on the Status of Women. Created by executive order as a successor to the President's Commission on the Status of Women, the council was directed to stimulate and evaluate the progress of organizations in advancing full participation of women in American life. This included reviewing the recommendations of the President's previous commission with respect to the child and dependent care deduction. As its predecessor had done, the council divided its work into task forces: health and welfare, women's rights and responsibilities, and social insurance and taxes.

The preamble to the report of the health and welfare task force set the tone for the remaining reports. The earlier commission's report "was unduly cautious" given the recent "surge of women into employment." Its findings "must be updated in varying degrees." The task force turned to its primary concern: the continued viability of families at all income levels. To this end the members believed it imperative that women have the fundamental right to decide whether to stay at home and care for their children or to seek employment and delegate child care to others. The task force emphasized this right to choose

because of increasing legislative attention to work and
training provisions for welfare mothers with preschool
children, specifically the Work Incentive Program.
"Generalizations," they concluded, "that all needy mothers
should work or that no mothers should work are equally
untenable." No principle was "more crucial" than ensuring
the mother's "right" in both middle- and low-income
families to choose "between employment and full-time
homemaking."[49]

This task force did not make any specific recommendations with respect to the child and dependent care deduction. The issue of choice, however, became central to
the council's deliberations. Integral to choice was
child care, and inseparable from child care was cost.
Two of the task forces assumed very different positions
on the nature of choice, child care, and the tax deduction. On one side was the task force on women's rights
and responsibilities. Its members stressed federal
assistance to middle- and upper-income groups. They
recommended that child and dependent care expenses
including amounts paid to a housekeeper, nurse, or
institution should be deductible. They explained that
categorizing child care as a business deduction would
help low-income families, who could not afford to itemize
deductions on their tax returns. Such a change would
also remove the income limitation and open the deduction
to higher-income families. "There seems," the task
force's report concluded, "to be no good reason for
limiting the deduction to low-income husband-wife
families."[50]

Another approach to strengthening a woman's right to
work was recommended by the task force on social insurance
and taxes. Its report suggested that Section 214 be
phased out. Rather than lose revenue through the deduction, the federal government should use these revenues to
develop day care and other human service programs. The
task force members based their recommendations on the
deduction's ineffectiveness as a relief provision for low-
income women and others in need. They found that women
in families with incomes under $6,000, particularly those
with several children, had little money available for
child care. In low-income families the mother was more
likely to care for her child while working. By contrast,
in higher-income families, the mother frequently worked
only during the child's school hours or employed a housekeeper to do housework and care for the children. Low-
income families with many children received little or no

benefit from the child care deduction because their exemptions and deductions exceeded their income. Moreover, for those families who did have sufficient income to benefit, the value of the $600 or $900 deduction was but a small part of the total cost of even the simplest type of child care. The $600 deduction was worth only $84 for a taxpayer in a 14 percent income bracket and $120 for one in a 20-percent bracket.[51]

In its report task force members extended their analysis of the effect on the deduction on low-income families. The number of taxpayers filing the deduction for child and dependent care expenses in 1966 revealed a decrease in the deduction's utility to low-income families. In 1960, 182,552 taxpayers with adjusted gross incomes under $5,000 claimed the deduction. Six years later only 99,151 taxpayers in this bracket claimed the deduction. In contrast, from 1960 to 1966 taxpayers with adjusted gross incomes over $5,000 increased their use of the deduction: 50,000 more taxpayers in the $5,000-$10,000 range claimed the deduction in 1966 than in 1960. Similarly, 1,400 more taxpayers with adjusted gross incomes of $10,000 or more took the deduction in 1966. The total number of returns claiming the deduction declined by 6.5 percent over these years.[52]

In light of the deduction's deficiencies, the social insurance and taxes task force carefully examined the possible effects of the amendments pending in the 90th Congress. Removing the income limitation on married women might divert attention from the question of higher salaries for women. "The significance of the benefits of such a deduction to the individual nurse, teacher, or social worker," they warned, "might well be exaggerated in the minds of the general public and of those who fix salary scales." In addition, removal of the limitation would help professional women defray the cost of their children's care, but give little or no help to service workers and other nonprofessional female workers with child care needs. Task force members criticized amendments that sought to make the deduction a tax relief measure for middle- and upper-income families. "Proposed revisions," they stated, "could result in significant revenue costs to the government while giving little help to the large proportion of working mothers who cannot afford to spend such amounts." Their report concluded that the present deduction is neither effective in giving assistance where it is most needed nor in encouraging better care of children of working mothers." The

proposed changes would "simply provide tax relief to
those families able to make expenditures for care of
children and disabled dependents."[53]

The task force took a firm position that it was the
government's obligation to provide relief in cases of
hardship. In this respect they supported a woman's right
to choose between formal employment and the maintenance
of her own household. They believed that federal aid to
low income mothers created new options for those women
and were willing to sacrifice the deduction as a middle-
income subsidy to offer more of a choice to the poor. By
refusing to extend to middle- and upper-income mothers the
benefits of a choice-enlarging deduction, the task force
implicitly confronted the large segment of the women's
liberation movement representing professional women.
Speaking for this segment of the movement, lawyer Grace
Blumberg attacked the task force's position in an article
on "sexism in the tax code." "While the Task Force's
consideration for the poor is commendable," she intoned,
"it is beside the point. Section 214 involves two
discrete problems: the cost of earning income (and
implicitly, the work disincentive arising from disallowance of a deduction for a necessary expense) and hardship
for low-income two-earner families." Blumberg concluded
that the "problem of the poor is an entirely separate
problem. It is not a valid objection to a provision
designed to allow deduction of business-related expenses
that the poor will not benefit from it."[54]

None of the recommendations of the task force were
formally discussed by legislators. Nevertheless, the
ideas and tensions of the various task forces concerning
the proper purpose and direction of the deduction persisted in Congress. Few legislators articulated the
specific explanations for the bills they introduced, but
several rationales were apparently operative. Some
members of Congress, who proposed an increase in deductible expenses, undoubtedly felt that present limits were
inadequate. The deduction was an insufficient incentive
for low-income mothers with many children to make use of
child care opportunities. Others believed that the amount
expended by middle-income mothers exceeded the present
deduction limit. The deduction was inadequate compensation for these women. Chairman Russell Long of the
Senate Finance Committee proposed a bill, the Child Care
Services Act of 1971, which represented an amalgam of
divergent interests concerned with the child care
deduction.[55]

Revision of the deduction had come to the Senate
Finance Committee's attention in the House-passed version
of the Nixon administration's Family Assistance Plan
(FAP). The FAP had a substantial child care provision of
$700 million in federally funded child care for welfare
recipients. It allowed an additional $50 million for
alteration and construction grants to create new care
facilities. The FAP stressed child care as a work
incentive. It changed the child and dependent care
deduction to liberalize the maximum income tax deduction
from $600 to $750 for one child, $900 to $1,125 for two
children, and $900 to $1,500 for three or more children.
Families with incomes up to $12,000 would be eligible to
take the deduction.[56]

In his bill Long separated the revised Section 214
from the FAP and amended its provisions by increasing the
deductible expenses from $600 to $1000 for one child and
from $900 to $1,500 for more than one child. He raised
the limitation on an eligible family income from $6,000
to $12,000 and changed the marginal reduction in the
deduction from dollar for dollar above the $12,000 income
limitation to 50¢ per dollar. "The key feature of my
bill," he told the Senate, "will provide greater tax
relief for the lower or middle income working woman who
needs child care services in order to work." His bill
had many other features relating to child care, most of
which were directed toward expanding the availability and
the variety of child care services. He was concerned
that lack of child care services prevented many mothers
from obtaining jobs. "There are few who would disagree,"
he asserted, "that the lack of availability of adequate
child care today represents perhaps the greatest single
obstacle in the efforts of poor families, especially
those headed by a mother, to work their way out of
poverty." Long was careful to add that middle-class
mothers as well were prevented from working. With the
exception of the child care deduction, however, all of
the provisions in his child care services bill were
targeted solely for welfare recipients and low-income
working women.[57]

The Finance Committee used Long's bill as a vehicle
to overhaul the entire deduction. They incorporated the
deduction into the Revenue Act of 1971 and renamed it the
"job development deduction" for household services and
child care. "The Committee has amended the bill," their
report explained, "to provide a new job development
deduction which is designed both to encourage the employ-

ment of individuals in child care and domestic service and to relieve hardship in certain cases where substantial extra expenses are incurred for such purposes." The revised bill included provisions that allowed a single working parent maintaining a household and a dependent under 15 years of age to deduct up to $400 a month for household services including those unrelate to child care. If child care were purchased outside the home, an eligible taxpayer could deduct $200 for one child, $300 for two children, and $400 for three or more. In families in which both parents worked, their total income could not exceed $12,000 in order for them to benefit fully from the deduction. Individuals maintaining households for themselves or for disabled dependents were also eligible for the deduction of household expenses.[58]

The committee pointed to several major needs addressed by the deduction. First, it would "give large numbers of individuals who are now receiving public assistance the opportunity to perform socially desirable services in [household and child care] jobs which are vitally needed." Deduction of household services was also justified by the original language of the 1954 measure. In certain families both parents required help not only with child care, but household chores as well. "The domestic help is needed in these cases because the adult members of the family are employed full time and in this sense the domestic help expenses can . . . be likened to an employee business expense." Second, the deduction would relieve hardship by helping to pay the "substantial extra expenses" that a single parent or parent with a disabled spouse incurred. Finally, in its liberalization of the income limitation for married couples and the inclusion of expenses for household services as legitimate deductions, the committee lightened the tax burden of two-earner families. The estimated revenue loss was $110 million in 1972 and $115 million in 1973.[59]

When the bill came to the floor, several senators proposed amendments to better what they already considered a good tax deduction. Senator John Tunney argued that child and dependent care expenses should be allowed as a business deduction. Furthermore, it would make the deduction available to those families that did not itemize their tax returns. Tunney pointed out that almost 70 percent of families with incomes under $10,000 took the standard deduction. Thus, the amendment would provide relief to more taxpayers in need. Long supported the amendment precisely because it would give relief to more

working mothers. In drafting the bill, he explained, the
committee had estimated its cost at $300 million. The
final estimate of cost was less than half this figure
because many taxpayers in the lower income ranges did not
itemize their returns. Long maintained that Tunney's
amendment merely improved on what the Finance Committee
and he himself had intended.[60]

Twelve other senators cosponsored Tunney's amendment.
Only Senator Wallace Bennett expressed any opposition to
the change. "We are tossing money around here pretty
freely," he noted. "[I] wonder when we will reach the
point where we consider that we must be responsible as
well as generous." Senator John Pastore was quick to
respond: "Every time we talk about little children and
retarded children, we start to talk about how much money
we will toss away." Tunney's amendment passed by a vote
of 74 to 1.[61]

On November 15, 1971, three days after the child and
dependent care deduction had been transformed into a
business deduction for job development, Tunney offered a
second amendment to the bill. The amendment proposed to
increase from $12,000 to $18,000 the point at which the
deduction for expenses of child care and household
services was incrementally reduced for married couples.
He argued that, since child care and domestic help are
work-related, they should be considered as business
expenses for families regardless of income level. Tunney
saw no reason to limit eligibility for the deduction to
families at or below the median income level "when we are
talking about work-related activities." Moreover,
families in the middle-income range face large tax
burdens. Federal, state, and local taxes consumed 16.7
percent of the income of families earning between $8,000
and $10,000 while taking 21.1 percent of the income of
families earning between $15,000 and $25,999. "[We]
ought" he insisted, "to have some additional form of tax
relief for families with incomes between $12,000 and
$18,000--particularly when that form of tax relief would
allow a mother to work, and at the same time . . . give
work to a babysitter."[62]

Long agreed fully that middle-income families merited
whatever tax relief the deduction could provide. "I
personally think," he drawled, "we should do more for
people who hire someone to do domestic work than we are
doing in this bill." He reaffirmed the deduction's two
major benefits: first to "a working woman by permitting
her to employ someone to help with domestic duties and

help look after her children; and second, [to] the people
who are being employed. The latter "are able to earn
enought to make their own way, or . . . supplement their
welfare payments so that the family, too, can live a
little better." And, of course, "Uncle Sam saves money
in the process."[63]

Bennett again raised objections to amending the bill.
He felt that it was not "necessary" for women from
families earning up to $27,000 (the income level at which
the deduction phased out completely) to work, and the
federal government had no business providing them with
any kind of tax relief. His point was that unless the
amendment further alleviated the child care problem of
low-income mothers, it had no legitimate purpose. He
punctuated his objections with an appeal to his fellow
legislators' sense of motherhood. How could they support
a measure that would encourage middle-income taxpayers to
"pass off the motherly duty of childrearing to an
employee"?[64]

Tunney and Long responded to Bennett's criticism by
stressing the idea that child care and household expenses
were business expenses. The only distinction, Tunney
quipped, was that in the first instance women were
involved, in the other the expenses were incurred
principally by men. Long told Bennett that his "idea
that a woman's place is in the home . . . is no longer
current. Rather, it is recognized as a right of women to
[work]." Long concluded that "the women's liberation
movement has caught on." This line of defense, however,
did not speak to the problem of how Tunney's amendment
would further ease the child care problems of low-income
women. Long admitted that the impact of the dedution was
greater at higher levels of income. Nevertheless, he
believed that the deduction's ability to create unskilled
jobs and help reduce the welfare burdens compensated for
its bias against low-income families. Such a justification seemed satisfactory to other senators as well, as
Tunney's second amendment passed by a vote of 59 to 24.[65]

The Tunney-Long amendment changed one of the central
purposes of the deduction to the employment of low-income
and welfare mothers rather than the relief of child care
expenses they incurred in working. Tunney's amendments
also came closer to a second, implicit purpose of the
deduction: that all mothers should be allowed the choice
of working and the costs for care of their children should
be legitimate business expenses. His amendments
transformed a tax deduction based on hardship into one

based on equity for working mothers regardless of economic
hardship. Much had changed since the last revision in
1964. There were several categorical day care programs
for the poor. Women's liberation and inflationary
pressures on real incomes had made mothers who worked
more prevalent. The FAP and the child development
legislation were still pending with large child care
programs for low-income families. These changes in the
deduction offered benefits to middle-income groups and
satisfied a constituency politically active and often
neglected in federal efforts on behalf of the poor and
needy.[66]

The Treasury Department's response to Tunney's amendments was less than enthusiastic. "We do not believe,"
the Office of Tax Analysis stated, "that an incentive for
domestic service meets a national need which deserves the
priority it is receiving in this legislation." Questions
arose over the deduction's ability to expand the domestic
work force. One analysis calculated that the proportion
of families in the $20,000-$25,000 income range eligible
to use the deduction under Tunney's amendment might employ
an additional 50,000 domestics. This increase, the
analysis concluded, was not enough to compensate for the
revenue loss of the bill. In addition, the deduction
opened opportunities for individuals on welfare in dead-
end jobs, thus undermining the usual objective of federal
programs to place welfare recipients in promising
occupations.[67]

The department also objected to Tunney's amendment to
raise the income limitation of married couples on the
grounds that the government should not subsidize dependent
care expenses when the family had the means to pay for
such care. It recommended that income limits apply to
single taxpayers as well as to married couples. The
department concurred with the task force on social insurance and taxes that the amended deduction offered no real
benefits to "the individuals who are most in need of
relief." Since low-income families often could not afford
to pay for child care and paid little or no taxes anyway,
the deduction was meaningless to them. The deducted
income would be better taxed, then allocated directly to
support child care centers to provide services to working
families at little or no cost.[68]

Finally the department objected to the equation of
child care and business expenses. Child care is personal
in nature; it is "the legal obligation of all parents"
that must be met irrespective of whether one, both, or

neither parent works. "In the absence of statutory
authority," it noted, "child care expenses are not
deductible as business expenses because in a tax system
which taxes income they are not directly related to the
production of income". In sum, the Treasury recommended
that the Senate's bill be changed to reduce the revenue
loss from $315 million to $100 million. The department
suggested that child care and dependent care expenses
remain an itemized deduction, that the income limitation
for married taxpayers be set at $12,000, and that the
income limitation be established for single taxpayers.
Treasury also suggested limiting qualified expenses to
those incurred primarily and directly for the care of
dependents that did not exceed the earnings of a
household's lowest-paid taxpayer. The department
estimated that these changes would reduce the revenue
loss by $215 million.[69]

It befell the conference committee to resolve the
differences among the House, Senate, and Treasury desires
for the deduction. In conference the members substantially retained the Senate's version. They did not,
however, allow the deduction "above line" and thus made
taxpayers electing the standard deduction ineligible.
The conference accepted a maximum deduction of $400 per
month for in-home child care and housekeeping expenses.
Out-of-home care expenses were graduated: $200 per
month for one child, $300 for two, and $400 for three or
more. It imposed the same $18,000 income ceiling on
single parents as on married couples with an incremental
phase out of 50 cents per dollar for incomes over the
ceiling. Children up to the age of 15 became eligible,
but payments to a relative of the taxpayer still did not
qualify as deductible expenses. It clarified the meaning
of household services to guard against possible abuses.
Such services were not to include those persons functioning principally as gardeners, chauffeurs, or bar-
tenders. In addition, a taxpayer had to be employed "on
a substantially full-time basis" in order to be eligible
to deduct service expenses. Finally, the conference
devised a complicated formula to calculate the portion of
disability payments applicable to the care of disabled
dependents.[70] On December 10, 1971, President Nixon
signed the Revenue Act of 1971 into law. The child and
dependent care deduction ceased to be a relief measure
for low-income families and became instead a child care
subsidy for working mothers in middle- and upper-income
brackets. Barely two weeks later the same President

vetoed the comprehensive child care bill in part to
preclude any "sovietizing" of middle-class children
through nonmaternal care.

FROM TAX DEDUCTION TO TAX CREDIT: 1971-1978

Passage of the 1971 deduction brought an unprecedented
outpouring of criticism from lawyers and economists.
They found that the inclusion of housekeeping expenses in
the deductible amount for households with children whose
parents worked discriminated against households without
children in similar circumstances. Both types of households had an equal claim to a deduction for housekeeping
expenses. "Equity between childless couples and couples
with children," one piece surmised, "is lost as long as
the household service deduction is available only to the
latter." Scholarly critics also asserted that the deduction excluded most low-income and many middle-income
households that did not itemize on their returns. Moreover, it discriminated against otherwise qualified part-
time workers, students, and vocational trainees who were
ineligible. Finally, the critics assailed the deduction's
failure to include payments to relatives for child care
services as allowable expenses. This failure further
limited the ability of the poor to deduct their care
expenses and unjustifiably restricted a taxpayer's choice
of employees.[71]
    Academic analysis of the deduction was virtually
unknown prior to the 1971 revision. In part its advent
reflects the growth in the dollar amount of the deduction
from $221 million in 1970 to $1.1 billion in 1972 and
$1.3 billion in 1973; the number of households claiming
the deduction tripled to 1.6 million. The increased
income level also moved it more into the purview of tax
lawyers and accountants serving higher-income taxpayers.
In part, too, the specificity of these analyses attest to
a change in attitudes toward working mothers. Their
narrow focus betrays a subtle but profound transformation
in perception: Working mothers in particular and working
women in general had become socially acceptable. The
issues now involved the less cosmic concerns of equity
across income classes and occupational pursuits. Broad
social policy designs and ideological appeals, so
prevalent in previous years, were becoming mute.
    Despite numerous arguments based on "equity," this
guiding principle of the overall tax system is to some
extent irrelevant to the enactment of specific provisions.

One might argue instead that the provisions are essentially the artifacts of those interests and ideologies victorious in the legislative decision-making process. Perhaps the changes in the power of women's lobbies and public mores better explain the incorporation of the child care deduction into the tax code and its subsequent vicissitudes than any growth in forensic enlightenment. Arguments for and against the deduction were still couched in concepts of equity, business expenses, personal expenses, etc.; this is the language of the tax policy-making process. These arguments, however, were perhaps merely overlays on a shifting political and social landscape whose changes molded tax policy.

In an article in Single Parent magazine, the leading proponent of a more liberal deduction, John Tunney, appears to substantiate this observation. He began his article by labeling the deduction a "discriminatory tax on single parents and working mothers who are making an effort to provide for themselves and their families." The tax structure, he continued, had failed "to respond to the changing realities of the times." The tax laws had not been written to take account of working mothers or fathers in single-parent families. Their numbers had not been "significant" and they had not yet organized "to make their presence felt." Since 68 percent of the families earning $10,000 or less use the standard deduction form, these families "who most need and deserve assistance from tax relief" did not receive the benefit of the child care deduction. "This is," he believed, "an inequity which must be removed." It was not a "personal expense" to make "sure your child is safe while you are away all day earning enough to keep your family together."[72]

In proposing to make child care expenses a business adjustment Tunney showed his concern for all working mothers, not only those who were in some way needy. He believed that subsuming child care under business expenses was a step toward equalizing the labor market conditions of men and women. He insisted that this "unnecessary and unjustifiable obstacle in the path of women who wish to enter the employment market" was not the result of "any positive attempt to discriminate against women." Rather, he suggested, it was a "relic of a time when it was not the normal or accepted thing for mothers to go out to work." In advocating his amendment to the deduction, he affirmed that times had changed, that all working mothers needed this help, and, finally, that the Senate in general

and John Tunney in particular were in step with the
women's liberation movement.[73]

Tunney had a great deal of support from other
senators. In February 1972 he introduced a bill to allow
the deduction of child care payments as business expenses;
23 senators volunteered to cosponsor the measure. In
October, however, when he resubmitted the bill for Senate
consideration in connection with H.R. 1, Senator Bennett
again came forward with objections. Bennett asserted
that the bill "is so loosely drawn that if a rich woman
had a maid and is making a fine living writing books, she
can decide that she can deduct all of her household
expenses." For Bennett, the allowance of "ordinary and
necessary expenses" in this context created a massive
loophole. If a mother "is presiding over a household
with half a dozen servants, to her those may be ordinary
and necessary expenses. There is not a thing here about
child care." Bennett retained the idea that the child
care deduction was only legitimate as a hardship provision. Changing the deduction into an "above-line" item
would effectively remove the $18,000 income ceiling and
extend benefits to individuals who, he believed, did not
need them.[74]

Despite Bennett's objections, Tunney's amendment
passed the Senate by 71 to 8. However, it encountered
strong opposition from the Treasury Department for many
of the same reasons that they had opposed the 1971
revision. Child care, the department insisted, was a
personal obligation of all parents and, thus, a personal
expense. Removing the income limitation "would generally
benefit only taxpayers in higher income levels who can
most afford to pay others to perform the household and
dependent care services which others must . . . perform
themselves." This effect ran against the basic hardship
justification for the deduction. The Treasury suggested
that the $200 million in lost revenue would better aid
the low-income taxpayer as a categorical child care
program than as a tax deduction: 80 percent of the
deduction's benefits would accrue to families earning
over $15,000 per year. Finally, to avoid abuses by
parents working part-time and still able to provide care
for their children, the department opposed dropping the
full-time employment restriction in Section 214. The
Treasury's position prevailed and Tunney's amendment was
deleted in conference.[75]

Defeat did not dampen efforts to restructure the
deduction. Over a dozen bills were introduced in the

House and Senate during the following three years. In
general they sought three changes in the provision: to
allow full-time students and part-time workers the deduction, to make payments to relatives for child care deductible, and the perennial proposal to subsume child care
costs under business expenses. The Treasury Department,
too, was working on changing the structure of the deduction. The department had discovered several administrative difficulties with the current law. Under the rubric
of simplification it proposed to eliminate three of the
most complex elements: the distinction between in-home
and out-of-home care, the requirement of a monthly calcu-
lation of expenses, and the disability income formula for
reducing the allowable deduction.[76]

In response to the continued congressional proposals
and the Treasury's administrative concerns, the staffs of
the Joint Committee on Taxation and the Office of Tax
Policy met to work out a set of revisions in drafting a
1974 tax reform measure. Under Laurence N. Woodworth,
the committee's chief of staff, participants took up
Treasury's proposals and the many congressional bills
involving the deduction. Treasury had explained their
suggestions for revision: an annual $4,800 ceiling on
the deduction, regardless of the number of dependents,
abolition of the distinction between in-home and out-of-
home care, limitation of the deductible amount to the
income of the "lesser compensated" spouse, elimination of
the disability income adjustment, and a dollar for dollar
phase-out of the deduction for taxpayers earning over
$22,000 per year.[77]

Woodworth agreed with most of the Treasury's proposals
and the Ways and Means Committee agreed with Woodworth.
By late spring 1974 they had drafted a bill incorporating
all of the department's major proposals. In addition, the
committee changed the maximum deduction from a flat $4,800
to $2,400 for one dependent and $4,800 for two or more.
The committee allowed full-time students and part-time
workers to take the deduction. The latter group was
subject to the "lesser compensated" spouse rule. This
rule eliminated objections that allowing a part-time
worker the deduction might open it to undetectable
abuses: deducting $4,000 worth of child care to earn
$2,000 in income. Deserted spouses were allowed the
deduction after 6 months instead of a year. In cases of
divorce or separation, the spouse maintaining the dependent's household was allowed the deduction regardless of
who claimed the dependent as an exemption. Finally, the

income limit was raised to $30,000--$8,000 above the
Treasury's recommendation.[78]

Although the bill incorporated several of the
revisions suggested by members of Congress, there were
two significant exclusions: changing dependent care
expenses to a business deduction and allowing payments to
relatives for care as deductible expenses. "The principal
reason," a Joint Committee on Taxation memorandum stated,
"for not permitting the deduction as a business expense
is that it is viewed by the committee, the Treasury
Department, and others as partly a personal expense."
The income limit was an expression of its character as a
personal expense since child care "is not quite as
'necessary' [at high levels] as it is at lower levels of
income." The memorandum concluded that the deduction
still retained the hue of a "tax relief measure for
widows and low-income married couples."[79]

The Treasury Department and Joint Committee staffs
also resisted any deduction for payments to relatives.
Here the issue was the possibility of abuse by taxpayers.
To one representative advocating such a measure, Woodworth
explained that it "would be difficult, if not impossible,
to verify whether payments to another family member . . .
were actually made . . . [and] whether these payments
were for a legitimate, deductible service or merely
represented a gift or transfer of income from one family
member to another." Even if the relative reported the
payments as income, he might not have sufficient total
income to be subject to tax. Moreover, Woodworth rejected
the idea that this revision "would increase the availability of child care services." Relatives receiving
payments "would probably care for the children even if
there were no payment or deduction."[80]

Ways and Means reported out their tax reform bill
with a limited revision of the child care deduction in
December 1974. Several events, however, intervened and
the bill never reached the floor. Wilbur Mills, the long-
standing pillar of tax legislation, had fallen victim to
alcoholism and puerile scandal. Without Mills, the Ways
and Means Committee lost its unequaled authority over tax
legislation. Long-time liberal foes of Mills convinced
the House Democratic caucus to strip Ways and Means of
its control over House committee assignments, increase
its membership by half, and make Mills's position as
chairman untenable. His removal and the new class of
liberal freshmen (artifacts of the November "Watergate"
election) gave tax reform proponents reason to believe

that they could restructure the present committee into
one more akin to their views. On the grounds that there
was insufficient time for deliberation before adjournment,
the House Rules Committee refused to rule the bill to the
floor.[81]

As a first order of business, the 94th Congress took
up the matter of tax reduction. In the trough of the
worst recession since the 1930s President Ford had
proposed and the Congress quickly enacted a $23 billion
tax cut. Barely a month into the session, Ways and Means
Committee reported a bill to reduce taxes by $20 billion.
In their haste they failed to include any measure revising
the child care deduction. The House-passed bill reached
the Senate Finance Committee in March. On the floor
Tunney again offered a bill to change the deduction into
a business adjustment to gross income and allow a deduction for payments to relatives. Russell Long, however,
persuaded Tunney to hold his measure until the Finance
Committee reported the House bill and then introduce a
modified version as amendment to the final bill.[82]

Presented during the Senate debate over the Finance
Committee bill, this modified version consisted essentially of Tunney's earlier proposal plus a provision
offering an optional tax credit for child care expenses.
A qualified taxpayer could elect to deduct child care
expenses from gross income as a business adjustment or to
credit 50 percent of those expenses up to $600 directly
against the tax liability. After introducing his revised
amendment, Tunney yielded the floor to Long. A consistent
advocate of "workfare" over welfare, Long defended the
credit as "especially helpful to a mother drawing welfare
payments who would like to go to work to improve the
condition of her little family." The tax credit, he
continued, "would cover about half the cost of providing
decent day care for her child while she . . . tries to
provide for a better situation in life for both herself
and the child." Long added that the credit accorded well
with the new earned income credit in making "honest
endeavor, honest work, more attractive than welfare."
Only Senator Carl Curtis objected to the Tunney-Long
amendment. Significantly, his objection did not extend
to the question of working mothers and nonmaternal child
care; he simply opposed the potential $1.7 billion in
lost revenues. Despite his reservations, the amendment
easily passed the Senate.[83]

The question of revenue loss, however, resurfaced in
the House-Senate conference. The Senate version of the

tax cut added $10 billion to the House bill--$1.7 billion
of which was contained in the child care deduction/credit.
The deduction/credit would increase by sixfold revenue
loss through the current deduction. Potentially, every
dollar expended for child care would be exempt from
federal income tax; business expenses had no restrictions
on income eligibility or ceilings on deductible amounts.
House conferees from Ways and Means balked at the magnitude of the Senate's tax cuts. For the same reasons they
had declined in 1974, House members refused to make the
child care deduction either a business expense or a
credit. The sole change in the existing deduction they
agreed to was an increase in the income ceiling to
$35,000. This revision reduced the revenue loss from
$1.7 billion to $100 million. Ford approved the measure
on March 29, 1975.[84]

Despite defeat of the tax credit, proponents believed
that they had discovered a method of expanding the child
care deduction without running afoul of Treasury and Ways
and Means. The credit offered the great advantage of a
business adjustment: an itemized return was unnecessary
to claim it. Yet, unlike the business adjustment, proponents argued that the credit provided proportionally
greater tax credit relief to lower-income groups and
circumvented the personal versus business expense debate
over the deduction. The credit also simplified Section
214 by replacing the income ceiling and the monthly
limitation on deductible expenses with a maximum dollar
amount. In September 1975 the Ways and Means Committee
began considering the credit as well as an extension of
the deduction to full-time students and part-time workers
up to the amount of their earnings and elimination of the
distinction between in-home and out-of-home care.

In committee three members assumed the lead in substi-
tuting the credit for the deduction: James Corman, Martha
Keys, and her husband, Andrew Jacobs. In this Congress
Ways and Means was a very different committee than it had
been previously. A larger membership, several subcommittees and, above all, the willingness of members to
appeal committee decisions to the Democratic caucus
served to loosen the grip of the chairman and conservative members on the purse strings. Corman took
advantage of these changes and the inherent attractive-
ness of the revision to move for substitution of the
child care deduction with a 15 percent credit of care
expenses up to $300 for one child and $600 for two or
more. It was adopted 19 to 13. Keys wanted a higher

credit, but the revenue loss precluded any credit near the Senate's 50 percent level. Such a credit simply had no chance in committee. She did, however, manage to persuade a majority of committee members to raise the credit to 20 percent of care expenses up to $2,000 for one child and $4,000 for two or more, a maximum credit of $400 and $800, respectively. She and Chairman Ullman agreed on a day when her amendment would be considered.[85]

In his rush to complete action on the overall tax bill and to minimize changes, Ullman brought up the Keys amendment earlier than he had promised. With several of its supporters absent, her amendment was defeated 17 to 12. Angered by their tactical defeat, liberals on the committee sought to illustrate the inequities of the committee's decisions on the bill. Jacobs arranged a little visual drama with the assistance of a staff member's two children. On the same day the committee had scuttled the Keys amendment, they had approved a generous provision for oil corporations. Jacobs costumed the children as oil wells and led them into the committee room. "If they look like oil wells," he explained to his colleagues, "perhaps they will be treated like oil wells." Although a few members protested that the dignity of the committee had been trod upon, the point had been made effectively to others.

In the earlier vote several supporters recognized their imminent defeat. Under committee rules a motion to reconsider could be granted any defeated measure, if that motion were made by a member voting with the majority. A few, therefore, voted against the amendment. When all the measure's advocates were present, Corman, a supporter who had voted against the amendment, moved to reconsider the Keys amendment. This time the committee adopted it by voice vote. Its passage reflected the basic appeal of the credit to the majority as a measure of the tax equity and simplification. Passage was also eased by the enhanced power of the House over decision making in Ways and Means and the presence of media representatives at mark-up sessions. Open sessions made opposition to popular tax measures, such as the child care credit, politically much more difficult.[86]

The committee also approved other changes in Section 214, including the ones related to students, part-time workers, and in-home and out-of-home care. They followed the earlier Tunney-Long proposal to allow a credit for payments to relatives who were not dependents of the taxpayers, who did not live in the taxpayer's home, and

"whose services constitute employment for Social Security
purposes." Committee members believed that relatives
often provided better care for children and a tax disincentive in this regard discriminated against low-income
taxpayers who frequently employed relatives as care
givers. Moreover, the qualifying provisions lessened the
possibility of abuse. In December 1975 the House approved
the entire tax bill--a 674-page tome of which 3 pages
comprised the child care credit. The House version then
went to the Senate Finance Committee. The committee heard
testimony and reworked the tax bill for the next 7
months. During this time the Treasury Department and
Senator Edward Kennedy advanced major proposals to revise
the new child care credit.[87] Treasury Secretary William
Simon testified against transforming the deduction into a
credit without any income ceiling. Though the department
approved simplification of the deduction, the "high cost
for the child care credit is entirely unjustified in terms
of the resultant benefits." Simon insisted that the
deduction be available "only to low- and moderate-income
taxpayers whose economic situation compels both spouses
to work." There was simply "no justification for allowing
the tax to subsidize high-income taxpayers in discharging
a personal obligation." The department's position was
somewhat ambivalent: it supported the "simplifying"
amendments but opposed the credit. It opposed extension
of the tax break to higher-income groups but supported
continuing the itemized deduction. Initially, Treasury
wanted to cut the $358 million revenue loss entailed in
the credit. It shifted ground, however, to confront the
greater revenue threat of Kennedy's proposal to make the
credit refundable.[88]

In his testimony before the Finance Committee on the
tax bill, Kennedy suggested that the credit be made
refundable in keeping with the earned income credit. To
contain the additional revenue loss of $35 million he
proposed to reinstate the $18,000 income ceiling with a
gradual phase-out to $27,000. The "poverty level families
who incur child care expenses to work would [then] be
eligible for the credit." His proposal was not brought
up in the Finance Committee mark-up. Other than removing
the House requirement that a relative caring for a
dependent not be a member of the taxpayer's household,
the Finance Committee had let stand the House version of
the credit. Kennedy again offered his refundability
amendment on the Senate floor. Calling it "an extremely
important work incentive," he defended refundability as a

benefit to low-income ($5,000-$7,000) families, particularly "the larger numbers of women represented in lower
income brackets." Kennedy recited statistics on the
number of single women with young children working in
very low-paying jobs. He said that he was "building
upon" Long's "brainchild," the refundable earned income
credit. Graciously, Long offered his support: "there is
no way on God's green Earth that we can consistently argue
against the amendment."[89]

Senator James Allen, however, found any credit dis-
tasteful, and a refundable one noxious: credits "eat up
the tax liability"; refundable ones were tantamount to
"putting an expensive social program in the tax laws
[which] would more properly be the subject of some added
social program." He warned against mixing social programs
and taxation. In response Kennedy restated the amendment's role in helping "working mothers" otherwise ineligible for tax benefits. Long took up Allen's charge that
the tax system was no place for a social program: "Sometimes we can use the tax system to bring about a good
result and sometimes we can use the appropriations system
better. We should use whatever is more appropriate at
the time." Majority leader Mike Mansfield "did not see
how we can differentiate between taxes and social
programs[;] . . . they complement each other." He
described Kennedy's statistics on the low incomes of
single working mothers as "startling" and "disheartening."
He commended Kennedy's amendment to the Senate; it passed
71 to 21.[90]

The Senate's final version of the tax was three times
the size of the House's original measure--the longest tax
bill to pass the Senate in 20 years. By the time the bill
went into conference Treasury had acquiesced in the child
care credit without an income ceiling, but did oppose the
refundability provision. This provision had "nothing to
do with the determination of tax liability; it is simply
an addition to the tax system which more properly serves
a welfare function." Otherwise the credit was "good" and
"significant." Since child care "may be considered a cost
of earning income," the credit "performs a legitimate tax
function" in determining tax liability. The House conferees concurred in the Treasury's assessment. They
deleted the refundability provision to avoid integrating
a "social program" into the tax code and to curb revenue
losses. They did retain the Senate's amendment allowing
the credit for payments to relatives who were residents
of the taxpayer's household. The provision that such

relatives be employees for social security purposes was
also retained. With Ford's signature the tax bill became
law in October 1976.[91]

Although designed to aid low-income groups, Treasury's
prediction of a windfall for upper-income groups better
described the effect of the credit without any income
ceiling. Households earning under $5,000 claimed the
credit at three times the rate they claimed the deduction.
In this income group returns claiming tax benefits for
child care rose from 8,000 in 1975 to 27,000 in 1976 and
tax savings from $1 million to $3 million. For middle-
income groups, earning $5,000 to $20,000, the credit made
little difference. Between 1975 and 1976 the number of
returns from these groups increased by 10 percent and the
tax savings by 3 percent. The big winners, however, were
those households with incomes over $20,000. Restricted
in 1975 by the $35,000 ceiling, only 134,000 households
in this group claimed the deduction for a tax savings of
$24 million. Under the credit households earning over
$20,000 increased their use of the tax benefit sevenfold
to 954,000 returns, for a tax savings of $196 million--an
eightfold increase. Indeed, 83 percent of the increase
in households claiming the benefit and 94 percent of the
additional tax savings were accounted for by families
earning over $20,000 per year. Even if the credit had
been made refundable, households earning over $20,000
would still have accounted for four fifths of the total
income transfer. Converting the deduction to a 20 percent
credit with no income ceiling was nearly 20 times more
beneficial in terms of income transfer to this income
group than was raising the income ceiling to $35,000.[92]

Part of the reason for this distribution pattern is
the distribution of tax liability across income classes.
In 1975 the median income of all taxpayers was $8,900.
Those below the median accounted for only 7 percent of
all income taxes paid. The upper 10 percent of taxpayers
had incomes over $23,400 and paid 49 percent of all
income taxes. In this respect the distribution of tax
liabilities biases any tax benefit toward upper-income
groups. Moreover, they generally pay more for their
child care and thus have larger expenses to reduce their
tax liability. Still, there remains a certain paradox
between what many of the credit's proponents believed
they were doing to aid low- and middle-income groups and
what actually resulted from the revision.

One possible explanation is that the proponents were
deliberately dressing up a loophole as an aid to the

middle- and low-income taxpayers. In this case, one
would then have to assume that the members of Congress
were dissembling (and continued to do so in subsequent
years). The more probable explanation involves a complex
mix of the structure of staff research, the complexity of
the tax legislation, and their intuitive sense of the
credit's impact. For every proposed change in the tax
code, staff of the Joint Committee on Taxation and the
Treasury Department calculate the revenue impact and
distribution of benefits. These calculations cover
numerous major proposals and nuances. The sheer quantity
of data combined with the complexity of tax legislation
itself results in most members of Congress dealing only
with "bottom line" figures, the total revenue loss of a
provision. The problem, one Treasury staffer notes, is
"informational overload."

This surfeit of information might cause a legislator
to use an intuitive sense of a measure's impact. A
member of Congress simply sensed that a child care credit,
particularly a refundable one, would benefit low- and
middle-income families more than a deduction with a high
income ceiling. That this was not the case eluded most
decision makers outside the Treasury and the tax committee
staff. Treasury opposed the credit's benefits to high-
income groups, but the department's greater institutional
concern was restraining aggregate revenue losses, not
tailoring every aspect of each provision in a 2,000-page
tax bill. Moreover, unlike other legislation, the
administration possesses no real veto threat; tax bills
represent too many compromises and too much negotiation
for that. The department would rather turn back attempts
to make structural changes in the tax code, such as a
refundable credit, and follow the politically popular
route of concurring in a tax break for upper-income
groups under the guise of a benefit to low- and middle-
income groups. Among relevant decision makers in Congress
this route was also easier. Only Kennedy offered the
refundability-income ceiling trade-off, and even he
dropped the idea of a ceiling in his floor amendment.

Since its passage, the only significant change in the
child care credit has been to abolish the clause on
employment for social security purposes in determining
the eligibility of payments to relatives. Designed to
avoid abuse of the credit through unverifiable intrafamily
income transfers, the effect of the clause was to preclude
a tax credit for payments to a child's grandparents.
Attention was focused on this effect by constituent

letters to members of Congress and an article by Ellen
Goodman on the editorial pages of the Washington Post:
"IRS Is Unfair to Grandma." Introduced by Representative
Barber Conable, the measure replaced the existing restriction with two specific limitations: a relative may not
be a dependent of the taxpayer and may not be a child of
the taxpayer under the age of 19. Conable asserted that
the present exclusion constituted a disincentive toward
the superior care that a grandparent might provide. It
also discriminated against low-income families who most
often paid relatives to care for their children.[93]
    The only opposition came from one member of Congress
who feared that potential abuse would evoke a Treasury-IRS
effort to eradicate the credit for payments to any relative. In a strong dissent, Ways and Means Committee
member Fortney H. Stark argued "that a measure billed as
aid for the poor or as an aid for working mothers will
prove to be mostly just another unadministrable and
unverifiable tax loophole." Despite this objection the
measure easily passed the Congress and became law in
November 1978. Effective for taxable year 1979 the
revenue loss was estimated at $36 million.[94]
    On the political horizon loom two possible revisions
in the child care credit: refundability and an increase
in the size of the credit. There appears to be substantial support for raising the 20 percent credit. Several
conservatives want to link this increase to a reduction
in Title XX funds earmarked for day care. Although
liberal members support a higher credit, they oppose the
Title XX trade-off unless a refundability provision is
enacted. Conservatives oppose refundability on principle
despite its relatively low estimated revenue loss of $38
million. The outcome of this policy debate is uncertain.

NOTES

    [1]Joseph A. Pechman, Federal Tax Policy (New York,
1971), 43. The best single work on tax policy making is
John F. Manley, The Politics of Finance (Boston: 1970).
See also Pechman, Tax Policy, 7-104; and Richard F.
Fenno, Jr., Congressmen in Committees (Boston: 1973),
passim for general discussions of tax policy.
    [2]The discussion of the history of the federal
income tax is drawn from Pechman, Tax Policy, 247-249;
Bureau of the Census, Historical Statistics of the United
States: Colonial Times to 1970 (Washington, D.C.:

255

1976), 1090-1096; and C. McCarthy et al., The Federal
Income Tax: Its Sources and Application (New Jersey,
1968), passim.
[3] Henry C. Smith v. Commissioner, 40 B.T.A. 1038.
[4] Alan Feld, "Deductibility of Expenses for Child
Care and Household Services: The New Section 214," Tax
Law Review, 27 (1972); and William Klein, "Tax Deductions
for Family Care Expenses," Boston College Industrial and
Commercial Review, 14 (1973).
[5] Bureau of the Census, Statistical Abstract of the
United States, 1954.
[6] Gilbert Steiner, The Children's Cause
(Washington, D.C.: 1976), 16-18; and Department of
Labor: Women's Bureau, Planning Services for Children of
Employed Mothers (Washington, D.C.: 1953), 10.
[7] Report of the Joint Committee on Taxation (April
21, 1953), 52-55.
[8] U.S. Congress, Hearings before the House
Committee on Ways and Means on General Revenue Revision,
83:1 (1953), 49-52.
[9] Ibid., 37-41.
[10] Representative Samuel W. Yorty, February 18,
1953, Congressional Record--Appendix, A937.
[11] Representative Louis B. Heller, Hearings before
. . . Ways and Means General Revenue Revision, 57-58.
[12] Representative James C. Davis, June 9, 1953,
Congressional Record--Appendix, A4191; Representative
Wesley D. Ewart, Hearings before . . . Ways and Means on
General Revenue Revision, 58-59; and Davis, ibid., 33-36.
[13] Representative Leonore K. Sullivan, Hearings
before . . . Ways and Means on General Revenue Revision,
31-33.
[14] Nancy Henderson, ibid., 61-63.
[15] Ibid., 37-41.
[16] Ibid., 49-52.
[17] Ibid., 53.
[18] Ibid., 63.
[19] Report of the (Treasury Department) Subcommittee
on Deduction of Expenses of Child Care (July 15, 1953),
Treasury Department Document (cited henceforth as TDD);
and The Budget: Message from the President, January 21,
1954, House Document 83-264.
[20] House Report 83-1337 (1954). The exact source of
the "available data" on child care costs and age is not
clear from the legislative record. Apparently, the
committee was referring to a study of child care
arrangements in Wichita, Kansas.

[21] Senate Report 83-1622 (1954).

[22] Ibid.

[23] Conference Report 83-2543 (1954). The revenue and household estimates are given in the respective reports of each chamber.

[24] Internal Revenue Code (1954), Section 214.

[25] HR12470, 87th Congress, 2nd Session (1962). The survey of bills related to the child care deduction is drawn from the Congressional Record--Indices (1957-1962).

[26] James Sundquist, Politics and Policy: The Eisenhower, Kennedy and Johnson Years (Washington, D.C.: 1968), 34-56.

[27] Message from the President (January 24, 1963), House Document 88-43.

[28] Although the commission issued its final report subsequent to the administration's proposals for tax reform, the commission's recommendations and general findings were known to the administration when it drafted the proposals.

[29] President's Commission on the Status of Women, Report of the Commission on Social Insurance and Taxes (Washington, D.C.: 1963), passim.

[30] Ibid.

[31] President's Commission on the Status of Women, Report of the Committee on Home and Community (Washington, D.C.: 1963), passim.

[32] U.S. Congress, Hearings before the House Committee on Ways and Means on the President's Tax Message, 88:1 (1963), 6-7, 42-43, 86-87, 202-208, 592-595.

[33] Ibid., 750-761.

[34] House Report 88-27 (1963); and P.L. 88-4.

[35] February 26, 1963, Congressional Record--House, 2999; and March 19, 1963, Congressional Record--Senate, 4544-4545.

[36] (Treasury Department) Subcommittee Report: Child Care Deduction (January 17, 1963), TDD.

[37] Surrey: Memo to Files (April 23, 1963), TDD; and Surrey: Child Care (June 5, 1963), TDD.

[38] House Report 88-749 (1964).

[39] Undersecretary Henry H. Fowler to Assistant Secretary of Labor Esther Peterson, August 28, 1963, TDD; and Bureau of the Budget--Legislative Reference File G3-6/63.6: Volume II (1963) Record Group 51, National Archives.

[40] October 3, 1963, Congressional Record--Senate, 23252-23253.

[41] Senate Report 88-830 (1964).

257

[42] Ibid.

[43] Conference Report 88-1149 (1964); and P.L. 88-272, Sections 212-214.

[44] Congressional Record--Indices (1965-1971); Statistics of Income: 1960, 1966.

[45] May 4, 1966, Congressional Record--House, 9845.

[46] Nolan to ABA, TDD.

[47] Schuldinger: Deduction for Child Care (November 24, 1971), TDD, discussed the Viorst proposal in detail.

[48] November 15, 1971, Congressional Record--Senate, 41251-41252.

[49] Citizens' Advisory Council on the Status of Women, Women and Their Families in Our Rapidly Changing Society (Washington, D.C.: 1968), passim.

[50] Citizens' Advisory Council on the Status of Women, Report of the Task Force on Women's Rights and Responsibilities (Washington, D.C.: 1970), passim.

[51] Citizens' Advisory Council on the Status of Women, Report of the Task Force on Social Insurance and Taxes (Washington, D.C.: 1968), passim.

[52] Ibid.

[53] Ibid.

[54] Grace Blumberg, "Sexism in the Tax Code: A Comparative Study of Income Taxation of Working Wives and Mothers," Buffalo Law Review, 21 (1971-72), passim.

[55] June 4, 1971, Congressional Record--Senate, 18106.

[56] For a discussion of the Nixon administration's Family Assistance Plan see Daniel P. Moynihan, The Politics of a Guaranteed Income (New York: 1973).

[57] June 4, 1971, Congressional Record--Senate, 18106.

[58] Senate Report 92-437 (1971).

[59] Ibid.

[60] November 12, 1971, Congressional Record--Senate, 40934-40935.

[61] Ibid.

[62] November 15, 1971, ibid., 41251-41252.

[63] Ibid., 41252.

[64] Ibid., 41253.

[65] Ibid., 41253-41256.

[66] Bird: Child Care Deduction (November 30, 1970), Joint Committee on Taxation Document (cited hereafter as JCTD); and Michael Bird, Joint Committee on Taxation, to Stanley S. Surrey, June 22, 1971, JCTD.

[67] Office of Tax Analysis: Treasury Position before the Conference Committee (November 24, 1971), TDD; and Re: Tunney Amendment (no date), TDD.

[68] Ibid.

[69] Ibid.

[70] Conference Report 93-708 (1971).

[71] Miriam Schwartz Alers, "Dependency and the Loss of Benefits Under Section 214 of the 1971 Tax Code," Case and Comment (November-December 1974), 44-50; Blumberg, "Sexism in the Tax Code," passim; Feld, "Deductibility of Expenses for Child Care," 415-447; Carol S. Greenwald and Linda G. Martin, "Broadening the Child Care Deduction: How Much Will It Cost?" New England Economic Review (September-October 1974), 22-30; Roland L. Hjorth, "A Tax Subsidy for Child Care: Section 210 of the Revenue Act of 1971," Taxes, 50 (1972), 433-445; John B. Keane, "Federal Income Tax Treatment of Child Care Expenses," Harvard Journal on Legislation, 10 (1972), 1-40; and Klein, "Tax Deduction for Family Care Expenses," 917-941.

[72] John V. Tunney, "You've Been Singled Out!" Single Parent (May, 1972), 3-5.

[73] October 5, 1972, Congressional Record--Senate, 33869.

[74] Ibid., 33870-33873.

[75] Frederic W. Hickman, Deputy Assistant Treasury Secretary to Long, April 28, 1972, TDD.

[76] Congressional Record--Indices (1972-75); and Oppenheimer to Hickman: Simplification, Prior Conference with Larry Woodworth (April 4, 1973), TDD.

[77] Balle to Hickman: Child Care Deduction (April 4, 1975), TDD.

[78] Canty: Child Care (May 21, 1974), TDD; and Joint Committee on Taxation Report 22-74 (November 18, 1974), 4.

[79] Bird to Woodworth: Further liberalization of the child care deduction (June 4, 1974), JCTD.

[80] Woodworth to Representative James R. Jones, October 20, 1975, JCTD.

[81] Congress and the Nation, IV, 89-90, 100.

[82] Ibid., 91-95; March 12, 1975, and March 21, 1975, Congressional Record--Senate, 53780-53781, 54651-54652.

[83] March 21, 1975, Congressional Record--Senate, 54652-54653.

[84] Senate Report 94-36 (1975); and Conference Report 94-120 (1975).

[85] Information provided by staff and members of the House Committee on Ways and Means.

[86] Ibid.

[87] House Report 94-658 (1975).

[88] U.S. Congress, Hearings before the Senate Finance Committee, 94:2 (1976), 94; and Tax Simplification: Credit for child care expenses (May 17, 1976), TDD.

259

[89] U.S. Congress, <u>Hearings before the Senate Finance Committee</u>, 94:2 (1976), 227; and July 21, 1976, <u>Congressional Record--Senate</u>, S12151-S12152.

[90] July 21, 1976, <u>Congressional Record--Senate</u>, S12152-S12154.

[91] Office of Management and Budget, Legislative Reference File G3-14/75.5 (1976); and Conference Report 94-1515 (1976).

[92] Calculations derived from Internal Revenue Service, <u>Statistics of Income: 1976</u> (Washington, D.C.: 1978), 86. All figures are rounded.

[93] House Report 95-1092 (1978).

[94] Ibid., and P.L. 95-600.

Legislative Changes in the Child Care

Date of Final Enactment	Eligible Households	Eligible Expenses	Size of Deduction
1954 itemized deduction	widowed or divorced mothers, widowers with children, mothers with incapacitated spouses, families in which both parents work and file a joint tax return	any expenses incurred in caring for a child or dependent physically or mentally incapable of caring for himself--if the care expenses allow the parent(s) to pursue gainful, full-time employment	$600 maximum regardless of number of children
1964 itemized deduction	(wives deserted by their husbands for one year were made eligible in 1963) single fathers and fathers with incapacitated wives added	unchanged	$600 for one dependent, $900 for two or more
1971 itemized deduction	unchanged	included expenses for housekeeping	$400 per month allowed for in-home care; out-of-home: $200 per month for one child, $300 for two, $400 for three or more
1975 itemized deduction	unchanged	unchanged	unchanged
1976 credit	a parent maintaining the household of a child, even if he is not eligible for the tax exemption, can credit care costs against his taxes; a spouse deserted for six months or more is eligible	care expenses to allow parent to attend school full-time, also for part-time work up to the amount of income made	20% credit for care expenses up to $2,000 per year for one child, $4,000 for two or more; maximum credit $400 for one child, $800 for two or more; all distinctions between in- and out-of-home care abolished
1978 credit	unchanged	unchanged	unchanged

Tax Deduction/Credit, 1953-1978

Income Limitation	Age Limit	Miscellaneous Provisions	Estimated Revenue Loss
$4,500, deduction reduced $1 for $1 over limitation-- phased out at $5,000	under 12	income limit applies only to households in which both parents worked	$140 million
$6,000, same marginal reduction	under 14	none	$20 million
$18,000, deduction re- duced 50¢ per $1 over limitation-- phase-out at $27,600	under 15	income limit applies to all households claiming the deduction	$145 million
$35,000 mar- ginal phase- out $44,600	unchanged	none	$107 million
none	unchanged	payments to non-de- pendent relatives, who are members of taxpayer's household, are deductible-- provided their services constitute employment for social security purposes	$325 million
unchanged	unchanged	all payments except those to a dependent or child under 19 of the taxpayer are eligible	$36 million

261

Appendix A   (continued)

Distribution of Households and Tax Savings by Income Class

1954	Under $5,000	213,000	$ 12 million	(67%)
	Over $5,000	60,000	$ 6 million	(33%)
	Totals	273,000	$ 18 million	

1966	Under $5,000	99,000	$ 7 million	(33%)
	$5 - $10,000	136,000	$ 12 million	(57%)
	$10 - $15,000	14,000	$ 1 million	(5%)
	Over $15,000	5,000	$ 1 million	(5%)
	Totals	254,000	$ 21 million	

1972	Under $5,000	47,000	$ 4 million	(2%)
	$5 - $10,000	455,000	$ 49 million	(24%)
	$10 - $15,000	625,000	$ 74 million	(36%)
	Over $15,000	442,000	$ 81 million	(39%)
	Totals	1,569,000	$208 million	

1975	Under $5,000	8,000	$ 1 million	(.4%)
	$5 - $10,000	344,000	$ 52 million	(19%)
	$10 - $15,000	604,000	$ 96 million	(35%)
	$15 - $20,000	575,000	$103 million	(37%)
	Over $20,000	134,000	$ 24 million	(9%)
	Totals	1,666,000	$275 million	

1976	Under $5,000	27,000	$ 3 million	(.7%)
	$5 - $10,000	365,000	$ 59 million	(13%)
	$10 - $15,000	600,000	$ 89 million	(19%)
	$15 - 20,000	709,000	$111 million	(24%)
	Over $20,000	959,000	$196 million	(43%)
	Totals	2,660,000	$458 million	

---

not available

262

Appendix B

Impact of the Child Care Deduction/Credit, Selected Years

	1954	1956	1960	1966	1970	1972	1973	1975	1976	1977
Totals										
Number of Returns ('000)	273	329	272	254	565	1,569	1,826	1,666	2,660	2,850
Amount Deducted ($ millions)	$ 89	$111	$103	$131	$221	$1,084	$1,292	$1,331	$2,290	$2,585
Revenue Loss ($ millions)	$ 18	$ 24	$ 22	$ 21	$ 37	$ 208	$ 249	$ 275	$ 458	$ 517
Under $5,000										
Number of Returns ('000)	213	237	183	99	137	47	52	8	27	5
Amount Deducted ($ millions)	$ 60	$ 82	$ 68	$ 48	$ 49	$ 27	$ 36	$ 6	$ 15	$ 4
Revenue Loss ($ millions)	$ 12	$ 16	$ 14	$ 7	$ 7	$ 4	$ 5	$ 1	$ 3	$ 1
$5,000-$10,000[a]										
Number of Returns ('000)	60	91	81	136	282	455	453	344	365	328
Amount Deducted ($ millions)	$ 20	$ 29	$ 31	$ 73	$128	$ 305	$ 334	$ 292	$ 295	$ 270
Revenue Loss ($ millions)	$ 6	$ 8	$ 7	$ 12	$ 21	$ 49	$ 53	$ 52	$ 59	$ 54

263

Appendix B (continued)

	1954	1956	1960	1966	1970	1972	1973	1975	1976	1977
$10,000-$15,000^b										
Number of Returns ('000)	--	--	9	14	92	625	715	604	600	560
Amount Deducted ($ millions)	--	--	$ 4	$ 7	$ 33	$ 429	487	$ 481	$ 445	$ 450
Revenue Loss ($ millions)	--	--	$ 1	$ 1	$ 6	$ 74	84	$ 96	$ 89	$ 90
$15,000-$20,000^c										
Number of Returns ('000)	--	--	--	5	55	442	605	575	709	647
Amount Deducted ($ millions)	--	--	--	$ 3	$ 11	$ 323	433	$ 461	$ 555	$ 315
Revenue Loss ($ millions)	--	--	--	$ 1	$ 3	$ 81	107	$ 103	$ 111	$ 103
Over $20,000										
Number of Returns ('000)	--	--	--	--	--	--	--	134	959	1,311
Amount Deducted ($ millions)	--	--	--	--	--	--	--	$ 90	$ 980	$ 1,345
Revenue Loss ($ millions)	--	--	--	--	--	--	--	$ 24	$ 196	$ 269

Median Income

Dual-Career Families	$5,336	$5,997	$6,900	$9,279	$12,276	$13,897	$15,237	$17,237	$18,731	$20,268
Female-headed Families	$2,294	$2,754	$2,968	$4,074	$5,093	$5,342	$5,797	$6,844	$7,211	$7,765

[a]For 1954, 1956, and 1960, this income category includes all returns of $5,000 or more.
[b]For 1960, this income category includes all returns of $10,000 or more.
[c]For 1966, 1970, 1972, and 1973, this income category includes all returns of $15,000 or more.

Source: Internal Revenue Service, Statistics of Income: 1954-1977; U.S. Bureau of the Census, Historical Statistics of the United States: Colonial Times to 1970; and Statistical Abstract of the United States: 1975, 1978.